AF538635
On your
Side

Published by :
FIREWALL MEDIA
(An Imprint of Laxmi Publications Pvt. Ltd.)
113, Golden House, Daryaganj,
New Delhi-110002

Phone : 011-43 53 25 00
Fax : 011-43 53 25 28

www.laxmipublications.com
info@laxmipublications.com

Economy Edition Price : **Rs. 125.00** *Only.* *Edition* : 2007

OFFICES

India

✆ **Bangalore**	080-26 61 15 61
✆ **Chennai**	044-24 34 47 26
✆ **Cochin**	0484-239 70 04
✆ **Guwahati**	0361-254 36 69, 251 38 81
✆ **Hyderabad**	040-24 75 02 47
✆ **Jalandhar**	0181-222 12 72
✆ **Kolkata**	033-22 27 37 73, 22 27 52 47
✆ **Lucknow**	0522-220 95 78
✆ **Mumbai**	022-24 91 54 15, 24 92 78 69
✆ **Ranchi**	0651-230 77 64

USA

Boston
11, Leavitt Street, Hingham,
MA 02043, USA
✆ 781-740-4487

ISBN : 81-7008-485-7
FOY-2774-125-OYS_WORD 2002

C—13275/06/11
Printed at : Sanjeev Offset Printers, Delhi.

*This is a book for anyone who uses **Word 2002**.*

It is designed so that you can look up the task you want to perform and find a clear description of how go about it.

The screens illustrated throughout add to the efficacy of the explanations, by showing the dialog box corresponding to a particular command, or by giving a precise example.

This book is made up of thirteen parts.

Miscellaneous features
p. 216 to 259

Getting the most out of Word: how to customise the interface, work with other users, create macros and use smart tags.

Internet/ intranet
p. 260 to 268

Publishing data from Word onto the Internet or your intranet and copying network data into Word.

A useful list of shortcut keys can be found in the ***Appendix****.*
You can find techniques and commands more quickly by using the comprehensive ***index*** *at the back of the book.*

Typographic conventions

To help you find the information you require quickly and easily, the following conventions have been adopted.

These typefaces are used for:

bold showing which menu option or dialog box to use.

italic giving an explanation of the command you are following, or of any changes on the screen.

Ctrl showing which keys you should press. When two keys are displayed together they must be pressed simultaneously.

The following symbols indicate:

♦ An action you should perform (activating an option, clicking with the mouse).

❑ A general comment on the command being used.

A useful tip.

A technique which involves the mouse.

A keyboard technique.

A technique which uses options from the menus.

TABLE OF CONTENTS

MICROSOFT WORD 2002

MANAGING DOCUMENTS

ENTERING/EDITING DATA

TABLE OF CONTENTS

STYLES/AUTOTEXT

TABLE OF CONTENTS

REVIEWING/MODIFYING TEXT

MANAGING LONG DOCUMENTS

TABLES

DRAWING OBJECTS AND CHARTS

TABLE OF CONTENTS

MAIL MERGE

MISCELLANEOUS FEATURES

INTERNET/INTRANET

Starting/leaving Word 2002

Starting Microsoft Word 2002

♦ Click the **Start** button.

♦ Move the mouse onto the **Programs** option.

♦ Click the **Microsoft Word** option.

An introductory screen appears, presenting the name of the software. Then the workscreen is displayed.

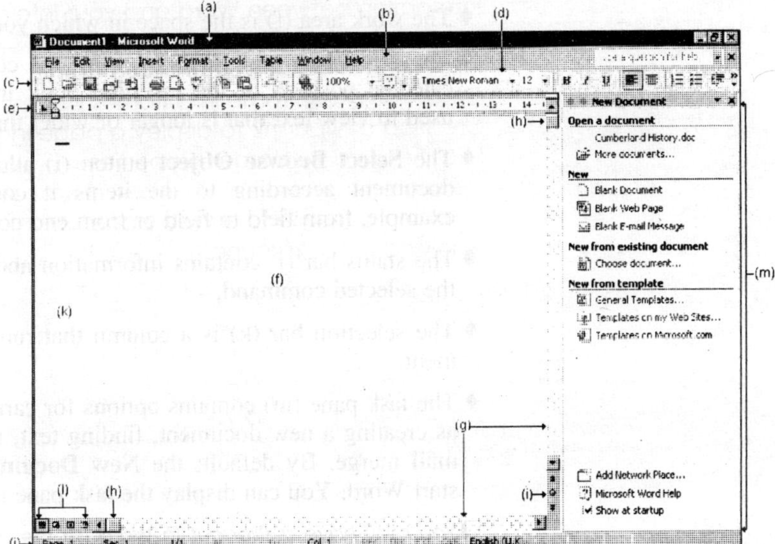

♦ The title bar and its icons (a): on the left is Word's **Control** menu icon ( ) followed by the name of the active document (here, **Document1** as it is a new document), itself followed by the name of the application (Microsoft Word).

♦ On the right are the **Minimize** ( ), **Restore** ( ) or **Maximize** ( ) buttons which you can use to reduce or restore the window size. Use the **Close** button ( ) to close the application or just the document.

♦ On the menu bar (b) are the names of the various menus in the Word application and the **Ask a Question** box. You can type a question or a keyword in this box to see the corresponding help topics. The document's **Close** button ( ) is to the right of this box.

- The **Standard** (c) and **Formatting** (d) toolbars share the same line. An extra tool button ( ) appears on the **Standard** toolbar if you have e-mail software installed on your computer.
  If these toolbars do not appear on your screen, you can activate the **Standard** and **Formatting** options in the **View - Toolbars** menu.
- The ruler (e) lets you change the presentation of your text quickly. Show the ruler using **View - Ruler**.
- The work area (f) is the space in which you enter and format your text.
- The scroll bars and cursors (g)/(h): the cursors in the scroll bars indicate the position of the insertion point in the document and are also used to view text that is longer or wider than the screen.
- The **Select Browse Object** button (i) allows you to move around the document according to the items it contains. You can move, for example, from field to field or from end note to end note.
- The status bar (j) contains information about the Word environment or the selected command.
- The selection bar (k) is a column that runs down the left of the document.
- The task pane (m) contains options for carrying out different tasks such as creating a new document, finding text, inserting clipart or creating a mail merge. By default; the **New Document** pane is open when you start Word. You can display the task pane using **View - Task Pane.**

❑ *You may have a shortcut to Word on the Windows Desktop. In this case, just double-click the Microsoft Word icon to start the application.*

Leaving Word 2002

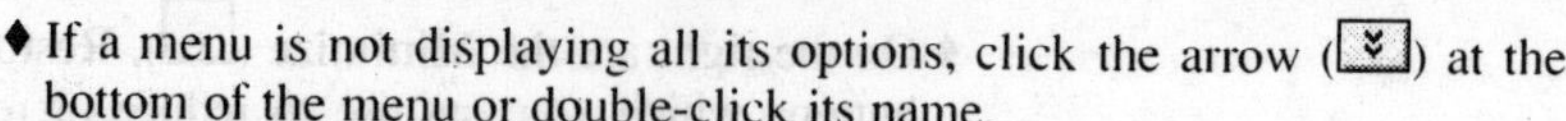

♦ **File** **Exit**	Click [X] in the application window	♦ Alt F4

- If a menu is not displaying all its options, click the arrow ( ) at the bottom of the menu or double-click its name.
- If you have left any documents unsaved, Word prompts you to save them.

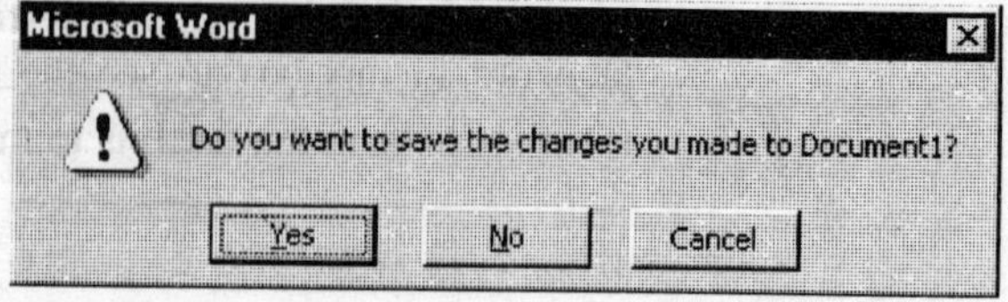

♦ Click **Yes** to save, **No** to leave Word without saving the document, or **Cancel** to stay in Word.

❑ *You can also close Word by double-cliking the application window's Control menu icon* .

Managing the task pane

♦ To display the task pane, use **View - Task Pane**.

*By default, the pane is anchored at the right of the application window. A tick appears to the left of the option in the **View** menu.*

♦ Different task panes are available, corresponding to different types of task. To change the task pane, click the button on the pane's title bar and click the name of the pane you want to display.

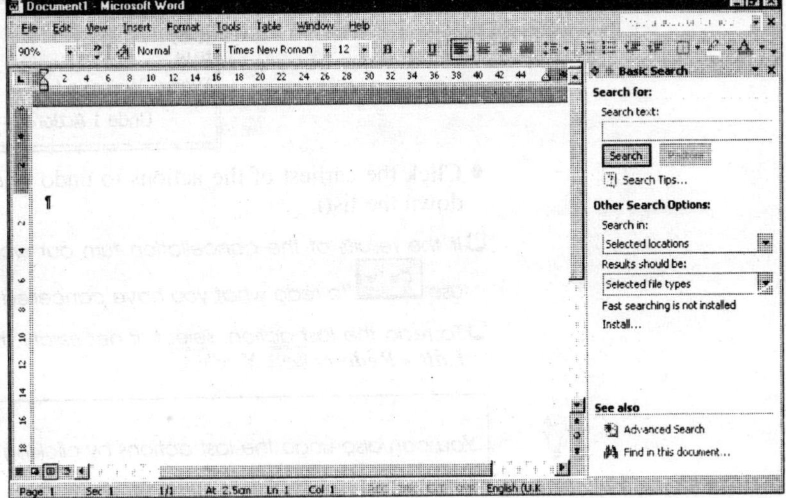

*The contents of the **Basic Search** can be used to search for a document.*

♦ Use the and/or buttons on the task pane title bar to see the contents of the previously shown panes.

♦ To undock the task pane, point to the pane's title then drag it to move it away from the edge of the window or double-click the pane's title. This floats the task pane.

♦ Dock the task pane by double-clicking it title or by dragging its title bar to the right edge of the application window.

♦ Close the task pane with the **View - Task Pane** command or by clicking the button on the pane's title bar.

Undoing actions

Undoing your last action

♦ **Edit**
Undo

♦ Ctrl Z

When Word is unable to undo anything, ***Can't Undo*** *replaces the command in the* ***Edit*** *menu.*

Undoing several actions

Word keeps in memory an archive of the last actions performed.

♦ **Open the list by clicking the down arrow on the tool button.**

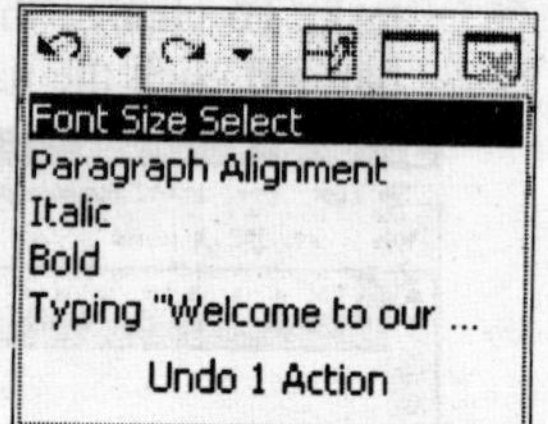

♦ Click the earliest of the actions to undo (the one which appears furthest down the list).

❑ *If the results of the cancellation turn out worse than the original mistake, use to redo what you have cancelled.*

❑ *To redo the last action, select, if necessary, the items concerned and use* ***Edit - Redo*** *or* Ctrl ***Y*** *or* F4.

You can also undo the last actions by clicking until you have undone all the actions concerned.

Using the help

First method

You can choose to go directly to the ***Microsoft Word Help*** *window without using the Office Assistant or the* ***Ask a Question*** *box.*

♦ Make sure the Office Assistant has been deactivated. Do this by displaying the Office Assistant using **Help - Show the Office Assistant** then click the Assistant and choose **Options**. Deactivate the **Use the Office Assistant** option then click **OK**.

♦ **Help**
Microsoft Word Help

♦ 

*You can also click the **Microsoft Word Help** link in the **New Document** task pane.*

♦ Click the **Contents** tab to search for a topic in the contents list. Click the plus sign (+) to expand the contents, double-click a book to open a category (or click the plus sign at the left of the book) then click a question mark to display the help topic you are looking for.

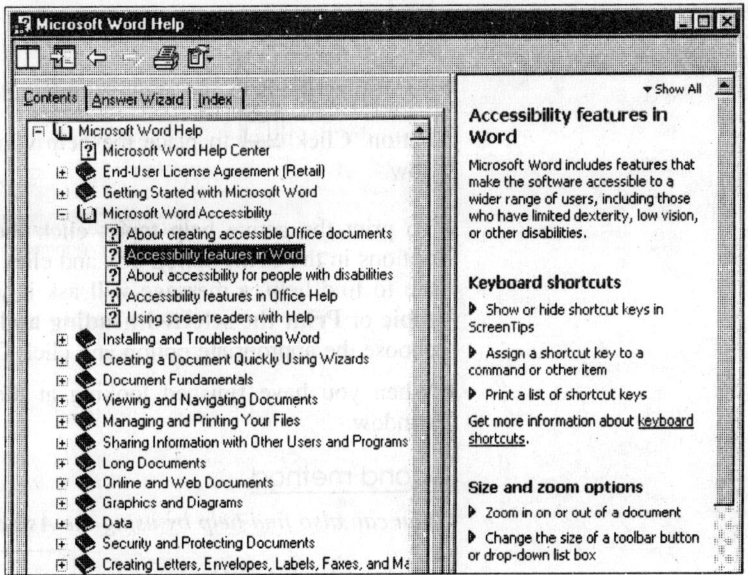

*The corresponding help appears in the pane in the right of the **Microsoft Word Help** window.*

♦ To display the topics that correspond to a question, click the **Answer Wizard** tab and type your question in the **What would you like to do?** box, click **Search** then select the topic for which you want to see the help in the right hand pane.

*The Answer Wizard's **Search on Web** button displays a new search pane on the right which contains a **Send and go to the Web** button. A click on this button starts your browser and takes you to a site that can give you more information about your question.*

♦ You can search for a topic in the index by clicking the **Index** tab. Type the first letters of the topic in the **Type keywords** box then click the **Search** button or double-click one of the words in the **Or choose keywords** list. Now select the topic for which you want to see the help in the right hand pane.

- To hide the left part of the window, containing the **Contents**, **Answer Wizard** and **Index** tabs, click the button. Redisplay this pane by clicking .
- Show the previous help topic by clicking the button and click the button to go to the next help topic.
- To display the help and application windows side by side, click the button. Click to place the help window over the application window.
- To print the active help topic, click the button, define the print options in the **Print** dialog box and click **OK**. If you used the **Contents** tab to find help, a message will ask if you want to **Print the selected topic** or **Print the selected heading and all subtopics.** If this happens, choose the appropriate option and click **OK**.
- When you have finished looking at the help, click to close the window.

Second method

*You can also find help by using the **Ask a Question** box.*

- Click in the **Ask a Question** box Type a question for help in the right of the menu bar, type your question or a keyword and press Enter.

*The corresponding help points appear. The **See more** option displays more points (if there are any more).*

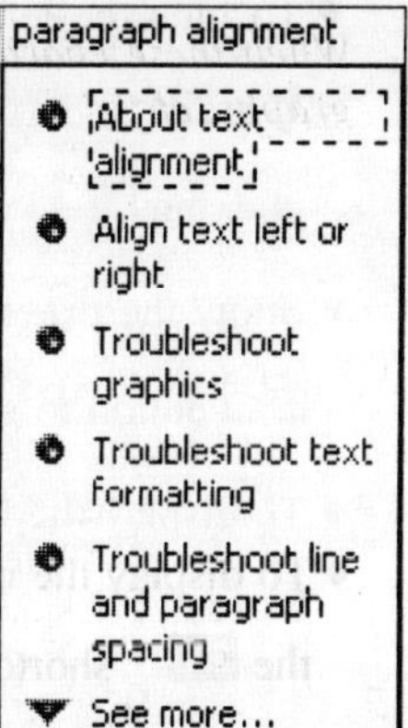

♦ Click the point that interests you to see the corresponding help.

*The **Microsoft Word Help** window opens.*

♦ Read the help then, if need be, click the button to show the **Contents**, **Answer Wizard** and **Index** tabs so that you can search again for help in the **Microsoft Word Help** window (see previous heading).

♦ Once you have finished using the **Microsoft Word Help** window, click to close it.

❑ *You can also find help using the Office Assistant. Display the Assistant using **Help - Show the Office Assistant**. Click the Assistant and type a keyword in the **What would you like to do?** box then click **Search**.*

❑ *You can hide the Assistant using **Help - Hide the Office Assistant** or by right-clicking the Assistant and choosing **Hide**.*

❑ *Deactivate the Assistant by first using **Help - Microsoft Word Help** (if the Assistant is hidden) or by clicking the Assistant (if it is not hidden). Click the **Options** button then deactivate **Use the Office Assistant** before clicking **OK**.*

*You can also look for help on the Internet by choosing **Office on the Web** from the **Help** menu.*

Showing/hiding nonprinting characters

When these characters are visible, it is easy to see spaces, ends of paragraphs, etc...

♦ To display the nonprinting characters, click the ¶ tool button or press the Ctrl * shortcut key.

*On the keyboard, use the * character on the main alphanumeric keyboard.*

The nonprinting characters become visible:
¶ represents the Enter key,
. represents the space bar,
→ represents the ⇄ key,
° represents a nonbreaking space.

❑ *To hide the nonprinting characters, deactivate the ¶ tool or press Ctrl *.*

❑ *You can choose which characters you want to display in the **Formatting marks** frame in the **Options** dialog box (**Tools - Options - View** tab).*

Changing the zoom

♦ Use the **Zoom** 100% list box on the **Standard** toolbar. It already displays the current percentage of zoom.

♦ Select one of the values proposed. The **Page Width** option displays the entire width of the page. You can also type in the value of your choice, and press Enter.

The new value is displayed on the toolbar.

You can also use the ***View - Zoom*** menu to change the zoom setting.

Changing the view

Normal view

♦ **View**
Normal

This view does not show the text as it really appears on the page (for example, page breaks are shown by a dotted line).

Print Layout view

♦ **View**
Print Layout

♦ Ctrl Alt P

Page Layout view displays the whole page, including margins, as it really appears (presented in columns, for example).

♦ To hide the blank spaces at the top and bottom of each page, point the mouse at the grey space at the top or bottom of one of the pages in the document and, when the pointer takes this shape, click the mouse button. You can show the white spaces again by pointing to the top or bottom of one of the pages and clicking when the pointer takes this shape: .

Displaying/ hiding toolbars

♦ **View**
Toolbars
or right-click one of the toolbars.

The standard version of Word has eighteeen different toolbars, and displays two of them: ***Standard*** *and* ***Formatting****.*

♦ Click the name of the bar you want to display or hide.

When a toolbar is displayed, a tick appears next to its name in ***View - Toolbars****.*

❑ *Some toolbars can be displayed by clicking a button on another bar (for example, displays the* ***Tables and Borders*** *toolbar).*

Moving a toolbar

♦ Point to the move handle (the vertical bar at the very left of the toolbar).

The pointer becomes a four-headed arrow.

♦ Drag this handle to the place where you want to position the toolbar.

If you drag a toolbar onto the workspace, it will become a floating toolbar, contained within its own window, which you can move or resize.

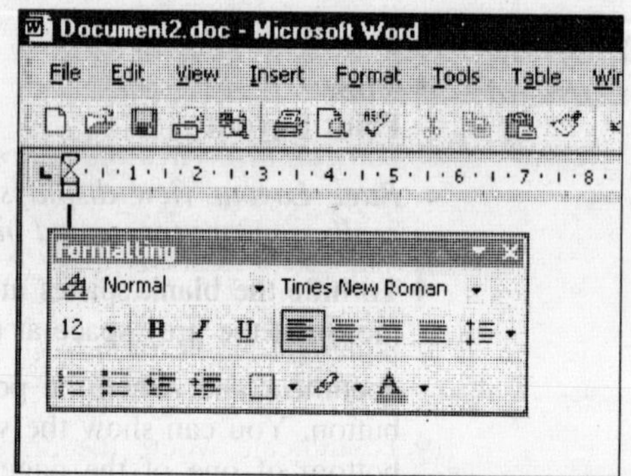

♦ To dock a floating bar, double-click its title bar, or drag it to an edge of the workspace.

The window becomes either a vertical or a horizontal bar.

You can also move a toolbar by double-clicking one of its edges.

.... Personal notes ....

Opening a document

♦ **File**
Open

♦  **O**

*You can also click the **More documents** link in the **New document** task pane.*

*The **Open** dialog box allows you to specify where to find the document you wish to open, as well as its name.*

When you point to an icon in the dialog box (without clicking), its name appear in a screen tip.

♦ To indicate where the document to open is located, click one of the buttons on the **Places Bar** (on the left of the dialog box) or open the **Look in** drop-down list. This list gives you access to all the drives on your computer (floppy drive, CD-ROM, hard disks etc) and to the folders they contain.

*The **History** button lets you view the 50 most recently used documents and/or folders.*

*The **My Documents** button shows the contents of the **My Documents** folder.*

*The **Desktop** button shows the shortcuts or documents installed on the Windows Desktop.*

*The **Favorites** button opens the **Favorites** folder.*

*The **My Network Places** button opens the **My Network Places** folder, where you can create shortcuts to the network locations you access most frequently.*

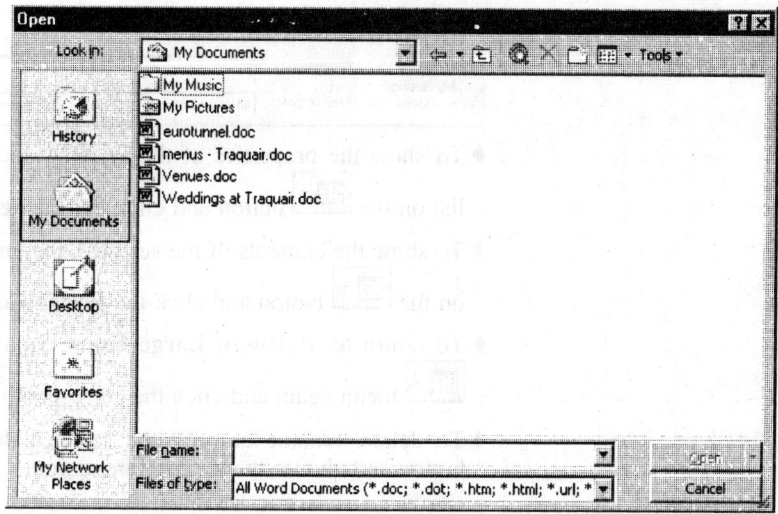

The list of folders and any documents contained on the folder or drive is displayed.

♦ Access the folder containing the document to be opened by double-clicking its icon ( ).

♦ Click the button to return to folders you have already used.

♦ To access the folder above, click the button.

♦ Open the drop-down list and click the **Details** option to display a detailed list.

The name of each document appears in the first column, followed by its size, its type and the date and time of its last modification.

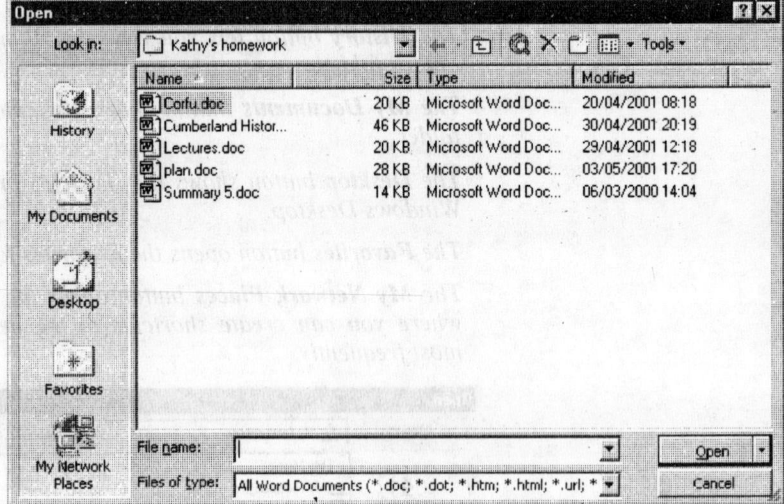

♦ To show the properties of the selected document, open the drop-down list on the button and click the **Properties** option.

♦ To show the contents of the selected document, open the drop-down list on the button and click the **Preview** option.

♦ To return to a view of **Large Icons**, **Small Icons** or a **List**, open the menu again and click the corresponding choice.

♦ To delete, rename or print the selected document(s), click the **Tools** button and choose the appropriate option.

♦ If you need to search for a document, click the **Tools** button then take the **Search** option to open the **Search** dialog box.

♦ Add a shortcut to a folder to the **Places** bar by selecting the folder, clicking the **Tools** button and choosing **Add to "My Places"**.

*The **Tools** button can also be used to add a document to the **Favorites** folder and map a network drive.*

♦ To manage the shortcuts on the **Places** bar, right-click the shortcut in question then activate the option for what you want to do (such as delete or rename).

♦ Open a document by double-clicking its name or clicking the **Open** button after having selected the document.

*The list on the **Open** button can be used to open a document in read-only mode, make a copy of it, open it in a browser or open and repair it.*

❑ *To open several documents at once, use the [Shift] key to select adjacent documents or the [Ctrl] key for non-adjacent ones.*

❑ *If you want to open a document that is open but not visible, click the document's button on the task bar or open the **Window** menu and click the name of the document you want to activate, at the bottom of this menu. The **Arrange All** option in the **Window** menu will display all open documents at once.*

*To open one of the last documents you worked on recently, open the **File** menu and click the document's name at the end of the menu or click the link to the document in the **Open a document** area in the **New Document** task pane.*

Closing a document

♦ **File**
Close

Click [X] on the menu bar

♦ 

When no documents are open, only the application window appears on the screen.

♦ Save the last changes made, if required.

*To close all open files at once, hold the [Shift] key down, open the **File** menu, then click **Close All**.*

Creating a new document

When you create a new document, a blank page opens in which you can enter new text.

Creating a blank document

- **File**
  New

*The **New Document** task pane opens.*

- Under **New**, click the **Blank Document** link.

*The tool button and Ctrl **N** keys let you create a new document without using the task pane.*

Creating a new document from an existing one

- If you need to, use **File - New** to open the **New Document** task pane.
- Under **New from existing document**, click **Choose document.**
- Select the drive and folder that contains the document you want to use to create the new document.
- Double-click the file in question or select it and click the **Create** button.

*The contents of the selected file appear in a new document called **Document [number]**.*

Creating a document from a template

You can create a new document which already contains the styles (or text) saved in a specific template.

- If necessary, open the **New Document** task pane using **File - New.**
- Click the **General Templates** link under **New from template.**

*The tool button and the Ctrl **N** shortcut do not open the **Templates** dialog box.*

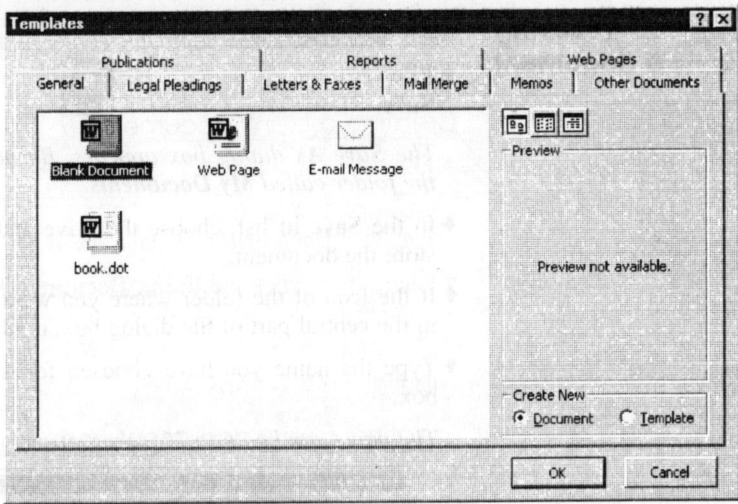

*In the **General** tab, the **Blank Document** template is already selected, as Word proposes you create a new document based on the **Normal** template. This tab shows all the templates in the **Templates** folder. The other tabs contain templates provided by Word.*

♦ Make sure that the **Document** option is active in the **Create New** frame.

♦ If need be, click the tab that contains the template you want to use.

♦ Double-click the name of the template you want to use.

A new document appears but nothing indicates that you are using a template other than the Normal one.

❑ The ***Templates on Microsoft.com*** link under ***New from template*** opens the Microsoft Office Template Gallery web page in your browser. This page contains a wide choice of templates you can download to Word.

❑ The ***Templates on my Web Sites*** link is for creating a new document based on a Web template.

The names of the last two templates you used appear in the top of the ***New from template*** zone. To use one of these templates to create a new document, simply click the name of the corresponding template.

Saving a document

Saving a new document

♦ **File**
Save

♦ Ctrl S

*The **Save As** dialog box appears. By default, documents are saved in the folder called **My Documents**.*

♦ In the **Save in** list, choose the drive and the folder where you want to store the document.

♦ If the icon of the folder where you want to store the document appears in the central part of the dialog box, double-click it.

♦ Type the name you have choosen for the document in the **File name** box.

The name can be up to 255 characters long, spaces included.

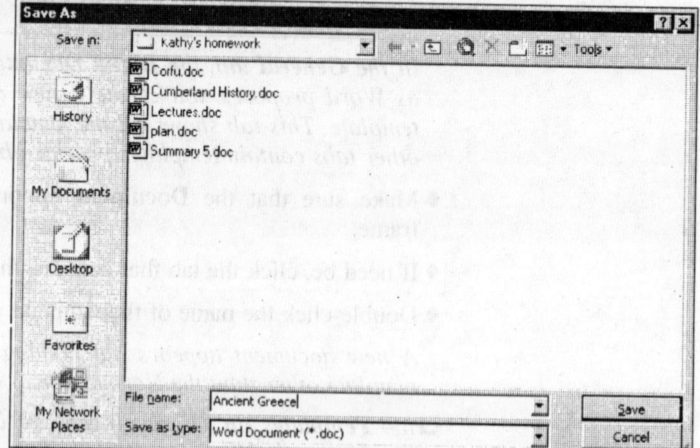

♦ Click **Save**.

The name and, possibly, the extension of the document appear on the title bar. A Word document always has the extension .DOC, even if this is not visible.

❏ *The command **File - Save As** can be used to duplicate the active document under a different name.*

❏ *To create backup copies (extension .BAK), activate the **Always Create Backup Copy** option in **Tools** dialog box (**Tools - Options - Save** tab).*

Saving an existing document

♦ **File**
Save

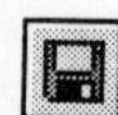

♦ Ctrl S

While the document is being saved, a floppy disk appears on the status bar.

❑ *To save all open documents, hold down the* ⇧Shift *key as you open the* ***File*** *menu, then click* ***Save All****.*

Activating/ deactivating automatic save

If this function is active, Word saves the document automatically every so often. It is you who decides how often.

♦ **Tools**
Options

♦ Click the **Save** tab.

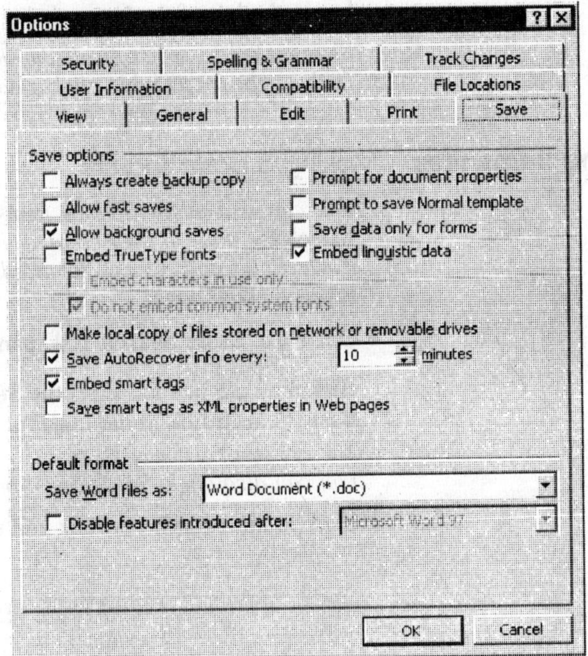

The save options are displayed.

♦ To activate the automatic save feature, make sure the **Save AutoRecover info every** option is active then enter the number of minutes that should pass between each automatic save in the **minutes** box.

♦ Switch off the automatic save function by deactivating the **Save Auto-Recover info every** option.

♦ Click **OK**.

Using the Favorites folder

*The **Favorites** folder is for storing shortcuts to documents or folders that you use frequently. The source documents or folders are not moved but you can access them quickly.*

♦ **File**
Open

♦  **O**

♦ You can also click the **More documents** link under **Open a document** in the **New Document** task pane.

♦ To add documents/folders to the **Favorites** folder, select them, click **Tools** and choose **Add to Favorites.**

♦ To use the **Favorites** folder, click the **Favorites** shortcut on the **Places** bar in the left of the **Open** dialog box.

*Straight away, a list of all the documents and folders in the **Favorites** folder appears. Double-click a document to open it.*

Finding items/files

Making a basic search

You can search for files or items that contain a specific text. You can search for data in files created using Office applications (Word, Excel, PowerPoint and Access), Outlook items (such as messages, contacts or tasks) or Web pages.

♦ Open the **Basic Search** task pane. Do this using **View - Task Pane,** click the button, select the **Search** option then, if need be, click the **Basic Search** link in the lower part of the window.

*You can also click the tool button on the **Standard** toolbar.*

♦ Click in the **Search text** box and type the text you want to find.

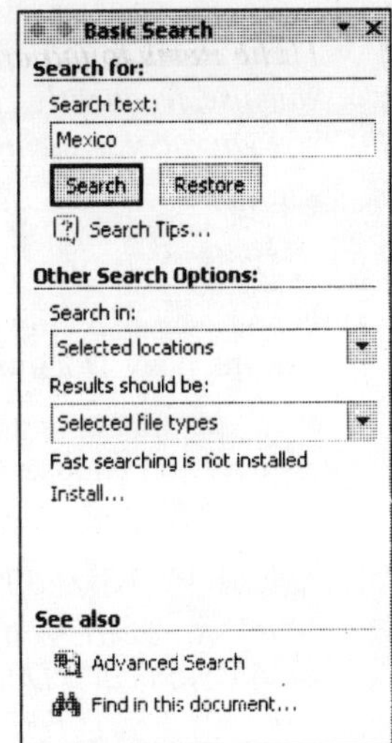

♦ Open the **Search in** list and choose where to search. To do this, type the path in the **Search in** box or open the drop-down menu and tick the check box in front of the folders in which you want to search. Click the box to select or deselect the folder, or double-click the box to select or deselect the folder and all its subfolders; click the plus sign (+) to expand the folder or the minus sign (-) to collapse it.

♦ Open the **Results should be** list and activate the options that correspond to the types of item you want to find and, if necessary, deactivate the others.

♦ Click **Search**.

The following message might appear if the component required for a basic search is not installed.

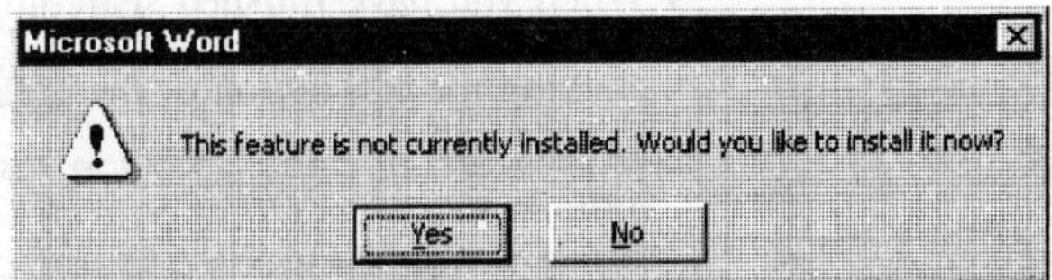

♦ If need be, put the Microsoft Office XP or Word 2002 CD in your drive and click **Yes** in the message: a window showing the progress of the installation appears briefly.

♦ If you want to suspend a search, click the **Stop** button at the bottom of the **Search Results** task pane. If you do not want to do this, wait until all the search results appear in the **Search Results** task pane: when the search is finished, the **Modify** button replaces the **Stop** button.

*The items found appear in the **Search Results** task pane.*

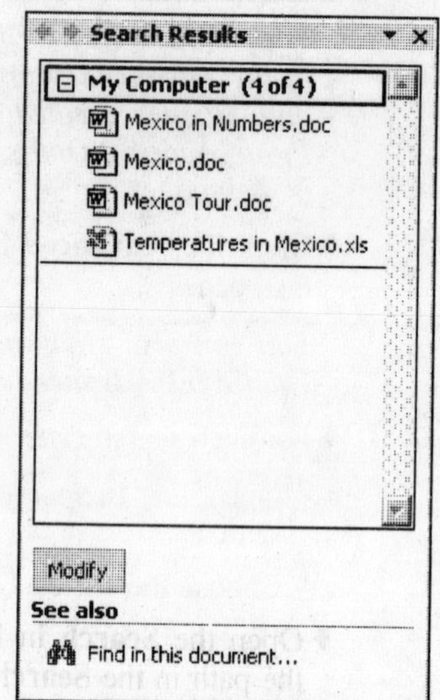

♦ To open one of the items in the results list (such as a file, web page or Outlook item), click it.

When you point to an item, you can see an arrow to the right of the item. If you click this arrow, you will open a list of options for opening the item in its application, creating a new item based on the current item, for copying a link to the item to the clipboard or for showing the item's properties.

♦ If you need to make a new search, click the **Modify** button to open the **Basic Search** pane again.

♦ When you have finished searching, if necessary, close the task pane by clicking the [X] button or the [tool] tool button on the **Standard** toolbar.

❑ *To activate or deactivate the fast searching function, click the **Search options** link under **Other Search Options** in the **Basic Search** task pane. In the dialog box which appears, activate or deactivate the Indexing Service. If you do not have a **Search options** link, install the missing component by clicking **Install** under **Other Search Options**.*

❑ *You can find the options in the **Basic Search** task pane in the **Basic** tab of the **Search** dialog box (**File - Open - Tools** button - **Search** option).*

Making an advanced search

*You can search for files or items using several search criteria defined in the **Advanced Search** task pane. As for a basic search, you can find data in files created using Office applications (Word, Excel, PowerPoint, Access), Outlook items (such as messages, tasks or contacts) or in web pages.*

♦ Click the **Advanced Search** link at the bottom of the **Basic - Search** task pane.

You can also click the [tool button icon] *tool button on the **Standard** toolbar, then choose the **Advanced Search** link.*

♦ For each search criterion you want to define:

– Open the **Property** list and choose the option appropriate to the search.

– Choose the search **Condition** from the corresponding drop-down list.

– Give the comparison value in the **Value** text box.

– Click **Add**.

– If you do not want to add any more conditions, click **Search**.

– If you have another condition to add, activate the corresponding connecting operator: **And** if the criteria should all be fulfilled or **Or** if only one of the criteria needs to be met.

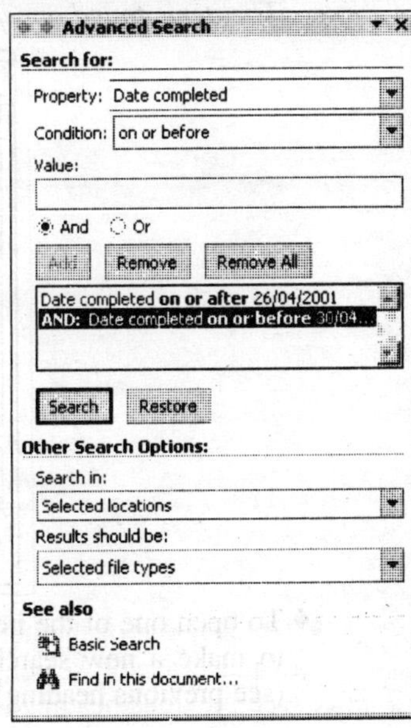

*Use the **Remove** button to delete the selected criterion from the list or the **Remove All** button to clear all the criteria.*

♦ Open the **Search in** list to choose where to search. To do this, type the path in the **Search in** box or open the drop-down menu and tick the folders in which you want to search. Click the box to select or deselect the folder. Double-click the box to select or deselect the folder and all its subfolders; click the plus sign (+) to expand the folder or the minus sign (-) to collapse it.

♦ Open the **Results should be** list and activate the options that correspond to the types of item you want to find and, if necessary, deactivate the others.

♦ Click **Search.**

A message might appear telling you that the component required for a basic search is not installed.

♦ If need be, put the Microsoft Office XP or Word 2002 CD in your drive and click **Yes** in the message: a window showing the progress of the installation appears briefly.

♦ If you want to suspend a search, click the **Stop** button at the bottom of the **Search Results** task pane. If you do not want to do this, wait until all the search results appear in the **Search Results** task pane: when the search is finished, the **Modify** button replaces the **Stop** button.

*The items found appear in the **Search Results** task pane.*

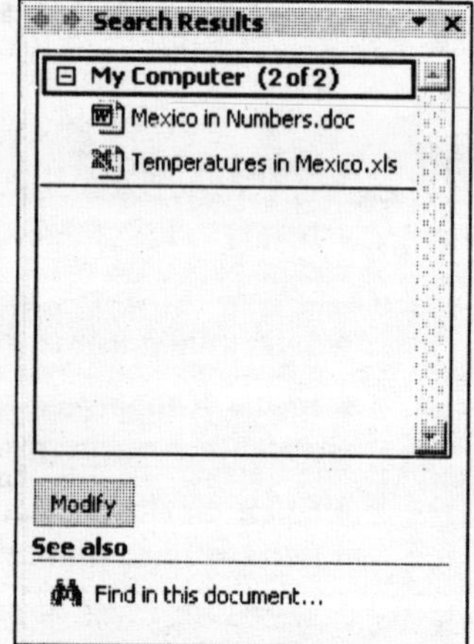

♦ To open one of the items (such as a file, web page or Outlook item), or to make a new search, use the same techniques as for a basic search (see previous heading).

♦ When you have finished searching, close the task pane, if you need to, by clicking its [X] button or by clicking the tool on the **Standard** toolbar.

❑ *Click the **Restore** button in the **Advanced Search** task pane to display previously defined search criteria.*

❑ *You can find the options in the **Advanced Search** task pane in the **Advanced** tab of the **Search** dialog box (**File - Open** - **Tools** button - **Search** option).*

Creating a summary of the properties of a document

If you specify the title, the subject of the document, the name of the author... it will be easier to find your document should you forget its name.

♦ Open the document concerned.

♦ **File**
Properties

♦ Click the **Summary** tab.

♦ Fill in the various boxes.

♦ Click **OK**.

*If you want Word to remind you to create a summary every time you save a new document, go into the **Tools - Options** dialog box, click the **Save** tab, then activate the choice **Prompt for document properties**.*

Inserting a file inside another

♦ Open the document in which you want to insert the file.

♦ Position the insertion point where you want to insert the document.

♦ **Insert**
File

♦ Select the document to be inserted.

♦ In the **Range** box, specify the name of a bookmark or a range (if, for instance, you are inserting a range of cells from a spread sheet).

♦ Click the **Insert** button, or open its list then click the **Link to file** option to create a link between the active and inserted documents.

Using e-mail

In Word you can send a document by e-mail, provided that e-mail software (such as Microsoft Outlook) is installed on your computer. You also need an Internet/intranet connection.

Sending a document as the message body

With this technique, the message recipients can view your document even if Word is not installed on their computers.

- Open or create the document you want to send.
- **File**
  Send To
  Mail Recipient

*A new toolbar appears, followed by four text boxes (**To**, **Cc**, **Subject** and **Introduction**):*

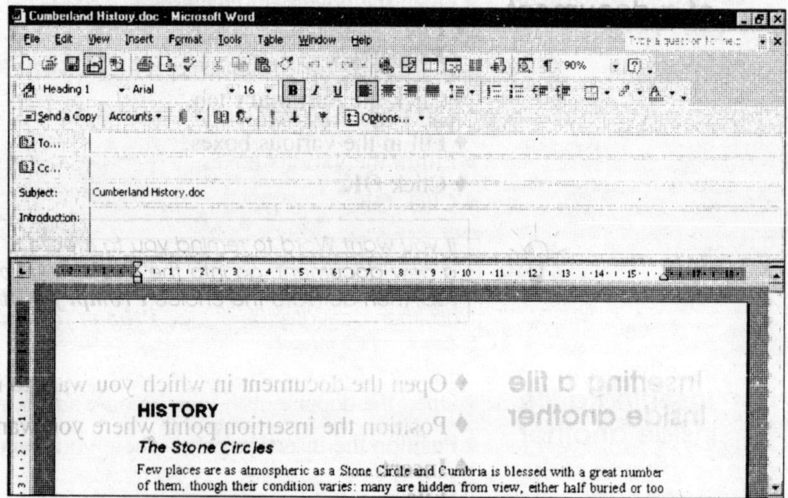

Your screen may differ slightly from the one shown here, depending on your e-mail program.

- In the **To** box, type the main recipient(s)'s address(es), using a semi-colon to separate them. You can also click the **To** button to select names from an address book.
- In the **Cc (Carbon copy)** box, enter the addresses of any people who are to receive a copy of the message or click **Cc** to choose names from an address book.

Sending a carbon copy of a message is done for information only and supposes that these recipients are not expected to reply.

♦ Type a subject for the message in the **Subject** box; the document's name appears here by default.

♦ If necessary, type a brief message in the **Introduction** box.

♦ Click the **Send a Copy** button.

A copy of the document is sent to the recipients. The document is the message body.

❑ *Close the message window without sending the message by clicking the tool button again.*

Sending a document as an attachment

This technique supposes that the recipients have Word installed on their computers and gives them the possibility of editing the document then keeping it or returning it.

♦ Open or create the document you want to send.

♦ **File**
Send To
Mail Recipient (as Attachment)

Your e-mail software's message window opens (Microsoft Outlook is the e-mail software in the illustration).
In rich text format, the attached document is shown as an icon in the big text box. Depending on the message format (rich or plain text or HTML) the attachment may appear differently.
*For example, in a plain text format, the attached document may appear as a link in the message header's **Attachments** field.*

♦ In the **To** box, type the main recipient(s)'s address(es), using a semi-colon to separate them. You can also click the **To** button to select names from an address book.

- In the **Cc** (**Carbon copy**) box, enter the addresses of any people who are to receive a copy of the message or click **Cc** to choose names from an address book.
- Type or edit the subject of the message in the **Subject** box.
- Type the main message text by clicking in the big text box (lower part of the window) so the insertion point appears, then type.
- Click **Send**.

To open and edit the attachment, the recipient must open the message then double-click the document's icon or link. Opening the file opens Word.

- Close the document.

❑ *You can close the message window without sending the message by clicking the* ☒ *button. You are asked whether or not you want to save the changes. If you click **Yes**, a copy of the message is saved in your **Inbox** or **Drafts** folder, depending on your e-mail software, and you can send the message later.*

. . . . *Personal notes* . . . .

Moving the insertion point

The insertion point is represented as a flashing vertical line. It marks your position in the document.

♦ Use the following keys to move the insertion point around:

Next/previous character
Beginning of the next/previous word
End/beginning of the line
Beginning of the next/previous paragraph
Bottom/top of the window
Next/previous window
Beginning/end of the document

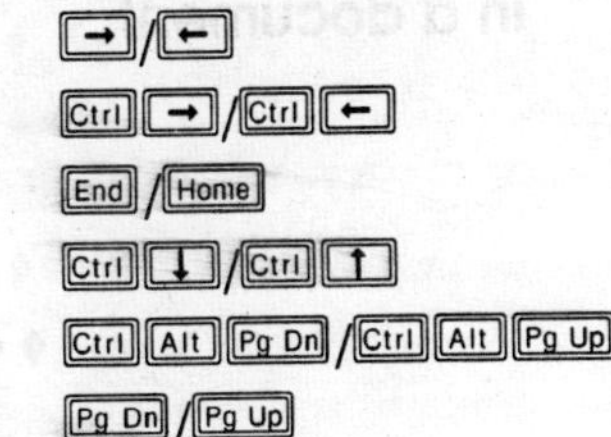

These keys do not allow you to go beyond the symbol marking the end of the document. Moreover, do not be surprised to reach blank lines when moving from paragraph to paragraph as each blank line is considered as a paragraph.

♦ Use the scroll bars to reach the text which interests you:

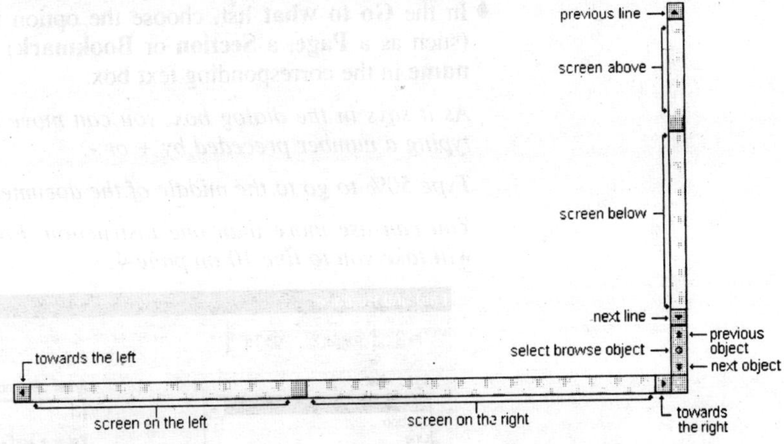

♦ To go straight to a specific point in the document, drag the scroll cursor along the scroll bar to that point's approximate position.

Word displays the page number as a ScreenTip.

♦ Now click in the text to place the insertion point.

Moving from object to object in a document

You can jump from field to field, note to note, table to table...

♦ Click the button on the vertical scroll bar.

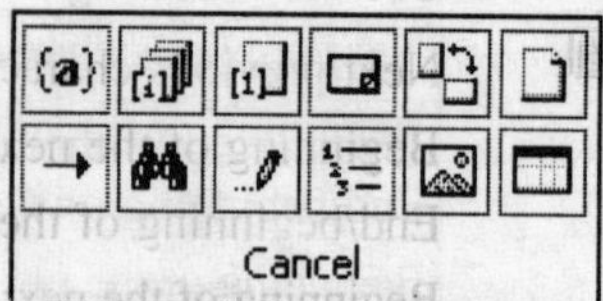

♦ Click the button representing the type of object which interests you.

The and buttons associated with the button appear in blue.

♦ Use the button and/or the button to move from object to object.

♦ **Edit Go To** — Double-click the **Page** information on the status bar — ♦ Ctrl **G**

*You can also click the button then the **Go To** icon.*

♦ In the **Go to what** list, choose the option for what you want to reach (such as a **Page**, a **Section** or **Bookmark**) then choose its **number** or **name** in the corresponding text box.

As it says in the dialog box, you can move up or down a few pages by typing a number preceded by + or -.

Type 50% to go to the middle of the document.

You can use more than one instruction. For example, entering P4L10 will take you to line 10 on page 4.

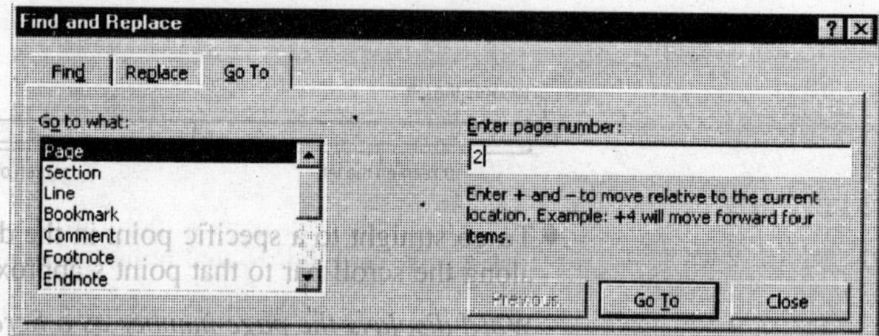

♦ Click **Next** or press Enter.

When you go to a page (or section), the insertion point is placed in the first line on the page (or in the section).

♦ Click **Close** to close the dialog box.

Using the Document Map

♦ View
Document Map 

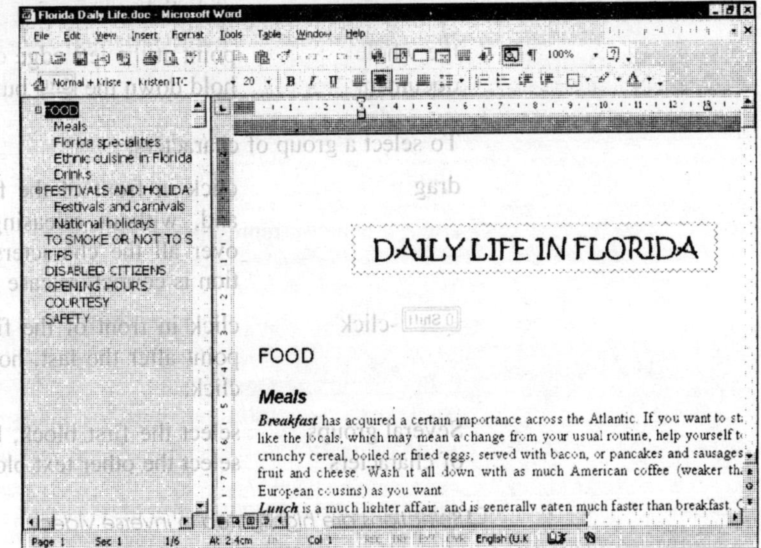

*A grey pane, called the **Document Map** or the **Document Navigator** appears at the left of the screen. It displays an outline of the document.*

♦ In the Document Map, click the part of the document you want to reach.

The part of the document you have chosen appears immediately in the pane on the right.

♦ Click [icon] to deactivate the Document Map.

Selecting text

As for moving around a document different techniques are available depending on the tool you use.

♦ To select:

a word	double-click the word.
a line	point at the left end of the line (the mouse pointer takes the form of an arrow pointing top right) and click once.
a paragraph	point at the left of the paragraph (the mouse pointer takes the form of an arrow pointing top right) and double-click.

a sentence	point at the sentence, hold down the Ctrl button and click once.
the whole document	point at the left edge of the text, and triple-click or hold down the Ctrl button and click once.

To select a group of characters:

drag	click in front of the first character to be selected and, without releasing the mouse button, move over all the characters required. When the selection is correct, release the mouse button.
Shift-click	click in front of the first character to be selected, point after the last, hold down the Shift key and click.
Several groups of characters	select the first block, hold down the Ctrl key and select the other text blocks with the mouse.

❑ *Selections are highlighted in inverse video.*

First method

- ♦ Position the insertion point before the first character required.
- ♦ Hold down the Shift key as you use the direction keys to select.
- ♦ When the selection is correct, release the Shift key.

Second method

- ♦ Position the insertion point in the text you wish to select.
- ♦ Press F8.

EXT appears in black on the status bar: the extension of selection mode is activated.

- ♦ Press F8 a second time to select the word,
a third time to select the sentence,
a fourth time to select the paragraph,
a fifth time to select the section,
a sixth time to select the whole document.
- ♦ To return to the previous selection, press Shift F8.
- ♦ Use the direction keys to make the selection more precise.

♦ Once the indicator **EXT** appears in black on the status bar, you can extend the selection by typing in the last letter you wish to select. For example, if you press [Enter], the selection is extended to the end of the paragraph.

♦ Press [Esc] to come out of extension mode.

You can also select the whole document by pressing [Ctrl] ***A*** *or using the* ***Edit - Select All*** *command.*

Selecting a column of text

This is a technique for selecting columns spaced using tabs.

♦ Drag to select (or hold down [Shift] as you click to select): hold down the [Alt] key at the same time.

♦ Activate the column selection mode by pressing [Ctrl][Shift][F8], then extend the selection as usual. Deactivate the selection mode by pressing [Esc].

When [Ctrl][Shift][F8] *is pressed, COL is displayed on the status bar.*

Personal notes...

Entering text

♦ Position the insertion point where you want to enter the text.

♦ Type the text: Word takes care of the line breaks (when the insertion point reaches the end of a line, Word repositions it at the beginning of the next line). At the end of a paragraph, press enter so that the insertion point begins a new line.

When you enter the first characters of today's date, a day of the week, a month or of certain set expressions which Word recognises, a ScreenTip appears displaying the full expression. This is one case where Word's ***AutoComplete*** *feature (semi-automatic data entry) comes into play.*

♦ Enter if you want to accept Word's suggestion; otherwise continue typing.

❑ *To deactivate* ***AutoComplete****, deactivate the* ***Show AutoComplete suggestions*** *option in the* ***AutoCorrect*** *dialog box (****Tools - AutoCorrect Options****,* ***AutoText*** *tab).*

❑ *You can use the Click and Type technique (see below) to place the insertion point anywhere in a document.*

❑ *To delete the previous character or the following character, press* [←] *or* [Del]*. To delete all the characters between the insertion point and the preceding space, press* [Ctrl][←] *and between the insertion point and the next space, press* [Ctrl][Del]*.*

Using Click and Type

This technique allows you to insert text, images, tables and other items quickly into an empty part of your document.

♦ Activate **Print Layout** or **Web Layout** view.

♦ Place the mouse pointer in an empty area where you want to insert text, images or a table then, if necessary, click once to activate Click and Type. The mouse pointer indicates the alignment of the text, image or table you will insert. The alignment proposed depends on the position of the pointer:

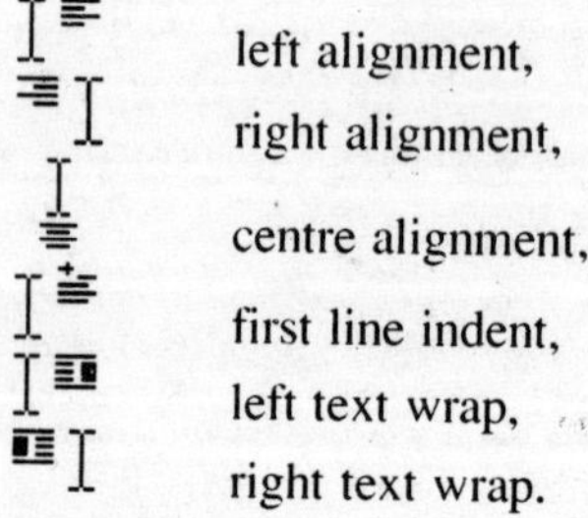

♦ Double-click.

Word inserts empty paragraphs and/or a tab so that the insertion point is positioned where you clicked.

♦ Type your text or insert the item (such as a table or graph) as you would normally.

❑ *If the Click and Type feature does not work, make sure the **Enable click and type** option is selected in the **Options** dialog box (**Tools - Options - Edit** tab).*

To undo a Click and Type position, press Esc *or double-click elsewhere.*

Correcting an error while you are typing

Whenever you make a spelling/typing error or type word that Word does not recognise, a wavy red line appears under the unrecognised word. If you type something that Word identifies as a grammatical error, the wavy line is green. The status bar displays a book icon marked with a cross.

♦ To correct the mistake, right-click the word concerned.

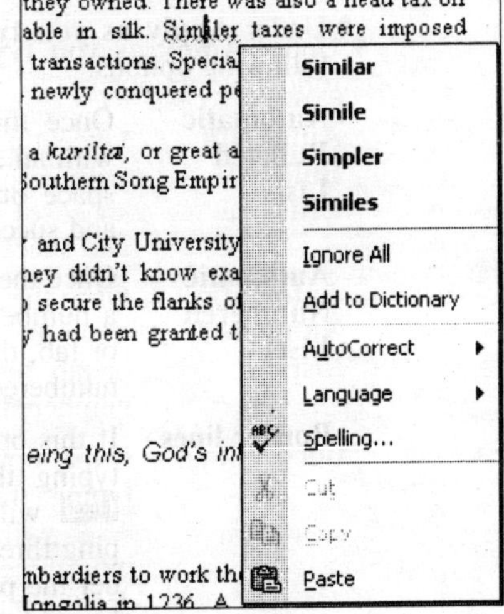

Word proposes possible replacements.

♦ Click the correct spelling (with the left mouse button).

The word is immediately replaced.

❑ *Most proper nouns are not recognised by Word. Any word typed twice in a row is queried.*

❑ *If you do not wish red lines to appear, activate the option **Hide spelling errors in this document** in the **Options** dialog box (**Tools - Options, Spelling & Grammar** tab). If this is done, only the icon on the status bar will indicate a mistake and no menu of possible corrections will be available. To stop the green lines from appearing, deactivate **Hide grammatical errors in this document**, also in **Tools - Options - Spelling & Grammar**.*

❑ *To turn off automatic spell checking altogether, deactivate the option **Check Spelling as you type** in the **Options** dialog box (**Tools - Options - Spelling & Grammar** tab).*

Activating/deactivating automatic formatting

♦ **Tools**
AutoCorrect Options

♦ Click the **AutoFormat As You Type** tab.

♦ Under **Replace as you type**, activate the options that correspond to the characters or symbols you want to replace or format automatically.

♦ Under **Apply as you type**, you can choose to activate any/all of the following options:

Automatic Bulleted Lists Once this option is active, if you begin a paragraph with an asterisk (*), the > sign or a dash followed by a space or a tab, then the beginning of that paragraph, and successive ones, will be marked with a bullet.

Automatic Numbered Lists Once the option is active, if you begin a paragraph with a number or letter followed by a full stop and a space or tab, then that paragraph and successive ones will be numbered.

Border lines If this option is active, at the beginning of a paragraph, typing three consecutive hyphens (---), followed by Enter will insert a single line under the paragraph. Typing three underscores (___) will insert a thick line under the paragraph. Typing three equals signs (===) followed by Enter causes a double-line to appear under the paragraph.

Tables If this option is active, typing +--+--+ followed by Enter will create a table with one column for each pair of plus signs (in this example, 2 columns would be created); the more hyphens you type between plus + signs, the wider the columns will be.

Built-in Heading styles If this option is active, typing a line then pressing Enter twice after it will cause the **Heading 1** style to be applied to the paragraph.

♦ Under **Automatically as you type**, activate or deactivate the following options:

Format beginning of list item like the one before it: if this option is active and if, for example, the first word in a list is in bold, Word will apply bold formatting to the first word or the following list item.

Set left- and first-indent with tabs and backspaces: if this option is active, when you press [Tab], you increase the left and first line indents and when you press [Backspace], you decrease the left and first line indents.

Define styles based on your formatting: if this option is active, Word creates new styles based on the formatting you apply.

♦ Click **OK**.

Using Insert/ Overtype mode

*When **Insert** mode is active, the characters you enter are inserted between existing characters.*

♦ Double-click the **OVR** indicator on the status bar or press the [Ins] key to deactivate insert mode.

*The letters **OVR** on the status bar change from grey to black. They indicate that you are now in overtype mode: the characters you enter replace existing characters.*

♦ To return to insert mode, double-click OVR or press the [Ins] key again.

Changing the case of characters

You may wish to put text written in upper case (capital) letters into lower case, or vice-versa.

♦ Select the text concerned.

♦ **Format**
Change Case

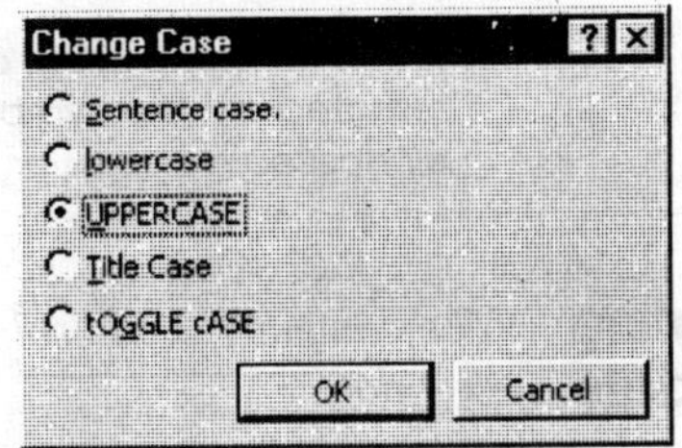

♦ Activate the option that corresponds to the case you want then click **OK**.

You can also double-click the option for the case you want.

> *The shortcut key* [Shift] [F3] *changes the case from upper to lower, then to title case.*

Splitting/merging paragraphs

♦ To divide a paragraph in two, position the insertion point just before the first character of what is to become the new paragraph and press the [Enter] key.

♦ To make two paragraphs into one, position the insertion point at the end of the first paragraph and press the [Del] key: the character marking the end of the paragraph is deleted.

Using tabs

♦ Enter any text which should appear at the beginning of the line.

♦ To go on to the next tab, press the [Tab] key.

Word tabs, set every 1.25 cm, are used by default. They are visible under the ruler as little, grey, vertical lines.

♦ To return to the tab stop before, delete the tab character by pressing [Backspace].

❑ *If the* [Tab] *and* [Backspace] *keys cause the left and first time indent to increase or decrease, deactivate the* ***Set Left - and first - Indent with tabs and backspaces*** *option in the* ***AutoCorrect*** *dialog box (****Tools - AutoCorrect Options - AutoFormat As You Type tab****).*

Inserting nonbreaking hyphens/spaces

Inserting one of these characters between two words prevents a line break between them.

♦ If the text is already entered, delete the existing space or hyphen.

♦ Insert a nonbreaking hyphen by [Ctrl] [Shift] _ or a nonbreaking space by [Ctrl] [Shift] [space].

❑ *When the nonprinting characters are visible, the nonbreaking space is represented by the symbol ° and the nonbreaking hyphen appears as an elongated hyphen.*

Inserting the current date

The computer's control date (current date) should be set to today's correct date.

♦ Position the insertion point where you want the date to appear.

♦ Press [Alt] [Shift] **D**.

The date appears in the format DD/MM/YY.

♦ To delete the date inserted, select it and press [Del].

❑ *If **AutoComplete** is active, type in the first characters of the date and Word will fill in the rest. Press* Enter *to insert the date.*

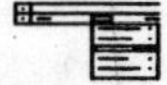

♦ Position the insertion point where you want the date to appear.

♦ **Insert**
Date and Time

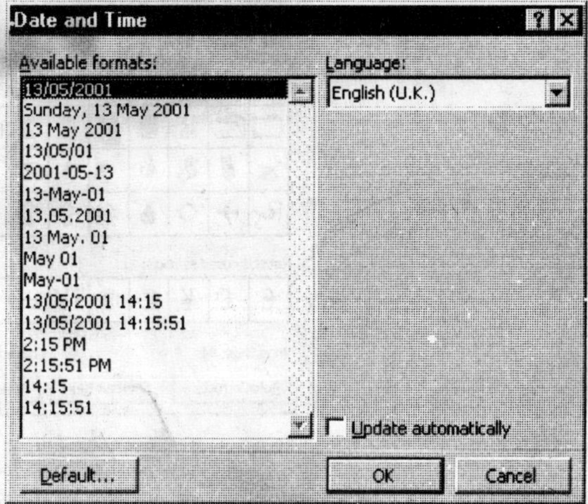

*Word shows you the **Available formats** list: it contains different presentations of the date (and time).*

♦ If required, open the **Language** list box to select another language for the date and time formats.

♦ Click the format you prefer, in the **Available formats list.**

♦ If you want the date printed in your document to be updated automatically, activate the choice **Update automatically.**

♦ Click **OK.**

❑ *Click the **Default** button to set the chosen format as the new default format.*

Inserting symbols into your text

This technique allows you to insert characters which do not figure on the keyboard.

♦ Position the insertion point where you want to put the symbol.

♦ **Insert**
Symbol
If necessary, activate the **Symbols** tab.

- In the **Font** list box, select the font containing the character you need. Depending on your printer, you may be able to use, for example, the **Zapfdingbats** or **Wingdings** font.
- To zoom in on one of the symbols, click it.

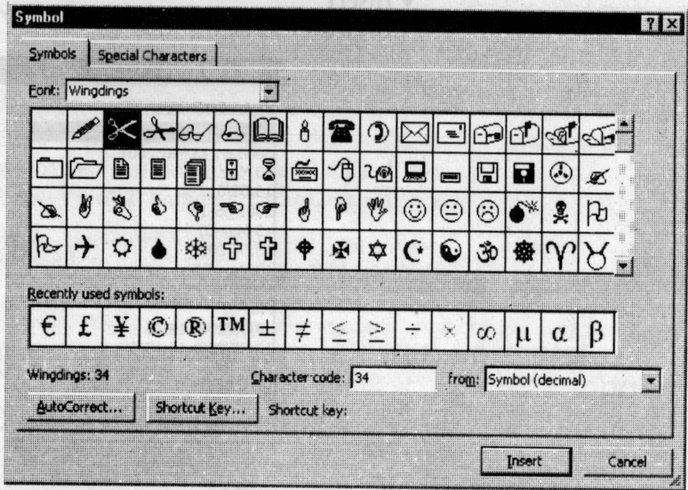

- Scroll through the symbols until you can see the one you want then double-click the character you want to insert or select it and click **Insert**. If the symbol you want is one of the **Recently used symbols**, you can select it from the symbols in this category.

  To select a symbol, you can also type its code (if you know it) in the ***Character code*** *box.*
- Click **Close** to close the dialog box.

> *If you have inserted a special character in the current document, double-click it to open the* ***Symbol*** *dialog box.*

Assigning a shortcut key to a symbol

You can use a shortcut key to insert a commonly used symbol quickly.

- If you need to, open the template or the document concerned.
- **Insert**
  Symbol
- Select the symbol in question.
- Click the **Shortcut Key** button.

  The insertion point flashes in the ***Press new shortcut key*** *box.*
- Enter the key combination you want to use to insert the symbol.

*The shortcut appears in letters in the **Press new shortcut key** box.*

♦ Make sure **[unassigned]** appears next to **Currently assigned to.**

*Depending on the font chosen, the **Description** frame displays either the character inserted by the shortcut key or the font and ANSI code of the character. A preview of the symbol may also appear underneath the **Press new shortcut key** box.*

♦ Click **Assign.**

*The shortcut is now visible in the **Current keys** list.*

♦ Check the name of the template or document in question in the **Save changes in** list then click **Close** twice.

❑ *To insert the symbol into the text, press the shortcut key(s) you have assigned to it.*

Inserting a page break

♦ Position the insertion point at the beginning of the line which is going to follow the page break.

♦ Press Ctrl Enter.

basement level is still being built. we except it to be occupied in ten days time. Meanwhile the hammering discourages us from occupying it in the daytime.

Page Break

|

Hotel

Well, I have said enough: it is a complex. About eight blocks like this are open so far, across a lovely large pool from the lovely large centre for bar, restaurant and administration.

In Normal view, if the nonprinting characters are visible, a dotted line appears on the screen. This is how Word represents a page break.

❑ *To remove this kind of "manual" page break, position the insertion point on the dotted line and press Del.*

❑ Ctrl Enter *is equivalent to the **Page Break** choice in **Insert - Break**.*

Inserting a line break

By this method, you can start a new line without changing paragraph.

♦ Position the insertion point at the end of the line.

♦ Press ⇧Shift Enter.

The insertion point moves on to the next line without starting a new paragraph.

♦ If you wish, activate the display of nonprinting characters ¶ to see the line break represented:

Each line of the address finishes with a line break.

Inserting a hyperlink

♦ Open the file in which you wish to insert the link.

♦ Position the insertion point where you wish to insert the link, or select the text which you are going to use as a link.

♦ **Insert**
Hyperlink

♦ 

♦ Click the **Existing File or Web Page** shortcut on the **Link to** bar.

The ***Create new document*** *shortcut allows you to create a link to a document that does not already exist.*

♦ Fill in the **Address** box using one of the following techniques:

– In the **Address** box, type the name and full path of the file or the URL of the Web page to which the link leads.

– Click the **Current Folder** shortcut, select the drive (using the **Look in** list) and folder in which the target file is stored then select the file in question. You can choose to target a folder, in which case, when the link is clicked, the folder will open in Windows Explorer.

– Click the **Browsed Pages** shortcut and select the link's target page from a list of recently viewed Web pages.

– Click the **Recent Files** shortcut to see a list of recently used files and choose the link's target file from among them.

♦ Use the **Text to display** box to enter or edit (if you need to) the text that is going to appear as the hyperlink.

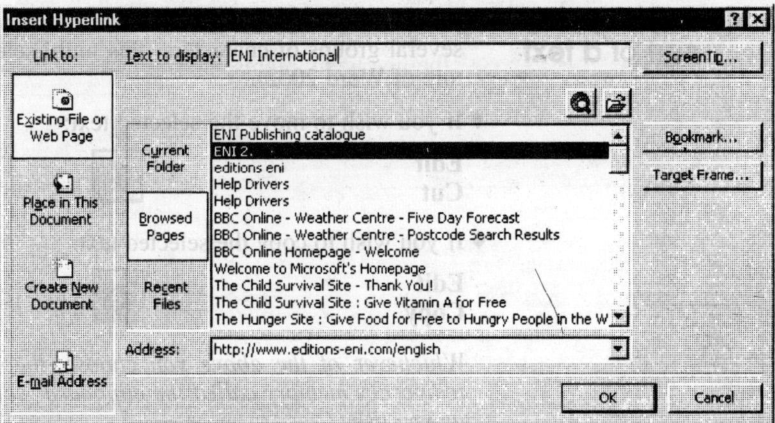

♦ To change the text that appears in the link's screen tip, click the **ScreenTip** button, type your text then click **OK**. By default, the screen tip contains the address of the target.

♦ The **Bookmark** button lets you select the named location in the document that is to be targeted by the link, if appropriate.

♦ If you are inserting a hyperlink into a frames page, click the **Target Frame** button to select the frame where you want the target page/file to appear (you can also choose to display it in a **New window**). If you intend to insert several hyperlinks, all of which will display their target document in the same frame, activate **Set as default for all hyperlinks** to avoid having to select the **Target Frame** each time.

♦ Click **OK**.

The hyperlink appears in blue. If you have not selected or specified a text, the link appears as the document's path. When you point to the link (without clicking), a screen tip appears (which is, by default, the file or web page's address).

♦ Activate a hyperlink by holding down the Ctrl key as you click the link.

The document or web page appears on screen.

❑ *Use the same technique to create more hyperlinks in the document, linking to other documents, such as Word or Excel documents or Web pages.*

Moving/copying part of a text

♦ Select the text you want to move or copy; use the Ctrl key to select several groups of characters (this multi-selection capacity is a new feature of Word 2002).

♦ If you wish to move the selected text:

Edit
Cut

♦ 

♦ If you wish to copy the selected text:

Edit
Copy

♦ 

Whichever of the above you choose, the selected text is stored in a temporary memory called the clipboard: you can paste it as many times as you like.

♦ Position the insertion point where the selected text is to go.

♦ **Edit**
Paste

♦ 

Straight away, the contents of the clipboard appear at the insertion point. The ***Paste Options*** *button appears just below the pasted text.*

♦ If need be, choose the format for the text you have just pasted. Do this by pointing to the **Paste Options** button, opening its lits and choosing one of the options:

Keep Source Formatting: Word does not apply the paragraph and character formatting of the destination paragraph to the pasted text, but leaves it with its original formats. However, if the text selected for copying or moving does not contain a paragraph mark (¶), Word does not conserve the paragraph formatting, only that of the characters. In this case, Word uses the formatting of the destination paragraph.

Match Destination Formatting: Word respects the source format of the characters and also applies the character formatting of the destination paragraph. The paragraph formatting of the destination paragraph is applied.

Keep Text Only: if you want Word to keep only the text. The source formatting is lost and the paragraph and character formatting of the destination paragraph are applied to the pasted text.

Apply Style or Formatting: opens the **Styles and Formatting** task pane so that you can select a style or format from the **Pick formatting to apply** list for the pasted text.

❑ *If the **Clipboard** task pane is open, you can also click one of the items in it to paste into your document (see below).*

❑ *You can determine whether or not the **Paste Options** button appears by activating or deactivating the **Show Paste Options** buttons check box in **Tools - Options - Edit** tab.*

Using the Office Clipboard

♦ If need be, open the **Clipboard** task pane. Do this using **View - Task Pane**, click [▼] then **Clipboard** or use **Edit - Office Clipboard** or press [Ctrl] **C** twice.

*The **Clipboard** task pane appears automatically after two consecutive copies or moves.*

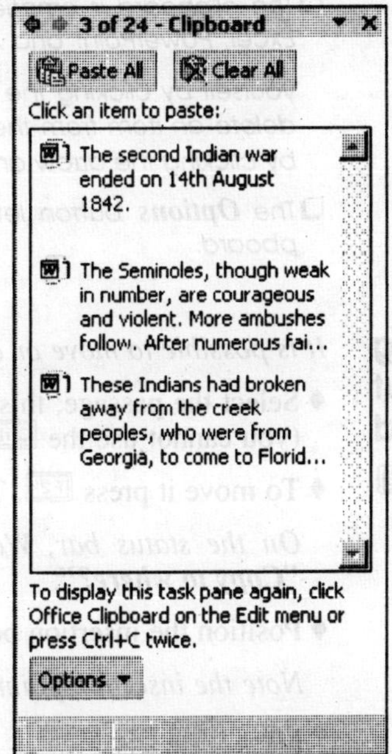

*The **Clipboard** task pane shows cut or copied items (up to a maximum of 24). You can see the first words of the text of each item.*

♦ Place the insertion point where you want to copy or move your text.

♦ In the **Clipboard** task pane, click the item you want to paste, or point to it, open the associated list and click **Paste**.

*The **Paste Options** button [icon] appears under the pasted text.*

♦ If need be, choose the formatting for the selection you have just pasted.

Do this by opening the list on the [paste options] button and choosing from the available options (these options are described above).

♦ Close the **Clipboard** task pane by clicking its [X] button or by deactivating the **Task Pane** in the **View** menu.

❑ *You can use this technique to paste a specific item from the clipboard, whereas the [Paste] button can only paste the last item placed on the clipboard.*

❑ *The [Paste All] button in the* ***Clipboard*** *task pane lets you paste all the items in the clipboard. They are pasted one after the other.*

❑ *The clipboard is emptied once all Microsoft applications (such as Word, Excel, PowerPoint and Access) are closed. You can empty the clipboard yourself by clicking the [Clear All] button in the* ***Clipboard*** *task pane. To delete an item from the clipboard, point to it, open the associated menu by clicking the arrow and choose* ***Delete****.*

❑ *The* ***Options*** *button lets you define the view options for the Office clipboard.*

Moving/copying text without the clipboard

It is possible to move or copy text without first storing it in the clipboard.

♦ Select the passage; this technique only works for a continuous selection (you cannot use the [Ctrl] key).

♦ To move it press [F2]. To copy it press [Shift] [F2].

On the status bar, Word writes the question ***"Move to where?"*** *or* ***"Copy to where?"****.*

♦ Position the insertion point in the required place.

Note the insertion point's new form.

♦ Press [Enter].

♦ Select the passage; use [Ctrl] to select several passages.

♦ Point to the selected text.

♦ To copy, press the [Ctrl] button and drag the text to its new position. To move text, just drag it to where you want it to be.

While the file is being moved, a rectangle appears attached to the mouse pointer; if the file is being copied, the rectangle contains a + sign.

♦ If need be, choose the pasted selection's format using the button below the pasted text.

Copying formatting

♦ To copy paragraph formatting, click in the paragraph whose formatting you want to copy or select it, including its paragraph marker (¶). Copy character formatting by selecting the text that has the formatting you want to copy.

♦ Click the tool on the **Standard** toolbar.

Notice that the pointer has taken the shape of a paintbrush.

♦ Copy paragraph formatting by clicking in the paragraph you want to format or, if several paragraphs are concerned, select them, without forgetting the paragraph markers. Copy character formatting by selecting the characters you want to format.

❑ *When you double-click the tool button, you can select several destination paragraphs for the formatting. Simply press Esc to leave the process.*

Copying Excel data to Word

♦ Open Excel then the workbook that contains the data you want to copy.

♦ Select the data in question.

♦ Use Excel's **Edit - Copy** command, tool button or Ctrl **C** shortcut key.

♦ If necessary, open Word and the destination document for the Excel data. If the Word document is already open, click its button on the task bar.

♦ Place the insertion point where you want to paste the data.

♦ **Edit Paste**  ♦ Ctrl **V**

You can also click the appropriate item in the **Clipboard** *task pane.*

♦ Click the **Paste Options** button under the pasted data and choose one of the options:

MEXICO	Jan	Feb	Mar	Apr	May
Maximum temperature	24.5	25	26.5	28	29.5
Minimum temperature	15	15	17	19.5	21.5
Average temperature	19.75	20	21.75	23.75	25.5

Keep Source Formatting
Match Destination Table Style
Keep Text Only
Keep Source Formatting and Link to Excel
Match Destination Table Style and Link to Excel
Apply Style or Formatting...

Keep Source Formatting: conserves the formatting applied to the Excel cells (such as borders and width).

Match Destination Table Style: to display the pasted data in a Word table; the formatting applied to the Excel cells is lost.

Keep Text Only: if you only want to keep the text. The data are not shown as a table and each item of data is separated by a tab.

Keep Source Formatting and Link to Excel: to keep the original formatting of the Excel cells and create a link: all changes (formatting or data) made to the source data in Excel are instantly applied to the linked data in Word.

Match Destination Table Style and Link to Excel: to display the data as a table in Word and create a link: all changes made to the source data in Excel are immediately applied to the linked data in Word.

Apply Style or Formatting: opens the **Styles and Formatting** task pane so that you can choose a style or formatting for the data from the **Pick formatting to apply** list.

❑ *If you are copying an object, such as a graph and you use the* ***Edit - Paste*** *command (or* *or* Ctrl *V) to paste the object in to Word, the object is pasted without a link and the button does not appear. Should you wish to paste the item with a link to the source application (Excel) from Word, use the* ***Edit - Paste Special*** *command, choose* ***Paste link*** *and click* ***OK****. This technique can also be used to create a link whilst copying data.*

Copying Excel data into Word as a hyperlink

This function creates a hyperlink in a Word document. The link targets one–or more cells from an Excel workbook. This cannot be a new workbook you are in the process of creating: it must have been saved on the disk.

♦ Open the Excel application then the workbook containing the data to be copied.

♦ Select the Excel cell(s) whose content will make up the hyperlink (a table name, a column heading etc).

However much of the worksheet you select, it will all be represented by a single hyperlink.

♦ Use Excel's **Edit - Copy** command, tool button or Ctrl **C** shortcut key.

♦ Open the Word application then the document into which the data is to be copied; if the Word document is already open, click the appropriate button on the task bar.

♦ Click the place where you want to insert the hyperlink.

♦ **Edit**
Paste as Hyperlink

The data appear as a hyperlink, with the text underlined. Ctrl-clicking the hyperlink will open the source document in Excel. Pointing to the hyperlink will display a ScreenTip naming the file to which the link refers.

Inserting an Excel object into Word

You can use this technique to construct a table using Excel.

♦ Click the place where you want to insert the object.

♦ Click the tool button, select the number of columns and rows and release the mouse button.

A worksheet appears in a rectangle with a hatched border. The Excel menus and toolbars replace those from Word.

♦ Create the table using the options and tools of the server application, Excel.

	A	B	C
1	Member	Fee	Paid?
2	Williams, P.	12.00	Y
3	Hatcher, G.	15.50	Y
4	Ferguson, J.	12.00	Y
5	Peters, J.	12.00	N
6	Watson, K.	12.00	Y
7	Fryer, L.	15.50	N
8			

Sheet1

- To view the spreadsheet in Word, click the Word document.
- To modify the spreadsheet, double-click the embedded object.
- Save then close the document.

❑ *To edit an Excel object when Excel is not installed on your computer, select the object and use **Edit - Worksheet Object - Convert** then choose a file format supported by one of the applications you have.*

*You can also click the object and use the **Edit - Worksheet Object** command and choose **Open** to edit the object directly in Microsoft Excel. Alternatively, choose **Edit** if you want to make the changes in Word.*

Personal notes

Printing a document

♦ Click the tool.

The document is printed according to the current page setup options and the default options in the ***Print*** *dialog box.*

Defining options for printing

Specifying which part of the text to print

♦ **File**
Print

♦  P

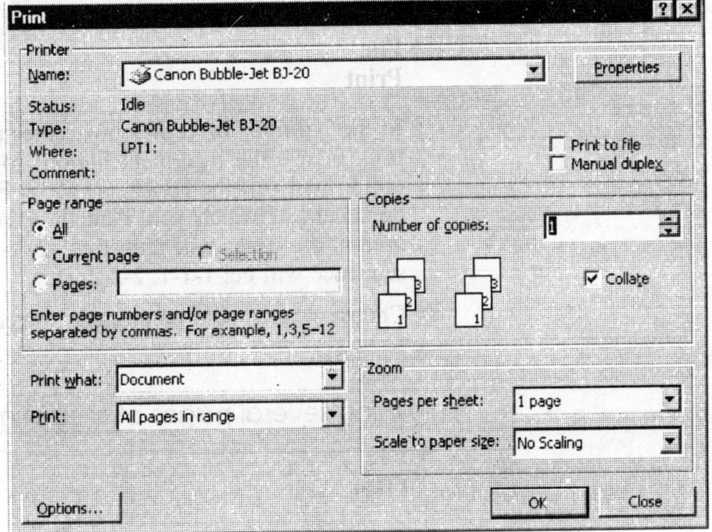

Notice that under ***Page range****, Word proposes to print* ***All*** *the document.*

♦ To print the page where the insertion point is, choose **Current page**.

♦ To print a previously selected passage, click **Selection**.

♦ To print certain pages, enter their numbers in the **Pages** box.

To print a series of consecutive pages, enter the number of the first, a dash then the number of the last (example: to print from page 5 to page 10, enter: 5-10).

If the pages are not consecutive, use commas to separate their numbers (example: to print pages 5 and 10, enter: 5,10).

♦ Click **OK**.

❑ *The* ***Manual duplex*** *option in the* ***Print*** *dialog box will print the document on both sides of a sheet of paper even if your printer is not capable of duplex printing. When Word is ready to print the second side of the sheet, a message appears to tell you to re-move the printed sheet, replace it in the feed then click* ***OK****.*

❑ *The* ***Print to file*** *option in the* ***Print*** *dialog box enables you to create a version of the document in a format that, for example, a high-resolution commercial printing machine can use.*

Printing several copies

♦ **File**
Print

♦ Ctrl P

♦ In the **Number of copies** box, enter the number of copies you want to print or use the increment buttons to choose the number. The **Collate** option will sort the copies properly. For example, you have a two-page document of which you want three copies. If you activate the **Collate** option, the pages will print as: 1-2, 1-2, 1-2. If it is not active, the print sequence will be: 1-1-1, 2-2-2, etc.

♦ Choose what should be printed, if necessary.

♦ Click **OK.**

Printing several pages of a document on each sheet

♦ **File**
Print

♦  P

♦ In the **Zoom** frame, open the **Pages per sheet** list and indicate how many pages of the document to print on each sheet.

♦ If the scale of your document needs adjusting open the **Scale to paper size** list and choose the paper format you are using. Word will increase or decrease the size of the fonts and graphics to fit the number of pages you chose onto one sheet of the format you choose here.

♦ If need be, choose what you want to print.

♦ Click **OK.**

Changing the page orientation

♦ Select the text in question or place the insertion point at the beginning of the section in question.

♦ **File**
Page Setup

♦ Click the **Margins** tab, if necessary.

♦ Click the **Orientation** you want: **Portrait** or **Landscape.**

*The page's orientation changes in the **Preview** frame.*

♦ Use the **Apply to** drop-down list to choose the text concerned:

Whole document applies the page setup to all the sections of the document.

Selected text inserts a section break before and after the selection.

This point forward inserts a section break before the insertion point.

Selected sections applies the formatting to all the selected sections.

This section applies the page setup to the section that contains the insertion point.

These choices are never all available at once.

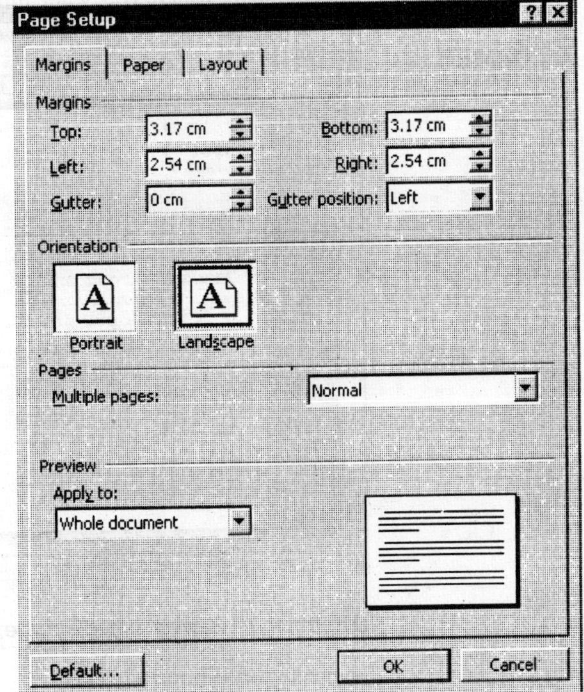

♦ Click **OK**.

❑ *When you change the page orientation, Word applies the values of the top and bottom margins to the left and right ones and vice versa.*

Making use of the print preview

Displaying a print preview

♦ **File**
Print Preview 

♦  Ctrl F2 or Ctrl Alt I

An image of the document appears as Word would print it. The percentage of magnification (zoom) applied to the page is visible on the toolbar. On the status bar, Word indicates which page you are viewing.

♦ To see another page, use the scroll bar, or the keys Pg Up and Pg Dn.

Viewing several pages at once

♦ Once in print preview, click [Multiple Pages].

♦ Drag to indicate the number of pages you wish to see and how they should be arranged.

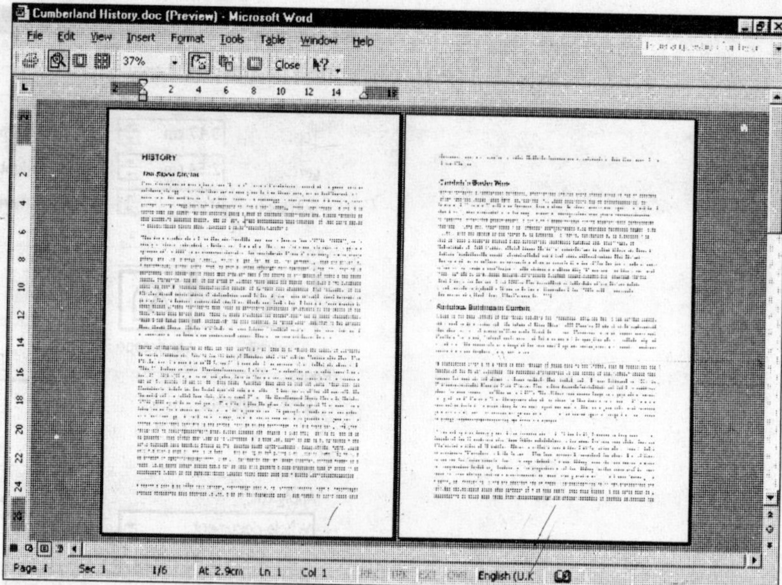

❑ *To return to viewing a single page, click* [One Page].

Zooming in on a preview

♦ Point to the part of the text you wish to see close up.

The mouse pointer takes on the form of a magnifying glass containing a + sign. This indicates that the current presentation is smaller than actual size.

♦ Click the text.

The passage is presented at 100 % zoom and the + sign in the magnifying glass is replaced by a -.

♦ To return to the scaled-down presentation, click the document again.

❑ *To decrease or increase the zoom of the current document, you can also change the value in the* ***Zoom*** *list on the* ***Standard*** *toolbar.*

Working in the preview

You can work in the preview as if you were in ***Normal*** *or* ***Print Layout*** *view.*

♦ Deactivate the tool button.

The insertion point flashes in the page. ***Magnifier*** *mode is inactive and replaced by* ***Insertion*** *mode.*

♦ Make the necessary changes (such as entering text, formatting, inserting a table).

♦ Return to **Magnifier** mode by clicking the tool button again.

Adjusting the length of a printed document

If there are just a few lines of text on the last page of a document, you may prefer Word to adjust the layout so that all the text fits into the previous pages.

♦ Click in the print preview.

Displaying the rulers in print preview

♦ Click in the preview.

Modifying the margins from within print preview

♦ Once in print preview, display the rulers.

♦ Drag the marker along the ruler until it indicates the margin width you require.

Printing from within print preview

♦ Once in print preview, click .

Returning to the workspace

♦ Click the **Close** button or press Esc.

Changing the margins of a document

♦ Select the text concerned, or position the insertion point towards the top of the passage.

♦ **File**
Page Setup

♦ Activate the **Margins** tab, if necessary.

*By default, Word leaves a **Gutter** (margin for binding) of 0 cm and allows you to choose the **Gutter position**. For a document in which both sides of each page are printed, the **Left** and right margins, (or **Top** and bottom) alternately are next to the binding.*

♦ If you want to adjust the margins for printing on both sides of the paper, open the **Multiple pages** list and choose **Mirror margins.**

***Inside** corresponds to the right margin of an even-numbered page (or left margin of an add-numbered one) and **Outside** to the right margin of an odd-numbered page (or left margin of an even-numbered one).*

♦ If the page format is smaller than the paper format used for printing and you want to print several pages on one sheet of paper, open the **Multiple pages** list and choose **2 pages per sheet.**

♦ Modify the margins as you require.

Remember to respect the minimum margins demanded by your printer.

♦ Use the **Apply to** list to choose the part of the document for which the margins need to change:

Whole document	applies this page setup to all sections of the document.
Selected text	inserts a section break before and after the selected text.
This point forward	inserts a section break before the insertion point.
Selected sections	applies this page setup to all sections selected.
This section	applies this page setup to the section that contains the insertion point.

These choices are never all available at the same time.

♦ Click **OK.**

*In **Print Layout** view, the margins can be altered by moving the corresponding markers along the horizontal and vertical rulers. In this case, the new margin format applies to the section containing the insertion point.*

Printing an envelope

- If the delivery address is already entered, select it.
- **Tools**
  Letters and Mailings
  Envelopes and Labels
- If necessary, activate the **Envelopes** tab.

*If you made a selection before opening the dialog box, the selected text appears in the **Delivery address** box.*

*If, when you installed the program, you entered address information, Word shows this information in the **Return address** box. You can see this information (and edit it if you need to) in the **Mailing address** box in the **Options** dialog box (**Tools - Options - User Information** tab).*

- If the **Delivery address** has not already been selected, enter it here.
- If you do not need the return address to appear, check the **Omit** box.
- Otherwise, enter an address under **Return address.**

You can use the [button] button to insert an address from your e-mail address book, if you have one.

- Click the **Options** button.
- Under the **Envelope Options** tab:
  - enter the **Envelope size,**
  - define the details of presentation for the addresses.

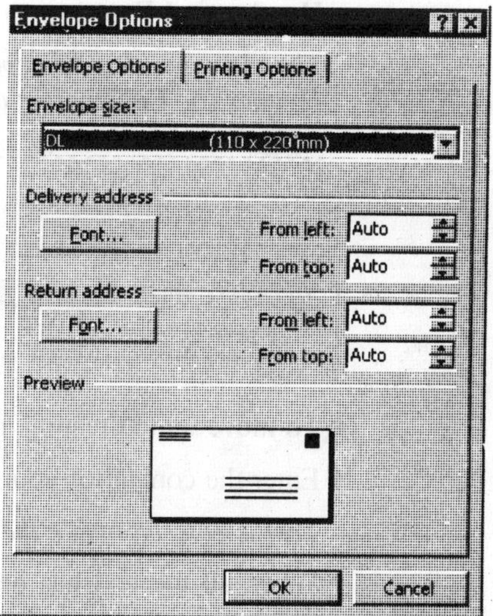

♦ In the **Printing Options** tab, choose:

– the **Feed method**: the way in which the envelope should be placed in the printer's paper tray.

– the **Feed from** option: which tray is used to place the envelope in the printer.

♦ Click **OK.**

♦ Choose whether to **Print** the envelope straight away or to **Add to Document.**

If you have modified the return address, Word prompts you to save.

♦ Click **Yes** if you wish the address entered to become the address by default, or click **No.**

When an envelope is added to a document, it is inserted at the top of the document as a new section; the double dotted line is visible underneath it on the screen. The new page created for the section is numbered 0.

Managing headers and footers

Headers and footers are lines of text appearing, respectively, in the upper and lower margins of a document.

Creating identical headers/footers for all the document

♦ Position the insertion point at the beginning of the document.

♦ **View**
Header and Footer

*The document text becomes grey. The insertion point flashes in the **Header** (or **Footer**) box and the **Header and Footer** toolbar appears.*

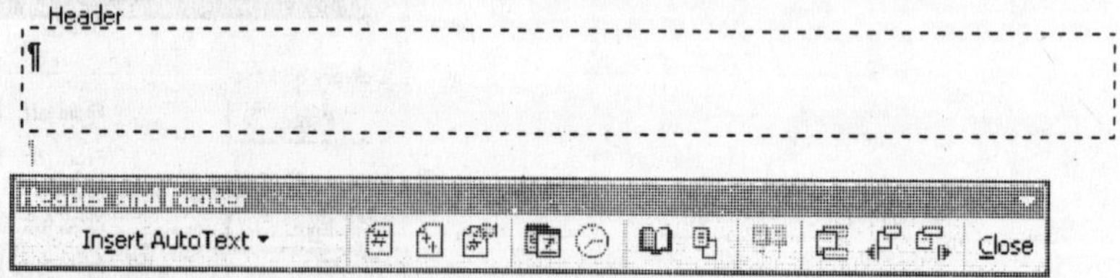

♦ To move on to creating a footer, and back again, click [icon].

♦ Enter the content of your header/footer and format it as you require.

Text is entered inside the dashed box.

♦ When all the text has been entered click the **Close** button of the **Header and Footer** toolbar.

❑ *Headers and footers are only visible on the screen when the document is displayed in Print Layout view, or in Print Preview.*

❑ *Unless otherwise specified, headers are printed 1.25 cm from the top of the sheet, and footers 1.25 cm from the bottom (**File - Page Setup - Layout** tab).*

❑ *If the upper and lower margins cannot contain the header/ footer, Word modifies them.*

Inserting variable data

♦ While creating or modifying the header or footer, click one of the following tools on the **Header and Footer** toolbar, to insert:

 page numbers.

 the total number of pages.

 the computer's control date.

 the current time, as set in the computer.

*You can also click one of the options from the **Insert AutoText** list on the **Header and Footer** toolbar.*

Defining the header/footer for the first page

♦ Position the insertion point at the beginning of the document.

♦ **View**
Header and Footer

♦ Click [icon].

♦ If necessary, activate the **Layout** tab.

♦ In the **Headers and Footers** box, activate the choice **Different first page.**

♦ Click **OK.**

♦ Define the header/footer for the first page.

♦ Click **Close** to finish.

Using different headers/footers for odd/even pages

♦ Place the insertion point anywhere in the document.

♦ **View**
Header and Footer

♦ Click [icon].

♦ In the **Layout** tab, activate the choice **Different odd and even.**

♦ Click **OK.**

♦ Enter the header/footer of the even-numbered pages, then click [icon] to enter the header/footer for the odd-numbered pages.

♦ Confirm your changes by clicking **Close.**

Creating several headers/footers

♦ Place the insertion point at the beginning of the section in which you want to use different headers and/or footers.

♦ **View**
Header and Footer

♦ Click the [icon] tool button to break the link between the previous headers and the current and following headers.

♦ Create the new header or footer.

The [icon] *and* [icon] *tool buttons can be used to go to the previous and next header or footer.*

♦ Finish your changes by clicking **Close.**

Numbering the pages in a document

Word has two methods for numbering the pages in a document.

First method

♦ Click anywhere in the document.

♦ **Insert**
Page Numbers

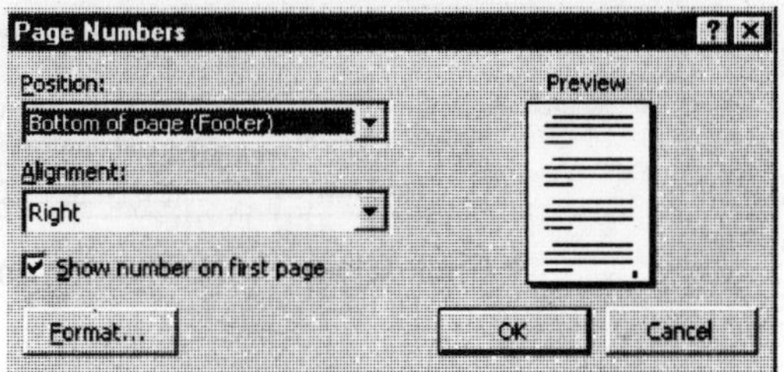

- Choose the **Position** of the page numbers from the corresponding list: **Top of page (Header)** or **Bottom of page (Footer)**.
- Select the option for the **Alignment** you want from the corresponding list:

Left	to align all the page numbers with the left margin.
Center	to centre the numbers between the left and right margins.
Right	to align all the page numbers with the right margin.
Inside	for odd page numbers to be aligned with the left margin and even ones with the right margin.
Outside	for odd page numbers to be aligned with the right margin and even ones with the left margin.

- Deactivate the **Show number on first page** option if you do not want a page number on the first page of your document.

  If this option is deactivated, Word does not print anything on the first page and prints the number 2 on the second page.

- Click **OK**.

Second method

This method involves creating a header/footer. This method allows you to add text to the page number (e.g. Page 1).

- You need to be creating or editing a header or footer (**View - Header and Footer**).
- Click the button on the **Header and Footer** toolbar to insert page numbers.
- Click to insert the total number of pages in the document.
- If you want to type a text to accompany the page number.
- If need be, format the page number and accompanying text.

♦ Click **Close** on the **Header and Footer** toolbar.

Changing the format of the page numbers

♦ If the document has several sections, place the insertion point in the first section where you are going to use the new number format. The new format will apply to the section containing the insertion point and to all the following sections.

♦ Use **View - Header and Footer** and click the button on the **Header and Footer** toolbar or use **Insert - Page Numbers** and click the **Format** button.

♦ Select the appearance of the numbers in the **Format** list.

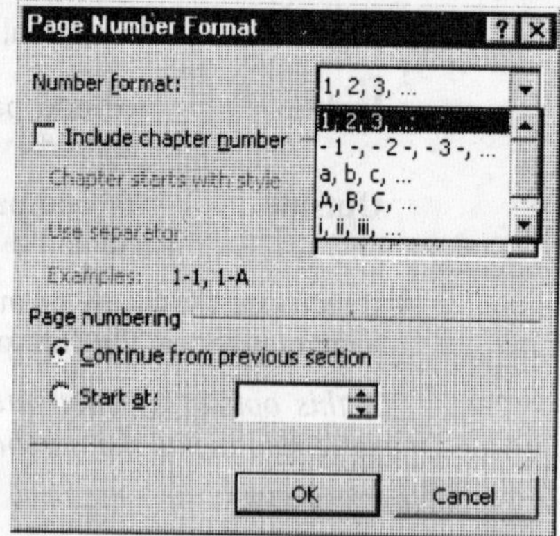

♦ If you do not want the page numbers of the current section (and any subsequent sections) to follow on from the numbers used in the previous section, activate the **Start at** option and enter a new starting value in the text box.

♦ Click **OK** then, if need be, **Close**.

Formatting characters

Characters can be put into bold type, italics, etc.

♦ If you have already entered the characters concerned, select them.

♦ Click one or more of the buttons on the **Formatting** bar to apply the attribute you require:

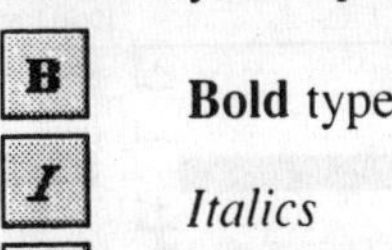

Bold type

Italics

Underlined

The selected characters take on the chosen format and the button of the active tool has a blue border.

♦ To deactivate an attribute, click its button again.

♦ If you have already entered the characters concerned select them.

♦ Use the following key combinations to apply the attributes you require:

Keys	Attribute
Ctrl B	**Bold**
Ctrl I	*Italic*
Ctrl U	Underlined
Ctrl Shift D	Double Underlined
Ctrl Shift W	Words only Underlined
Ctrl Shift K	SMALL CAPITALS
Ctrl Shift A	CAPITALS
Ctrl Shift +	in Superscript
Ctrl =	in Subscript
Ctrl Shift H	Hidden text

❑ *To put characters into superscript, you must use the + key on the main (alphanumerical) keyboard.*

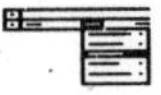

♦ If the characters have already been entered, select them.

♦ **Format**
Font

♦ Ctrl D

♦ If necessary, activate the **Font** tab.

♦ Make your choice from the **Font style** and **Underline style** list boxes and the **Effects** frame.

*In the **Preview** box, Word shows the text selected in the format chosen.*

Font

Font | Character Spacing | Text Effects

Font: Impact
Haettenschweiler
Helvetica
Helvetica-Narrow
Impact
Lucida Console

Font style: Bold Italic
Regular
Italic
Bold
Bold Italic

Size: 12
8
9
10
11
12

Font color: Automatic
Underline style: (none)
Underline color: Automatic

Effects
Strikethrough
Double strikethrough
Superscript
Subscript
Shadow
Outline
Emboss
Engrave
Small caps
All caps
Hidden

Preview
MORE THAN MEETS THE EYE

This font style is imitated for display. The closest matching style will be printed.

Default... OK Cancel

The illustration below shows the result of each effect:

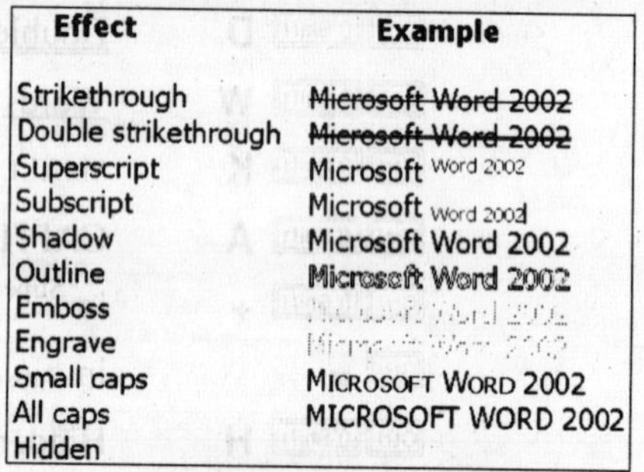

Effect	Example
Strikethrough	~~Microsoft Word 2002~~
Double strikethrough	~~Microsoft Word 2002~~
Superscript	Microsoft Word 2002
Subscript	Microsoft Word 2002
Shadow	Microsoft Word 2002
Outline	Microsoft Word 2002
Emboss	Microsoft Word 2002
Engrave	Microsoft Word 2002
Small caps	MICROSOFT WORD 2002
All caps	MICROSOFT WORD 2002
Hidden	

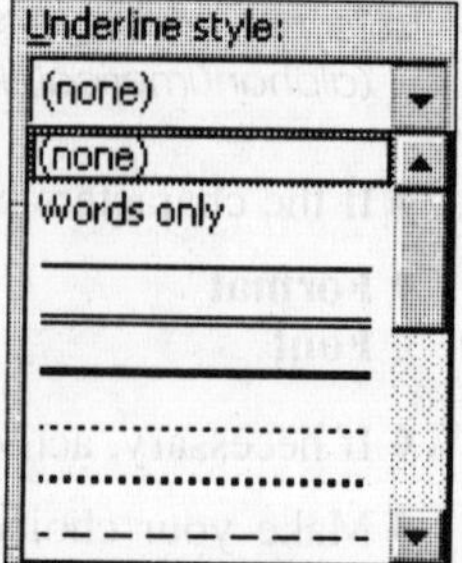

*The **Underline Style** list offers several possibilities.*

♦ Click **OK**.

❑ *You can activate the character format before you start to type. In this case, the new characters you type automatically take the format you have activated.*

❑ *To undo all the character formatting, select the characters in question and press* Ctrl space *or* Ctrl ⇧Shift **Z** *or click the* ***Clear Formatting*** *choice in the* ***Pick formatting to apply*** *list in the* ***Styles and Formatting*** *task pane. You can undo just one format by selecting the characters in question and deactivating the tool for the formatting you want to remove.*

❑ *Each different character format is stored in the* ***Pick formatting to apply*** *list in the* ***Styles and Formatting*** *Task pane. You can use this list to apply formatting to other characters in the document (see the FORMATTING chapter).*

Changing the character font/size

♦ If the text has already been typed, select the characters.

♦ Open the **Font** or **Font Size** list (in points) on the **Formatting** toolbar.

Word lists the fonts or sizes available for the characters you have chosen:

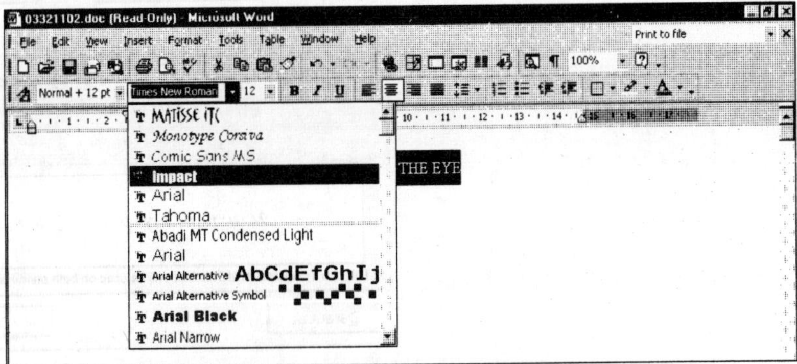

At the top of the list, Word shows the last 10 fonts used.

♦ Click the font or size you want.

You can also change the font and/or size of the characters using the ***Font*** *and* ***Size*** *lists in the* ***Font*** *dialog box (****Format - Font - Font*** *tab).*

Modifying the space between characters

- If necessary, select the characters concerned.
- **Format**
  Font

- Activate the **Character Spacing** tab then open the **Spacing** list.
- Activate the spacing you require:

  Expanded more space between characters.

  Condensed less space between characters.
- If need be, in the **By** box, enter the value (number of points) for the character spacing, or select it using the increment buttons.

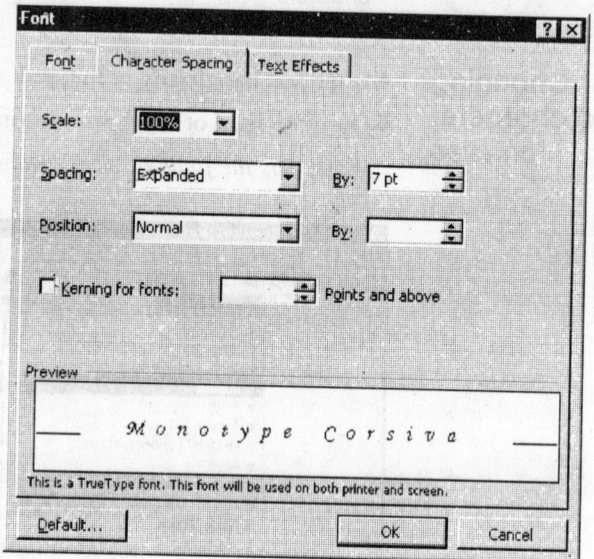

- Click **OK**.

Colouring or highlighting characters

- Select the characters concerned.
- Open the appropriate list by clicking its down arrow:

  to change the colour of the characters.

  to highlight them with a band of colour.
- Click the colour you prefer.

> *To apply the last colour selected, simply click the tool button [A] or [pen] without opening the list.*

Applying an animation effect

- Select the characters concerned.
- **Format** — Ctrl D
  Font
  Text Effects tab
- Choose the effect you require from the **Animations** list.

  *You can see the effect of the animation in the **Preview** box.*
- Click **OK**.

  An animation effect can be viewed but not printed. Animation effects are generally used in Web pages.

Applying a border to characters

- If necessary, select the characters you want to surround with a border.
- If need be, open the **Tables and Borders** toolbar by clicking the button.

  *If you are working in **Normal** view and you click the tool button, Word switches to **Print Layout** view automatically.*
- Open the list on the tool and choose the line style you want for the border.
- Open the list on the ½ tool and click the thickness you want.
- Click the border colour you want in the list on the tool button.

  *Click this tool button to open the **Borders and Shading** dialog box.*
- Click the tool button to apply an external border to the selected text. If this tool shows a different border type (top or right border, for example), open the list on the tool button and click .

❑ *If you do not open the list on the tool button but simply click it, the border visible on the tool is applied.*

Changing the standard presentation of characters

You can change the default font, style, attributes, spacing, etc.

♦ Whatever the position of the insertion point, define the new standard presentation in the **Font** dialog box (**Format - Font** or Ctrl **D**).

♦ Click the **Default** button:

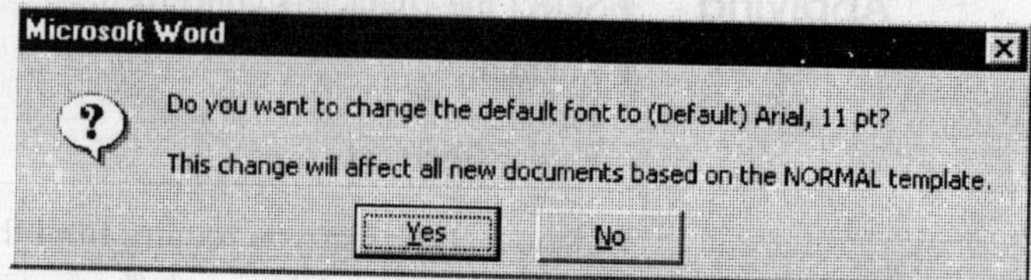

Word displays the choice just made, and reminds you that, if you go ahead, the template on which the document is based will be modified.

♦ Confirm by the **Yes** button.

All characters adopt the new standard presentation (except those to which you had already applied a specific font or style, etc).

Personal notes

Setting a tab stop

When you change the paragraph formatting options, the new options apply to the current paragraph or to the paragraphs selected when the changes were made. If you want to change the formatting of all paragraphs with a particular style, it is the style itself that you should modify (cf. STYLES).

Tabs are used for aligning text in various ways. If you set a tab stop then press the ⇄ *key before you type the text (or in front of an existing line of text) the text aligns itself with the tab stop.*

Here are examples of the effects produced with different types of tab stop:

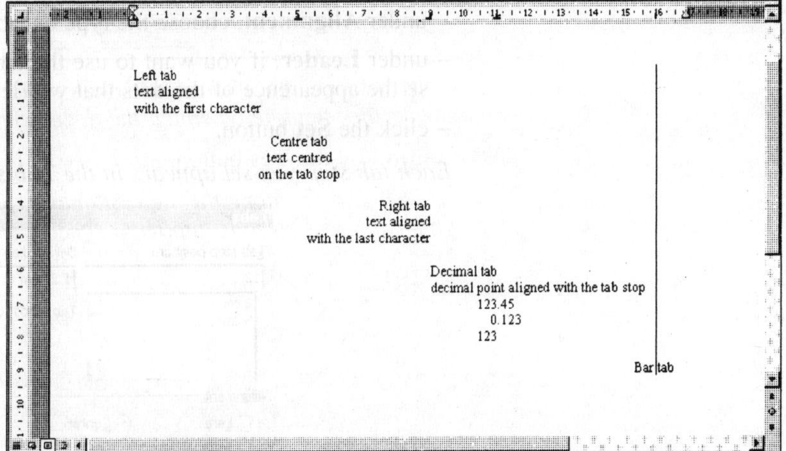

When you create a new document, the tab stops are set every 1.27 cm by default.

♦ Select the paragraphs concerned, or position the insertion point inside the paragraph.

♦ Activate the type of tab required, by clicking once or several times on the button to the left of the ruler:

- left tab
- centre tab
- right tab
- decimal tab
- bar tab (draws a bar on the screen wherever the tab stop is placed).

♦ Click the mark on the ruler corresponding to the position you intend for the tab.

The tab stop appears on the ruler.

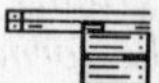

♦ Select the paragraphs concerned or place the insertion point in the paragraph.

♦ **Format**
Tabs

♦ For each tab you wish to set:

– enter the **Tab stop position** in the corresponding text box,

– under **Alignment**, choose the type of tab you require,

– under **Leader**, if you want to use the tab to insert a dotted line, choose the appearence of the dots that will lead up to the tab stop,

– click the **Set** button.

Each tab stop you set appears in the ***Tab stop position*** *list.*

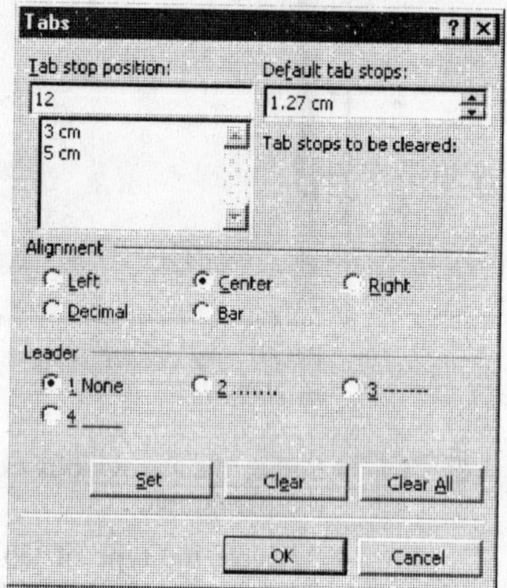

♦ Once you have finished setting tab stops, click **OK**.

You can see the markers for the tab stops on the ruler.

The ruler shows the tab stops for the active paragraph.

❑ *Custom tab stops override all Word's tab stops placed before their position.*

❑ *To change the interval between each default tab stop, change the value in the* ***Default tab stops*** *box in the* ***Tabs*** *dialog box (****Format - Tabs****).*

Once a custom tab is displayed on the ruler, just double-click it to activate the ***Tabs*** *dialog box from the* ***Format*** *menu.*

Managing existing tabs

♦ To move a tab stop, drag its marker to a new position.

♦ To delete a tab stop, drag its marker right off the ruler.

As soon as the marker has crossed the top or bottom line of the ruler, it disappears.

> *If all the custom tab stops are to be deleted, the quickest way to do this is to open the* ***Tabs*** *dialog box (****Format - Tabs****) and click the* ***Clear All*** *button.*

Setting tab stops with leader lines

A leader line is a dotted line inserted in front of the tab stop with which it is associated.

♦ Select the paragraphs concerned or place the insertion point in the paragraph.

♦ **Format**
Tabs

♦ In the **Tab stop position** box, give the position of the new tab stop or select an existing tab stop that is to have a leader line.

♦ Activate the option **Alignment** that corresponds to types of tab stop you want.

♦ Under **Leader**, click the option that corresponds to the type of dotted line you want.

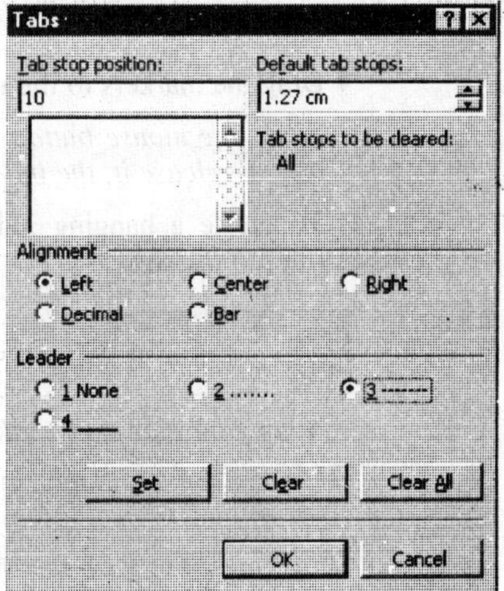

♦ Click **Set**.

♦ If need be, set more tab stops.

♦ Click **OK** when you have finished.

Indentation of paragraphs

These examples show the effect of the four types of indent proposed on the presentation of paragraphs:

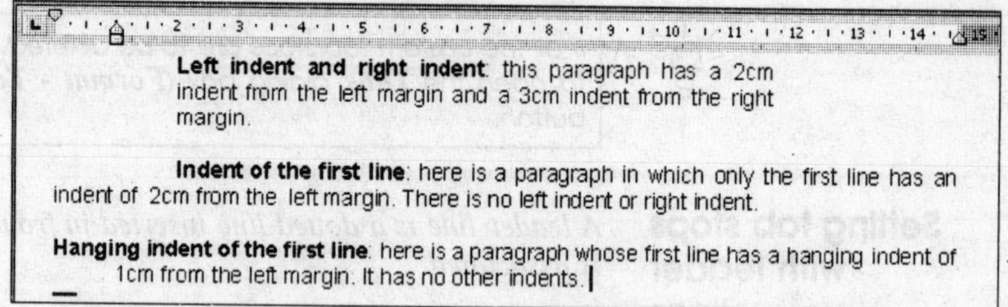

♦ Select the paragraphs concerned, or place the insertion point in the paragraph.

On the ruler there are four indentation markers, corresponding to the four types of indent:

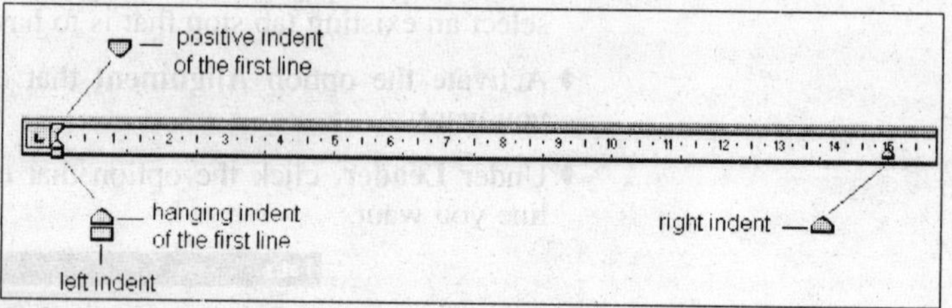

♦ Drag the markers to the required position.

While the mouse button is held down, you see a vertical line; as soon as you release it, the indent you have defined is taken into account.

♦ To create a hanging indent, move the hanging indent marker on the ruler to the right.

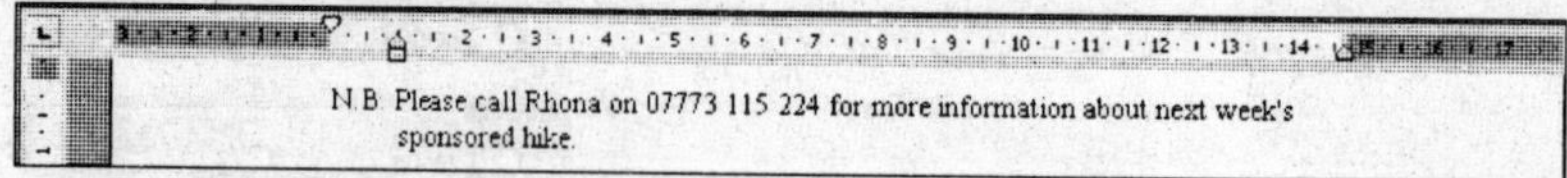

A hanging indent gives this sort of presentation.

❑ *Moving the left indent marker also moves the right and hanging indent markers.*

❑ *If you want to type text in the left margin and make paragraphs appear there without changing the document's margins, drag the left indent marker to the left.*

❑ *If you want to make a hanging or positive first line indent, you can also click several times on the [L] button on the left of the ruler until the [▽] button (first line indent) or [⊔] button (hanging ident) appears. Once the correct button is displayed, click the position on the ruler where you want to set the indent.*

> *The [button] and [button] buttons on the **Formatting** toolbar can also be used to move the left indent to the next tab stop, or the preceding one.*

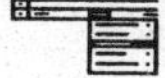

♦ Select the paragraphs in question or place the insertion point in the paragraph.

♦ If the text is already entered, select it.

♦ **Format**
Paragraph
Indents and Spacing tab

Double-click one of the four indentation markers

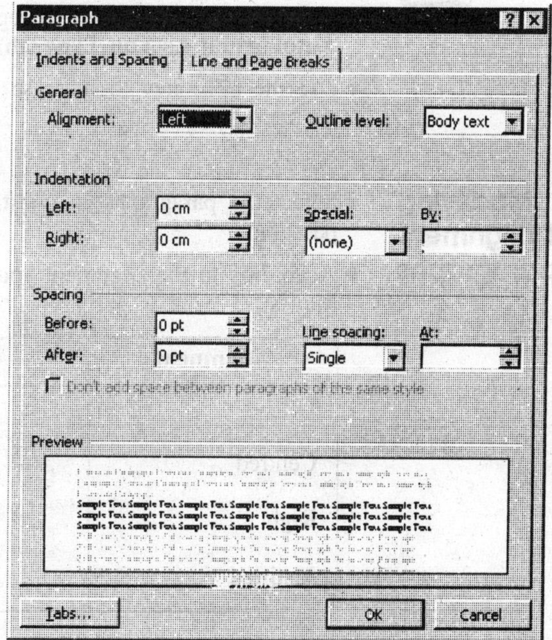

*In this dialog box, the **Indentation** frame contains options for **Left** and **Right** indents and for **First line** and **Hanging** indents (available in the **Special** list).*

♦ Using the given unit of measurement, choose the value of the indents you want to apply.

♦ To create a hanging indent, select the **Hanging** option from the **Special** list and type the indent value in the **By** box.

♦ If you only want to indent the first line, choose **First line** from the **Special** list and type the indent value in the **By** box.

♦ Click **OK**.

❑ *The default unit of measurement is the centimetre. If you want to enter a value using another unit, type the following: **pt** for points, **"** for inches, **cm** for centimetres, **mm** for millimetres or **pi** for picas.*

*To change the default unit of measurement, select the appropriate unit from the **Measurement units** list in the **Options** dialog box (**Tools - Options - General** tab). The document's ruler displays the unit you choose.*

♦ Activate the **Set left- and first- indent with tabs and backspaces** option in the **AutoCorrect** dialog box (**Tools - AutoCorrect Options - AutoFormat As You Type** tab).

♦ Use the [Tab] key to increase the left indent and/or the [Backspace] key to decrease it.

Modifying text alignment in paragraphs

♦ Select the paragraphs in question or place the insertion point in the paragraph.

♦ According to the alignment you require, use one of the following techniques:

Alignment	(mouse)	(keyboard)
Left	[button]	Ctrl L
Centred	[button]	Ctrl E
Right	[button]	Ctrl R
Justified	[button]	Ctrl J

❑ *These alignments can also be accessed using the **Alignment** drop-down list in the **Paragraph** dialog box (**Format - Paragraph**).*

Changing the line spacing

The line spacing is the gap between the lines of a paragraph. By default, it is calculated according to the size of the paragraph characters.

♦ Select the paragraphs concerned or place the insertion point in the paragraph.

♦ **Format** **Paragraph** **Indents and Spacing** tab	Double-click one of the four indent markers

♦ From the corresponding list, choose the **Line spacing**:

Single	the line spacing corresponds to the height of the line.
1.5 lines	the line spacing equals one and half times the height of the line.
Double	the line spacing equals the height of two lines.
At least	give the minimum line spacing value in the **At** box.
Exactly	give the fixed line spacing in the **At** box. Word will not change this value, no matter what the size of the characters.
Multiple	give the basic value you want in the **At** box. Each individual line will adapt to this tallest character.

♦ Click **OK**.

Modifying the spacing of paragraphs

You can unpack your text without having to insert blank lines, by leaving space before and/or after paragraphs.

♦ Select the paragraphs concerned or place the insertion point in the paragraph.

♦ **Format** **Paragraph** **Indents and Spacing** tab	Double-click one of the four indentation markers

♦ Under **Spacing**, define the value of space to be left **Before** and/or **After** a paragraph.

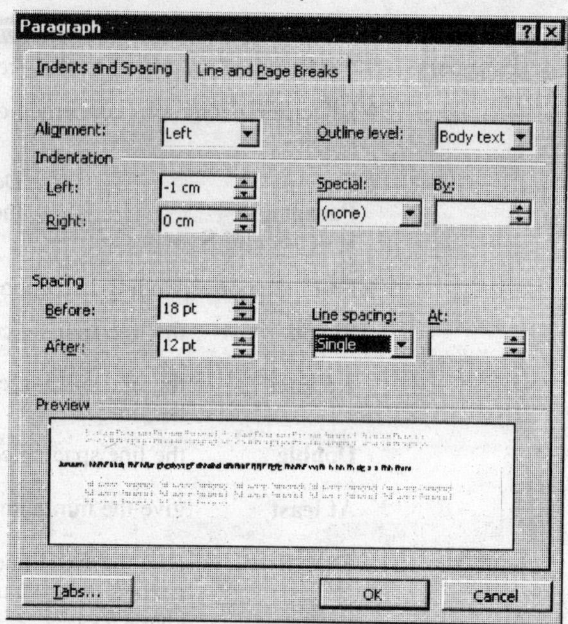

♦ Click **OK**.

❑ *By default, these text boxes propose values in points. Here too, you can use a different unit of measurement providing you indicate, after the value,* ***cm*** *for centimetres,* ***li*** *for lines,* ***"*** *for inches,* ***pi*** *for picas.*

If you prefer to work from the keyboard, press Ctrl ***0*** *(on the alphanumerical keyboard) to leave a blank line (12 pt) above each selected paragraph.*

Preventing a break within/between paragraphs

Page breaks or column breaks are often undesirable in the middle of a paragraph, or between complementary paragraphs.

♦ If the page/column break is to be avoided within a paragraph, select that paragraph; if it is to be prevented between two paragraphs, select the first; if it is to be prevented between several paragraphs, select all except the last.

♦ **Format Paragraph** — Double-click one of the four indentation markers

♦ Activate the **Line and Page Breaks** tab.

♦ To avoid a page/column break within a paragraph, activate the choice **Keep lines together**; to avoid a page/column break between paragraphs choose **Keep with next**.

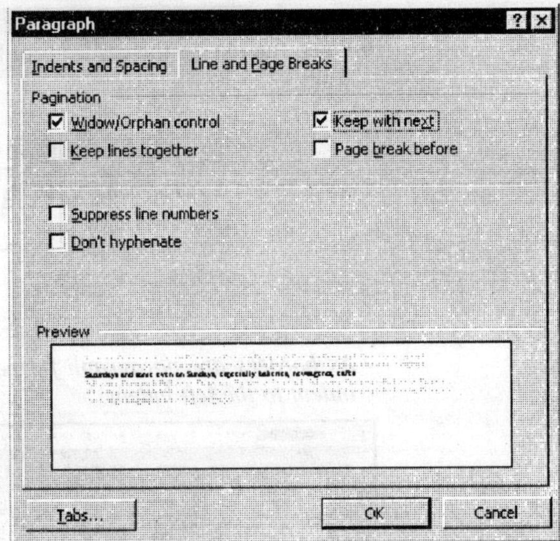

♦ Activate the **Widow/Orphan** control option to prevent the last line of a paragraph appearing at the top of a page (widowed) or the first line of a paragraph appearing alone at the bottom of a page (orphaned).

♦ Click **OK**.

Putting a border around a paragraph

♦ Click the paragraph concerned, or if there are several paragraphs, select them.

♦ Display the **Tables and Borders** toolbar by clicking [button].

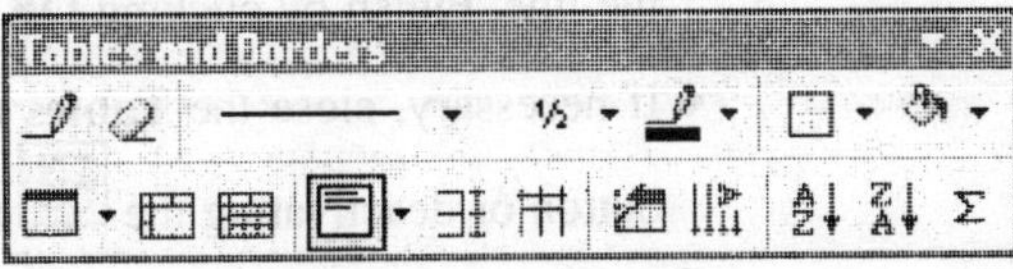

♦ Open the list on the [button] tool button and click the border style you want.

♦ Open the list on the [½ button] tool button and choose the line weight you want.

♦ Open the list on the [button] tool button and choose the colour you want for the border. Click this tool to open the **Borders and Shading** dialog box.

♦ Open the list on the [icon] tool button and click the type of border you want:

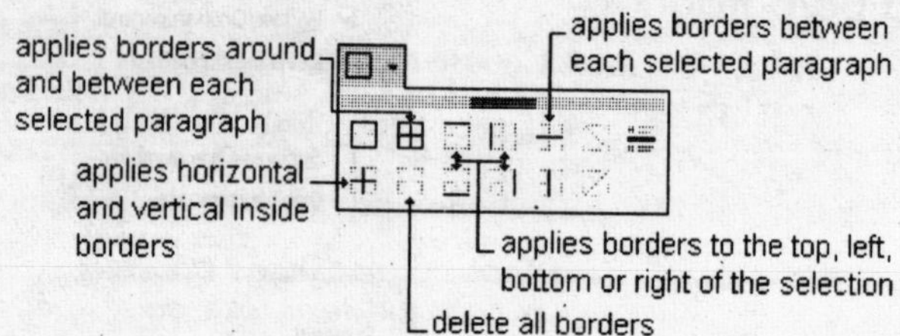

As borders are paragraph formatting, border stretches from the right indent to the left indent:

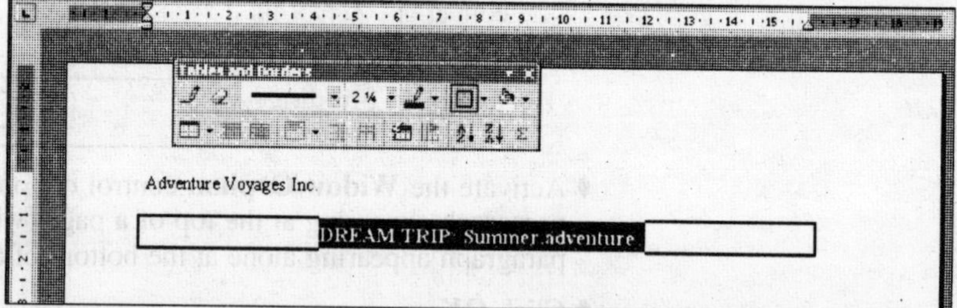

♦ To change the width of the border, change the left and/or right indents.

♦ You can define the spacing between the text and the border by using **Format - Borders and Shading** and clicking the **Borders** tab. Click the **Options** button then, in the **Top**, **Bottom**, **Left** and/or **Right** text boxes, give the values for the spacing you want between the text and the line. Finish by clicking **OK** twice.

♦ If necessary, close the **Tables and Borders** toolbar by clicking the [icon] button or deactivating the [icon] tool button.

❑ *You can also apply borders using the* ***Format - Borders and Shading*** *menu.*

❑ *The spacing between the lines and the text cannot exceed 31 points.*

Applying a background colour to a paragraph

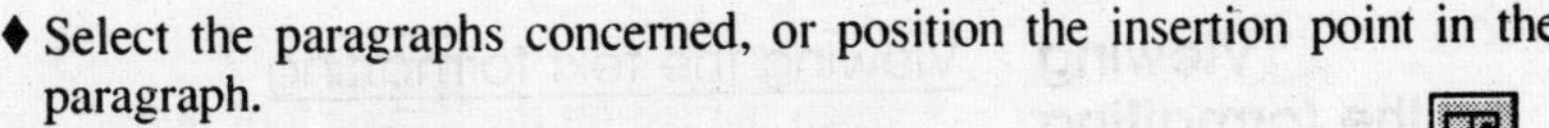

♦ Select the paragraphs concerned, or position the insertion point in the paragraph.

♦ If necessary, display the **Tables and Borders** toolbar by clicking .

♦ Choose the shading from the list.

♦ If necessary, close the **Tables and Borders** toolbar by clicking the button or deactivating the tool button.

❑ *Applying a coloured background to a paragraph tends to affect the legibility of the text: take care when choosing colours, style and the size of characters.*

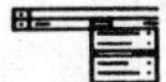

♦ Position the insertion point in the paragraph or, if several paragraphs are concerned, select them.

♦ **Format**
Borders and Shading
Shading tab

♦ In **Fill**, indicate the background colour you require.

♦ In **Style**, indicate the density of the pattern you want to apply over the fill colour.

♦ Choose a colour for the pattern from the **Color** list.

♦ Click **OK**.

Personal notes

Viewing the formatting applied to a text

Viewing the text formatting

- Open the **Reveal Formatting** task pane. Do this using **View - Task Pane**, click the ▾ button and choose **Reveal Formatting.**
- Click the paragraph whose text formatting you wish to see or select the text in question.

 *A preview of the selection appears in the **Selected text** box.*
 *The formatting details, given in the categories **Font**, **Paragraph** and **Section**, appear in the **Formatting of selected text** box in the **Reveal Formatting** task pane.*

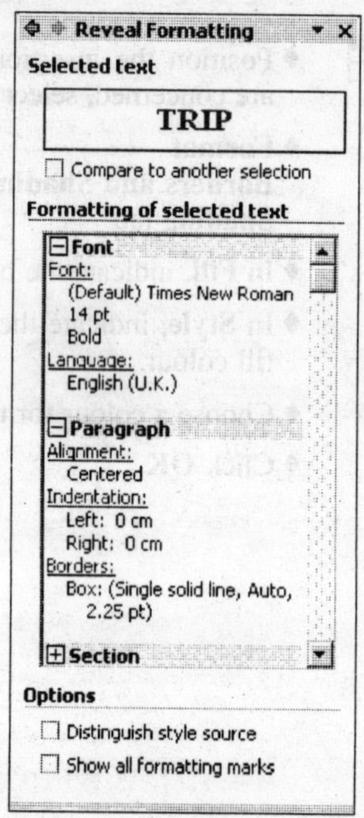

- You can expand or collapse the contents of a category (**Font, Paragraph** or **Section**) by clicking the ⊞ (expand) sign or the ⊟ (collapse) sign.
- To display the name of the style applied to the paragraph, activate the **Distinguish style source** option.
- To select all the paragraphs or text that have the same formatting as the active paragraph or selected text, point to the **Selected text** preview frame, open the associated list and choose the **Select All Text With Similar Formatting** option.

*You can also select text with similar formatting in the **Styles and Formatting** task pane (cf. Selecting all text with the same formatting below).*

♦ You select text then apply the formatting of the text to the left of the selection by pointing to the **Selected text** box, opening its list and choosing **Apply Formatting of Surrounding Text.**

♦ To remove formatting from the selected text or the active paragraph, point to the **Selected text** preview, open the associated list, and choose **Clear Formatting.**

♦ Close the **Reveal Formatting** task pane by clicking [X].

❑ *Activate the **Show all formatting marks** option in the **Reveal Formatting** task pane to show the non-printing characters (such as paragraph markers and spaces) in the document.*

Comparing the formatting of two texts

♦ Open the **Reveal Formatting** task pane using **View - Task Pane** then click the [▾] button and choose **Reveal Formatting.**

♦ Select the first of the two texts. You can also click in a paragraph if you want to compare paragraph formatting.

*You can see the formatting in the **Reveal Formatting** task pane.*

♦ Activate the **Compare to another selection** option.

*Two example frames, with identical contents, appear in the top part of the pane (in the **Selected text** box).*

♦ Select the text you want to compare or click in the paragraph if you are comparing paragraph formatting.

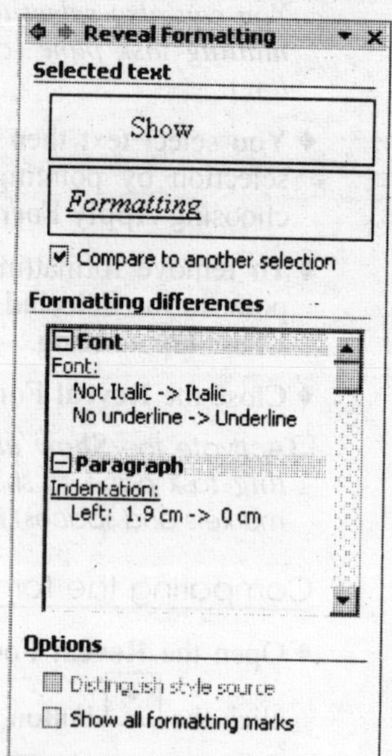

*The details of the formatting differences, by category, appear in the **Formatting differences** box. If Word does not find any formatting differences, the text **No formatting differences** appears here.*

- You can apply the formatting of the first text you selected (which can be seen in the first frame under **Selected text**) to the active selection by pointing to the second frame under **Selected text**, opening the associated list, and choosing **Apply Formatting of Original Selection.**
- When you have finished comparing the texts, deactivate the **Compare to another selection** check box then close the **Reveal Formatting** task pane by clicking its [X] button.

Applying formatting

*All character or paragraph formats are in the **Pick formatting to apply** list in the **Styles and Formatting** task pane. You can apply this formatting to other text in the document.*

- Open the **Styles and Formatting** task pane using **View - Task Pane**, clicking the [▼] button and choosing **Styles and Formatting** or by clicking the [A] tool on the **Formatting** toolbar.

*By default, the **Pick formatting to apply** list shows the document's formatting and its styles.*

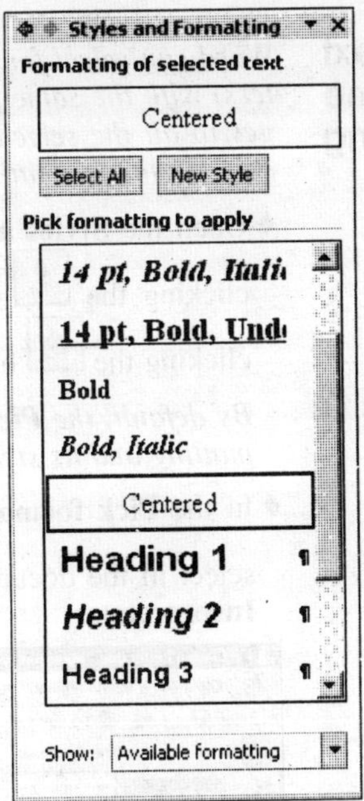

- ♦ If you only want to see the **Formatting in use**, select the corresponding option from the **Show** list at the bottom of the pane.
- ♦ Select the characters you want to format or click in the paragraph concerned. If you want to format several paragraphs, select them all. You can use the Ctrl key if you want to select several sections of text.
- ♦ In the **Pick formatting to apply** list, click the formatting you want to use.

*The formatting appears in the **Formatting of selected text** box.*

- ♦ Close the **Styles and Formatting** task pane by clicking ☒ or by clicking button on the **Formatting** toolbar to deactivate it.

❑ *If you remove formatting in the document, it disappears from the **Pick formatting to apply** list in the **Styles and Formatting** task pane.*

❑ *To remove paragraph or character formats, select the text concerned then click the **Clear Formatting** option in the **Pick Formatting to apply** list.*

Selecting all text with the same formatting

Word can select for you all the blocks of text (paragraphs and/or characters) with the same formatting attributes. This allow's you to make changes to all the selected text blocks simultaneously (as a rule, the changes concern the formatting applied).

♦ Open the **Styles and Formatting** task pane using **View - Task Pane**, clicking the button and choosing **Styles and Formatting** or by clicking the button on the **Formatting** toolbar.

*By default, the **Pick formatting to apply** list shows the document's formatting and its styles.*

♦ In the **Pick formatting to apply** list, point to the format you want to select in the document, click the button then choose **Select All n Instance(s).**

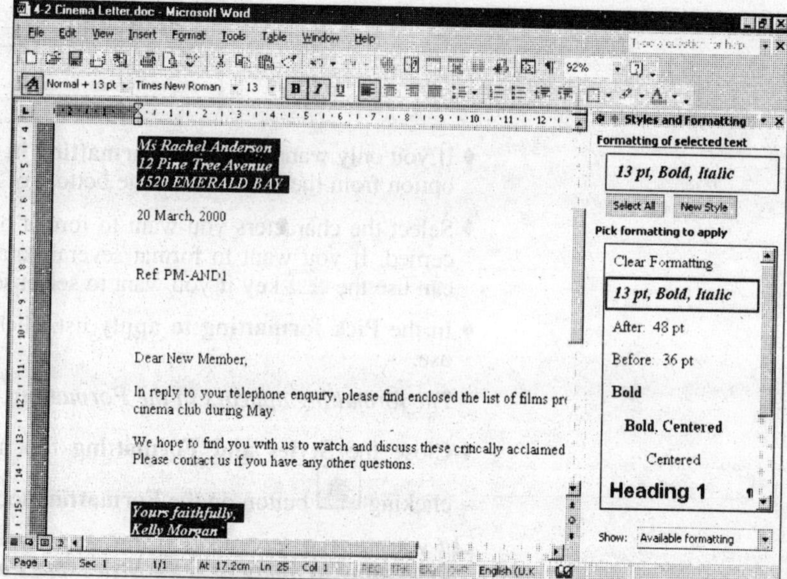

In this example, all the text in the document that is 13 points, with bold and italic formatting, has been selected.

♦ If need be, make changes to the selection's formatting or carry out other actions.

♦ Close the **Styles and Formatting** task pane by clicking or click on the button on the **Formatting** toolbar to deactivate it.

Deleting a type of formatting

♦ Open the **Styles and Formatting** task pane using **View - Task Pane**, clicking the [▾] button and choosing **Styles and Formatting** or by clicking the [A] button on the **Formatting** toolbar.

♦ In the **Pick formatting to apply** list, point to the formatting you want to delete, click the [▾] button and choose **Delete**.

A confirmation message appears.

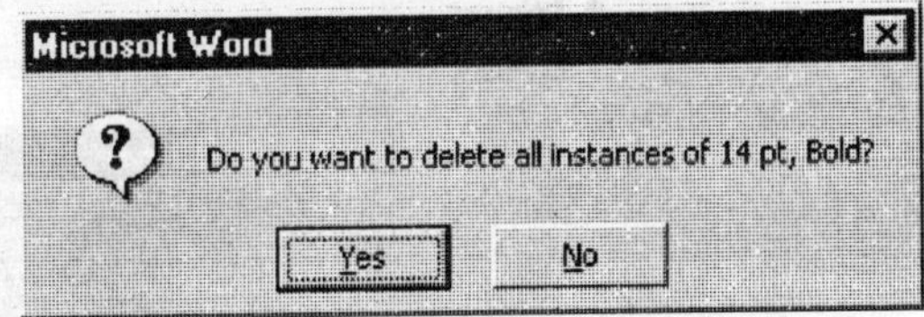

♦ Click **Yes**.

Word removes this formatting from all the text in the document to which it has been applied.

♦ Close the **Styles and Formatting** task pane by clicking [X] or by deactivating the [A] button on the **Formatting** toolbar.

. . . . *Personal notes*. . . . .

Creating and formatting a section

A section is part of a document which has a particular layout (such as columns, a different orientation, specific headers and footers and so on). Before formatting sections, you must separate them with section breaks to differentiate then.

Inserting a section break

- Place the insertion point at the beginning of the new section you wish to create.
- **Insert**
  Break

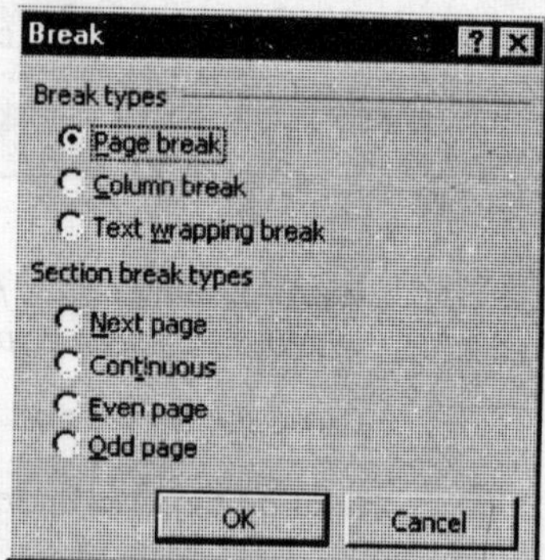

- Under **Section break types**, choose the type of separation you want between the sections:

Next page	A page break occurs between sections.
Continuous	The new section begins straight after the previous one.
Even page	Word will start to print the new section on the next even-numbered page.
Odd page	Word will start to print the new section on the next odd-numbered page.

- Click **OK**.

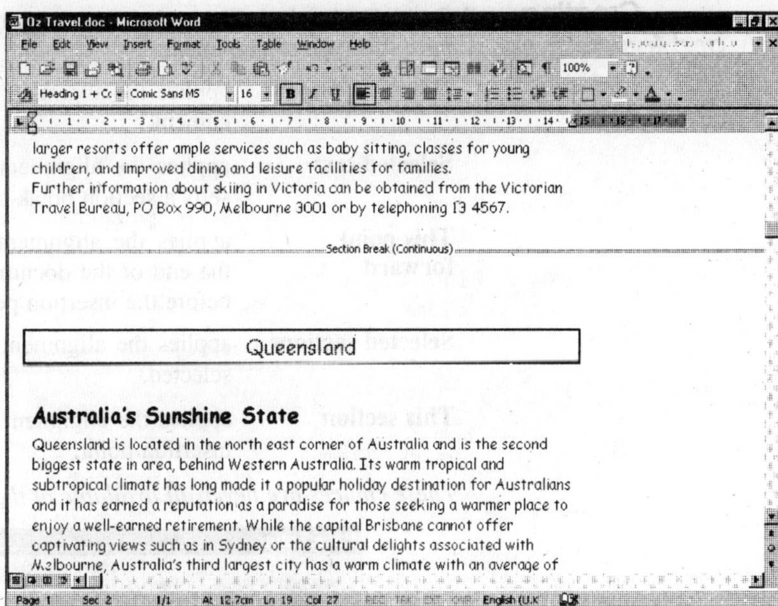

*In Normal view, Word shows the term **Section Break** followed by the type of break. The status bar gives the number of the new section (**Sec 2** in the example above).*

Formatting a section

- Place the insertion point in the section you wish to format.
- Go to the required dialog box (**Page Setup**, **Borders and Shading**, **Columns** etc) and make your presentation changes.
- In the **Apply to** list, choose **This section.**
- Click **OK.**

Aligning text vertically

- Select the text that you wish to align vertically or click the section concerned.
- **File**
  Page Setup
- Click the **Layout** tab.
- Open the **Vertical alignment** list and click one of the options: **Top**, **Center**, **Justified** (to distribute the text down the length of the page) or **Bottom.**

*The default vertical alignment is **Top**.*

♦ Open the **Apply to** list and choose which part of the document should have this type of alignment:

Whole document applies the alignment to all the sections of the document.

Selected text applies the alignment to the selected text and inserts a section break before and after the selection.

This point forward applies the alignment from the insertion point to the end of the document, inserting a section break before the insertion point.

Selected sections applies the alignment to all the sections you have selected.

This section applies the alignment to the section containing the insertion point.

These choices are never all available at the same time.

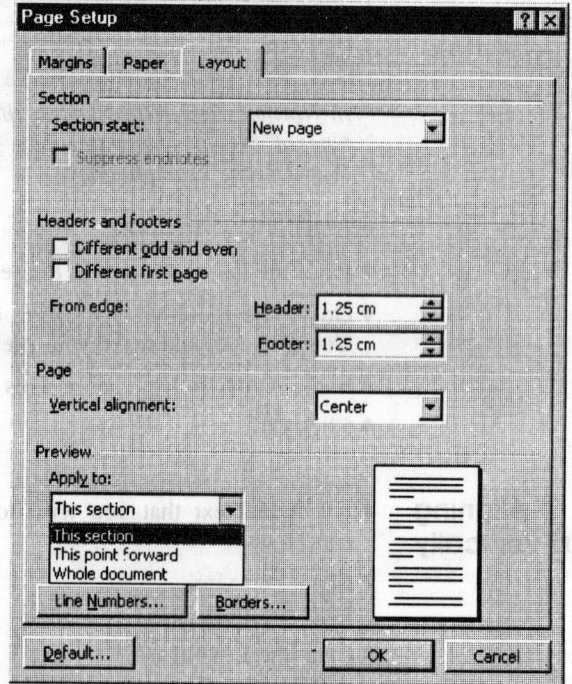

♦ Click **OK.**

Applying a border to a page

♦ Position the insertion point in the section concerned.

♦ **Format**
Borders and shading
Page Border tab

♦ Under **Setting**, choose the type of border you require: **Box, Shadow, 3-D** or **Custom.**

*The **Custom** option applies a different style of border to each side of the page.*

♦ Choose the **Style** and **Color** of the border, or if you prefer, choose a pattern from the **Art** list.

*When you open the **Art** list, you may see a message informing you that the art patterns have not been installed. If this occurs, insert the Microsoft Office XP or Word 2002 CD-ROM in the CD-ROM drive and click **OK**.*

♦ If necessary, modify the **Width** of the border.

♦ If you only wish to add borders to certain edges of the page, click on the diagram to specify where the borders should be placed.

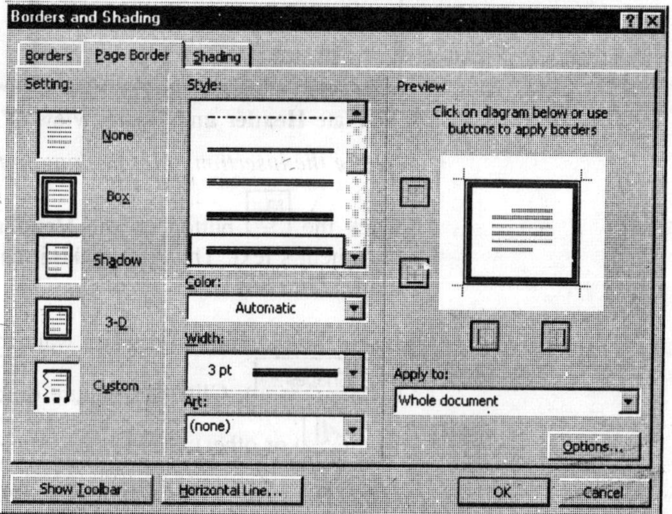

♦ In the **Apply to** list, choose the part of the document to which you want to apply the border.

*In the **Apply to** list, the **This section - First page only** option applies the border to the first page in the active section and the **This section - all except first page** option applies the border to all the pages apart from the first page.*

♦ Click **OK**.

Creating a watermark

A watermark is a drawing object which is usually printed as a background to the text on all the pages of a document.

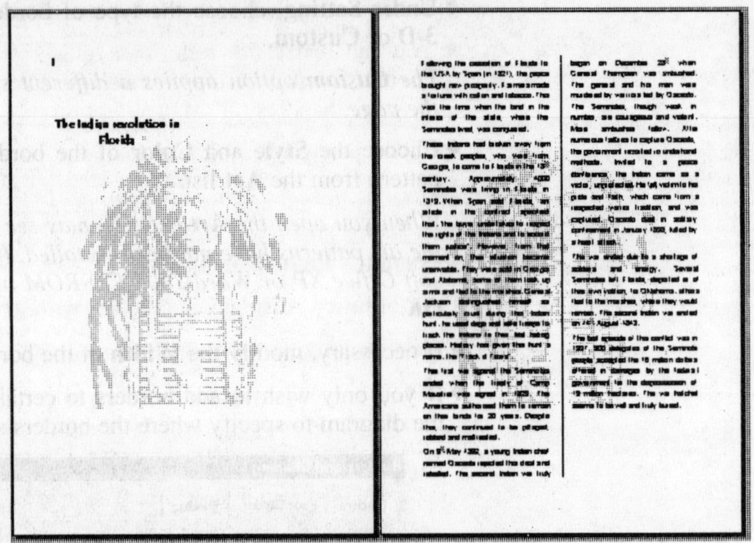

♦ Activate **Header and Footer** view (**View - Header and Footer**).

*Notice the insertion point flashing in the **Header** box.*

♦ Click the button on the **Header and Footer** toolbar to hide the document's text. This will make it easier to concentrate on your watermark.

♦ Insert the drawing object you want to use (**text box**), **AutoShape** (AutoShapes), **Clip Art** picture ( ), **Picture** ( ), **Word Art** object ( ) or other).

*The object you insert appears automatically at the insertion point in the **Header** box.*

♦ To reposition the watermark, select it, point to one of its edges and wait until the mouse pointer takes the shape of a four-headed arrow. Drag the object to its new position in the document then release the mouse button.

♦ If you need to change the watermark's **Text Wrapping** options, select the object and activate the last option in the **Format** menu (the name of the option depends on the type of object) or use the button on the object's toolbar (**Picture, WordArt**...).

The usual wrapping option for a watermark is ***Behind Text*** *().*

♦ You can resize the watermark object either via the last option in the **Format** menu (the one named after the object) or by dragging one of its sizing handles (cf. Managing objects).

♦ If you are using a picture for your watermark, you can adjust the colours in the picture by clicking the tool on the **Picture** toolbar or choosing an option from the **Color** list on the by **Picture** tab of the **Format - Picture** dialog box:

Automatic displays the picture with its original colours.

Greyscale displays the picture in black, white and shades of grey.

Black & White displays the picture in pure black and white.

Washout decreases the brightness and contrast of the colours (the usual choice for a watermark).

If the colours used in the watermark are too dark, the text will be difficult to read.

♦ If you are using a picture for the watermark, you will be able to use the buttons on the **Picture** toolbar to edit it:

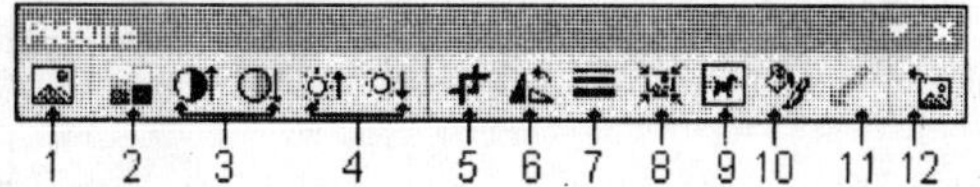

1 click to choose a picture to insert
2 options for adapting the colour
3 increases/decreases the contrast
4 increases/decreases the brightness
5 cropping tool
6 rotation tool
7 options for changing the outline
8 compression options
9 text wrapping options
10 opens the Format picture dialog box
11 tool for making individual colours transparent
12 restores the original settings

♦ When you are satisfied with the watermark, click the **Close** button on the **Header and Footer** toolbar.

❑ *Before you can edit or delete a watermark, you need to go into* ***Header and Footer*** *view.*

A quick and easy way of adding a watermark (picture or text) to a document is to use the ***Printed Watermark*** *option in* ***Format - Background****. This method does not, however, give you access to all the options described above.*

Creating a drop cap

A drop cap is an illuminated initial opening a chapter or paragraph.

♦ Select and format the future drop cap (font and size of character).

♦ **Format**
Drop Cap

♦ Under **Position,** choose the effect you prefer.

♦ Customise the presentation by changing the **Font**, the number of lines taken up by the drop cap (in **Lines to drop**) and the **Distance from text.**

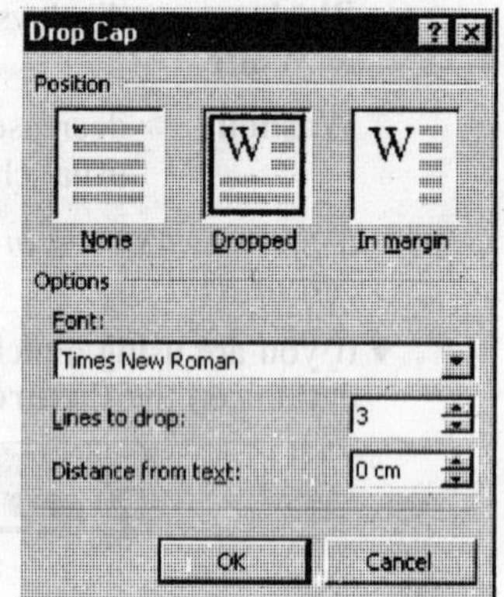

♦ Click **OK.**

The drop cap is created in a frame represented by a grey outline.

Numbering paragraphs or putting bullets in front of them

Two options are proposed on the toolbar, but other choices are accessible via the menu.

♦ Select the paragraphs you wish to format, if they are already entered.

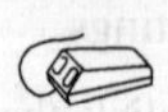

♦ Click [numbering button] to number the selected paragraphs or [bullets button] to put a bullet before each paragraph.

- **Location:** The Isle of Man is located approximately halfway between the north-west coast of England and the east coast of Northern Ireland.
- **Capital City:** Douglas, located 54.1° N and 4.5 ° W.
- **Population:** 73 000 approximately (one of the lowest population densities in Europe).

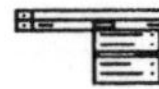

♦ Enter the paragraphs and select them.

♦ **Format**
Bullets and Numbering

♦ Click the tab dealing with the type of list you wish to create: **Bulleted** or **Numbered.**

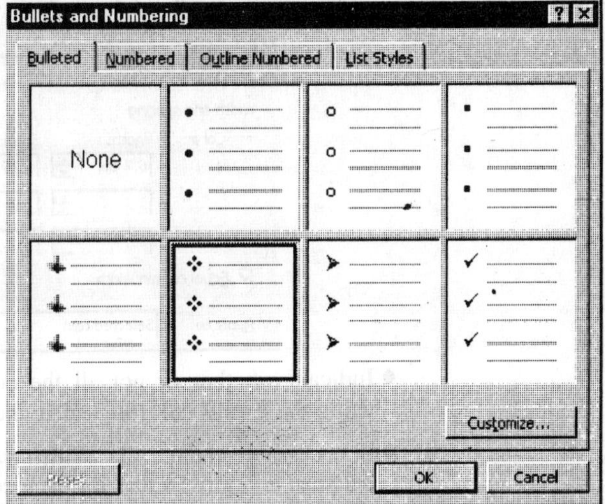

♦ Click the style of your choice.

♦ If you wish, click the **Customize** button to modify the position of the bullets (or numbers) and/or the position of the text relative to the bullets (numbers).

♦ In the **Customize Bulleted List** dialog box, the **Character** button opens the **Symbol** dialog box so you can select a new bullet and the **Picture** button opens the **Picture Bullet** dialog box so you can choose a picture for the bullet.
In the **Customize Numbered List** dialog box, the **Number style** list can be used to select a new numbering style and the **Start at** box indicates the starting number for the list. Once you have made your changes, click **OK**.

❑ *When you click* [icon] *or* [icon] *you activate the previous type of bullet or numbering chosen in the* ***Bullets and Numbering*** *dialog box.*

Presenting text in columns

♦ Place the insertion point in the section concerned, or select the required text.

♦ **Format**
Columns

♦ Under **Presets**, choose the basic presentation you require.

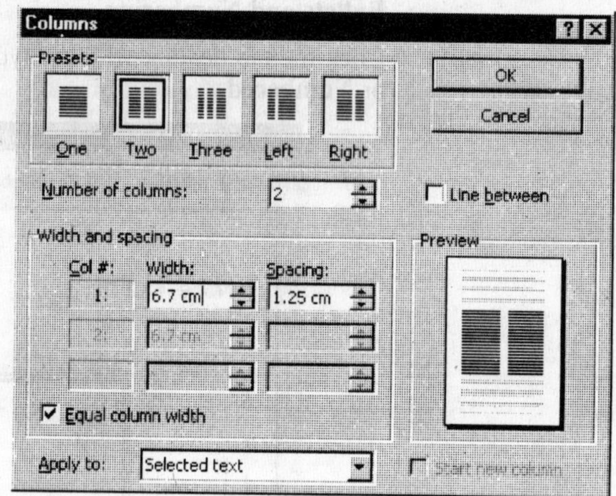

♦ Indicate whether or not all the columns are to be of identical width, using the **Equal column width** check box.

♦ If necessary, change the **Width** value and the **Spacing** (the space left between columns) value for each column or all columns.

♦ Check the box to draw a **Line between** the columns.

If you have activated support for a language that reads from right to left, such as Arabic, an additional check box will appear above ***Line between*** *so that you can order the columns from right to left.*

♦ Use the **Apply to** list to define the part of the text to be presented in columns.

♦ Click **OK**.

❑ *In* ***Normal*** *view, only one column of text can be seen. To view the presentation in columns, you must be in* ***Print Layout*** *view.*

❑ *The*  *tool button may be used but, in this case, you can neither define the width of the columns, nor draw a line between them.*

> *To present text in columns, without having previously inserted section breaks, you can select the text concerned and activate columns. Word will create its own section breaks before and after the selection.*

Inserting a column break

♦ Place the insertion point at the beginning of the line which will become the first line of the new column.

♦ **Insert**
Break

♦ Ctrl Shift Enter

♦ Activate the **Column break** option.

♦ Click **OK**.

You can also insert a column break with the Ctrl Shift Enter *shortcut key.*

❑ *When non-printing characters are displayed, a dotted line and the words* ***Column Break*** *indicate the position of the break.*

. . . . Personal notes. . . . .

Creating a document template

A template is a document in which you can save presentation styles and/or text in order to reuse them. Any new document is based on a template, the default template being Normal.dot.
You can create your own template from scratch, adding styles, text and so on, or you can create a template from a document already containing the required styles and/or texts.

Creating a template based on an existing template

- If it is not on the screen, show the **New Document** task pane with the **File - New** command.
- Click the **General Templates** link in the **New from template** section.

Do not use the tool button on the ***Standard*** *toolbar or the* Ctrl ***N*** *shortcut or you will not be able to access the* ***Templates*** *dialog box.*

- Click the **Template** option under **Create New**.

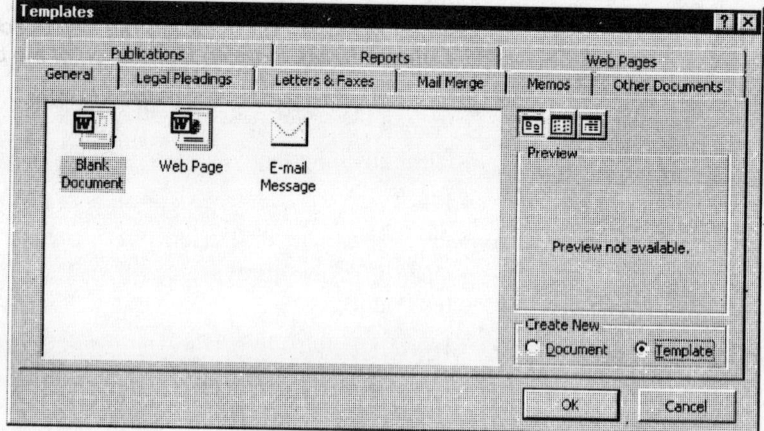

- To base your new template on the Normal.dot template, make sure the **Blank Document** icon is selected on the **General** page. Otherwise, activate the appropriate tab and click the template on which you wish to base the new one.
- Click **OK**.

The title bar reminds you that you are creating a new template.

- Set out the styles, text and layout for your new template.
- **File Save**  ♦ Ctrl **S**

*Word offers to save the template in the **Templates** folder. The **General** page in the **Templates** dialog box shows the templates that exist in this folder.*

♦ In the **File name** box, give the name of the template.

Templates have a .dot file extension.

♦ Click the **Save** button.

❑ *Templates that you create are stored by default in the **Templates** folder (C:\Windows\Application Data\Microsoft\Templates). To save templates in a different folder, you must create a subfolder of the Templates folder. When you do this, an extra tab, of the same name as the subfolder, appears in the **Templates** dialog box. Click the tab to see the templates saved within the new subfolder.*

❑ *The predefined templates in Word (for letters, faxes, brochures and so on) are not stored in the same Templates folder but in subfolders of the Templates folder which is located in C:\Program Files\Microsoft Office\Templates.*

Creating a template from an existing document

♦ If necessary, open the document concerned.

♦ Set out the styles, text and layout you require.

♦ Clear anything that you do not want to save with the template.

♦ **File**
Save As

♦ Open the **Save as type** drop-down list and click **Document Templates (*.dot).**

*Word offers to save in the **Templates** folder.*

♦ If necessary, open the folder in which you wish to save the template.

♦ Modify the **File name** if you wish.

♦ Click the **Save** button.

Modifying a document template

You can open a template to modify its contents.

♦ **File**
Open

♦ 

*You can also click the **More documents** link on the **New Document** task pane if the pane is open.*

♦ Open the **Files of type** drop-down list and choose **Document Templates (*.dot).**

The list of documents disappears and a list of templates appears in its place.

♦ Activate the folder where the template is saved (by default C:\Windows\Application Data\Microsoft\Templates for your own templates or C:\Program Files\Microsoft Office\Templates for Word's ready-made templates) and activate one of its subfolders if you need to.

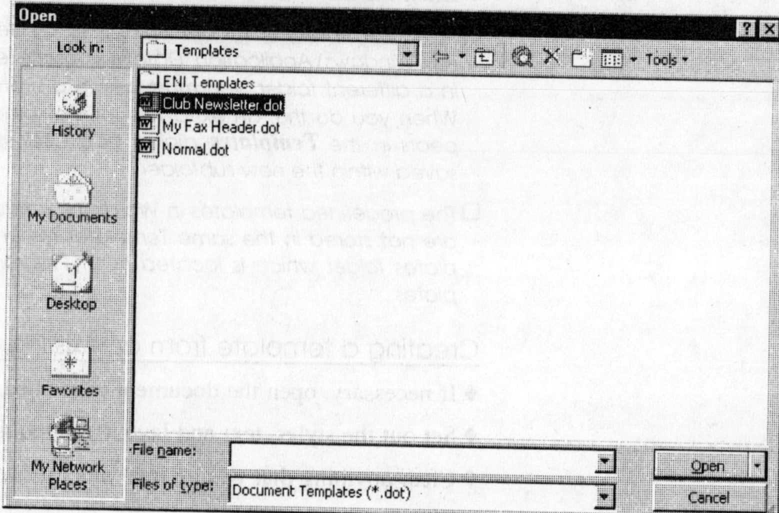

♦ Double-click the name of the template you wish to open.

♦ Make your changes and save the template.

❑ *The next time you try to open a document, remember to change the **Files of type** option so the dialog box will show **All Word Documents** again and not the templates.*

Linking a template to an existing document

This allows you to use the styles from another template than the one used to create the current document.

♦ Open the document that you want to link to another template.

♦ **Tools**
Templates and Add-Ins

♦ Click the **Attach** button in the **Document template** frame.

A list of all the template files opens.

♦ If necessary, double-click the name of the folder containing the template.

♦ Double-click the name of the template you wish to use.

♦ Activate the **Automatically update document styles** option if you want to update the styles in the document and use the same as those in the attached template.

♦ Click **OK**.

*The **Style** list on the toolbar now contains the styles attached to the template.*

♦ Apply the template's styles as you wish.

.... *Personal notes* ....

Creating a style

A style contains character, paragraph and/or table formatting properties. Creating a style saves these presentations so you can apply them easily at another time. Styles are saved with a document or in a template.

Based on existing formatting

With this technique you can only create paragraph styles, not character or table styles.

- If necessary, open the document or template to be used.
- Do the formatting which is to be included in the style.
- Place the insertion point in the formatted paragraph.
- Click the name of the active style in the **Style** list box on the **Formatting** toolbar.
- Type the name of the new style and press Enter.

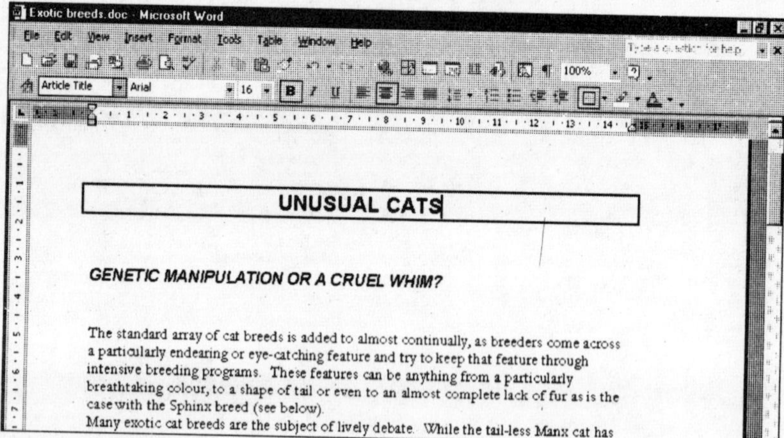

In this example the new style is named Article Title. It is applied immediately to the current paragraph.

❑ *You can also create a style based on existing formatting with the* ***Styles and Formatting*** *task pane. Open the task pane, point to the formatting type, click the [▼] button and choose* ***Modify****. Enter a* ***Name*** *for the style in the corresponding text box and click* ***OK****. The formatting is saved as a style and this style is applied to all the paragraphs in the document (or template) which have that type of formatting.*

Without existing formatting

- **Format**
  Styles and Formatting

*The **Styles and Formatting** task pane opens.*

♦ Click the **New Style** button.

♦ Enter a **Name** for the style in the corresponding text box.

♦ If the style concerns a **Character**, **Table** or **List** presentation, choose that option in the **Style type** list. The default **Style type** is **Paragraph**.

♦ If you wish, choose a style on which to base your new style in the **Style based on** list.

♦ If you are creating a paragraph style, you may want to open the **Style for following paragraph** list and choose the style that will be applied automatically to the next paragraph. When you press Enter at the end of a paragraph to which the new style is applied, Word will give the next new paragraph the style you choose in this list.

♦ Using the tools in the **Formatting** frame or the **Format** button, modify the formatting options for the style. If you are creating a table style, you should specify, before changing the formatting, which part of the table the style should be applied to (use the **Apply formatting to** list for this).

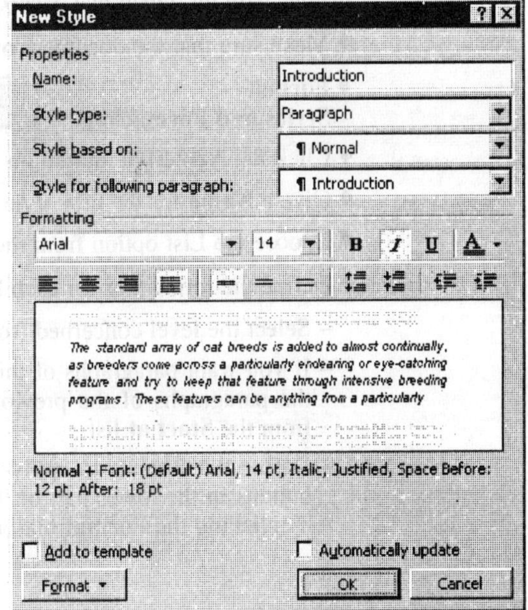

♦ Tick the **Add to template** option if you are not working in a template but you want to add the style to the template associated with the active document.

♦ Tick the **Automatically update** option if you want any changes made to a paragraph presented with that style to be carried over into the style itself.

This option is not available for character or table styles.

♦ Click **OK.**

The name of the style now appears in the ***Styles and Formatting*** *task pane. The names of paragraph styles are followed by a ¶ symbol, the names of character styles by a* **a** *symbol and table styles by a* ⊞ *symbol.*

Creating a list style

The particularity of a list file is that it contains different levels of formatting. When you apply a list style, the formatting applied to each paragraph depends on its level. The level of a paragraph is defined by the value of the left indent: as a rule, the more a paragraph is indented, the lower its level (for example, if a left indent of 1.5 cm is identified with level 2, the list style will apply level 2 formatting to all the selected paragraphs with an indent of 1.5 cm).

♦ Make sure that the document or template concerned is the active one.

♦ **Format**
Styles and Formatting

♦ Click the **New Style** button on the **Styles and Formatting** task pane.

♦ Give a **Name** for the new style in the dialog box which appears.

♦ Choose the List option from the **Style type** list.

♦ Define the formatting for each level:

- Select the level concerned from the **Apply formatting** to list.
- If you want paragraphs of this level to be numbered independently of the paragraphs of the previous level, choose a new starting number from the **Start at** list.
- Define the formats to apply to paragraphs of this level: use the tool buttons in the lower part of the dialog box and access further options by clicking the **Format** button.

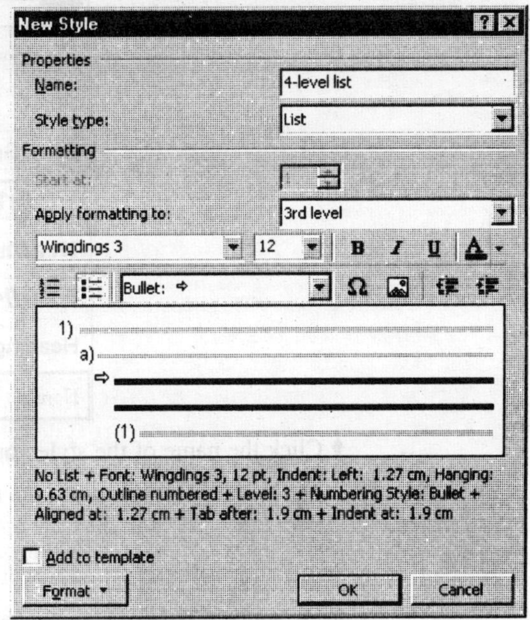

♦ If you are not working in the template itself, but would like the list style to be included in the template on which the current document is based, tick the **Add to template** check box.

♦ Click **OK**.

The name of the new style appears in the ***Styles and Formatting*** *task pane.*

Applying a style

There are two different ways of applying a style's presentation to text or a table.

First method

♦ To apply a character style, select the text concerned; to apply a paragraph style, select the paragraphs or click the paragraph concerned; to apply a table style, click the table concerned.

♦ Open the **Style** list on the **Formatting** toolbar.

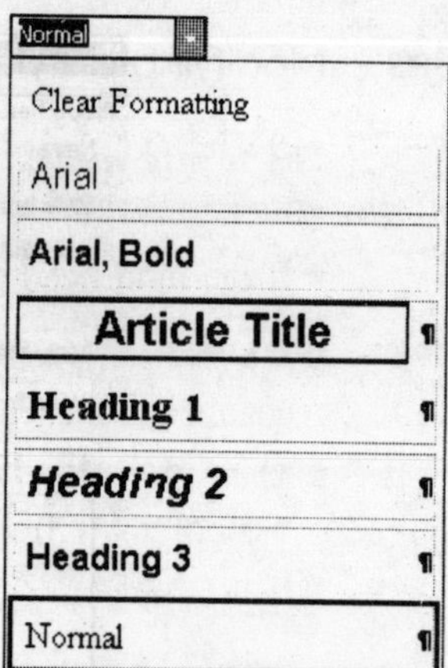

♦ Click the name of the style you wish to apply.

The formatting contained in the style is applied automatically to the selection.

Second method

♦ To apply a character style, select the text concerned; to apply a paragraph style, select the paragraphs or click the paragraph concerned; to apply a table style, click the table concerned.

♦ If it is hidden, show the **Styles and Formatting** task pane by clicking the  button on the **Formatting** toolbar.

♦ Click the name of the style you wish to apply.

*If the insertion point is in a blank paragraph and you click the name of a table style, Word offers to insert a table by opening the **Insert Table** dialog box.*

❑ *When you point to a style name in the **Styles and Formatting** task pane, a description appears in a ScreenTip.*
If a keyboard shortcut is associated with that style, you can use that shortcut to apply the style to the selected character(s), paragraph(s) or table(s).

❑ *Whatever the method used, using a style never limits the formatting applied to a paragraph. You can always add other types of formatting to those characters and/or paragraphs.*

*To cancel the use of a style, open the **Style** list on the **Formatting** toolbar or show the **Styles and Formatting** task pane. Click **Clear Formatting** to cancel a character or paragraph style or **Table Grid** to cancel a table style.*

Managing styles

Modifying a style

The mouse technique can only be used to modify character and paragraph styles.

♦ If the modifications are only to affect the active document, make them in the document. On the other hand, if you want the modifications to carry over into any new documents made from the template, make the changes in the template.

♦ Make the formatting changes on text that already uses the style you wish to modify (character or paragraph styles only).

♦ If it is hidden, show the **Styles and Formatting** task pane by clicking the button on the **Formatting** toolbar.

♦ In the **Pick formatting to apply** list, point to the style you want to modify, click the button and choose **Update to Match Selection.**

The changes made to the style are carried over to all the characters or paragraphs to which the style has previously been applied.

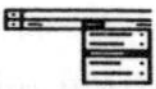

♦ Activate the document or template containing the style you wish to modify.

♦ If it is hidden, show the **Styles and Formatting** task pane by clicking the button on the **Formatting** toolbar.

♦ In the **Pick formatting to apply** list, point to the style you want to modify, click the button and choose **Modify.**

♦ Using the tool buttons in the **Formatting** frame or the **Format** button, modify the formatting options for the style. Tick the **Add to template** option if you are not working in a template but you want to add the style to the template associated with the active document.

♦ Click **OK.**

The changes made to the style are carried over to all the characters or paragraphs to which the style has previously been applied.

To modify the standard presentation of characters, you should modify the style called ***Normal.***

Deleting a style

♦ Activate the document or template containing the style you wish to modify.

♦ If it is hidden, show the **Styles and Formatting** task pane by clicking the button on the **Formatting** toolbar.

♦ In the **Pick formatting to apply** list, point to the style you want to modify, click the button and choose **Delete**.

♦ Confirm that you want to delete the style by clicking **Yes**.

❑ *If you delete a style in a template, the style is not deleted in existing documents based on that template and vice versa.*

❑ *Word's own predefined styles such as **Normal, Heading 1, Heading 2** and so on cannot be deleted.*

Printing the list of styles

♦ Open the template, or a document containing the styles to print.

♦ **File**
Print ♦ Ctrl P

♦ Open the **Print what** list and choose **Styles**.

♦ Click **OK**.

The styles are printed in alphabetical order, along with their attributes.

❑ *To see the styles in a document, activate **Normal** view, use the **Tools - Options** command and click the **View** tab. Enter a width (1.5 cm for example) in the **Style width area** box and enter: the names of the styles used in each paragraph appear on the left side of the screen.*

Using styles from another template

♦ Open the document concerned.

♦ Apply to your document the styles already defined.

♦ **Format**
Theme

♦ Click the **Style Gallery** button.

♦ Choose a **Template**.

♦ Activate the option corresponding to the content you wish to see in the **Preview of** screen:

Document	to show a preview of the current document formatted with the styles from the selected template.
Example	to show the list of styles from the selected template and examples of the formatting they produce.

Style samples to show a sample of text from the current document as it would look with the styles from the selected template.

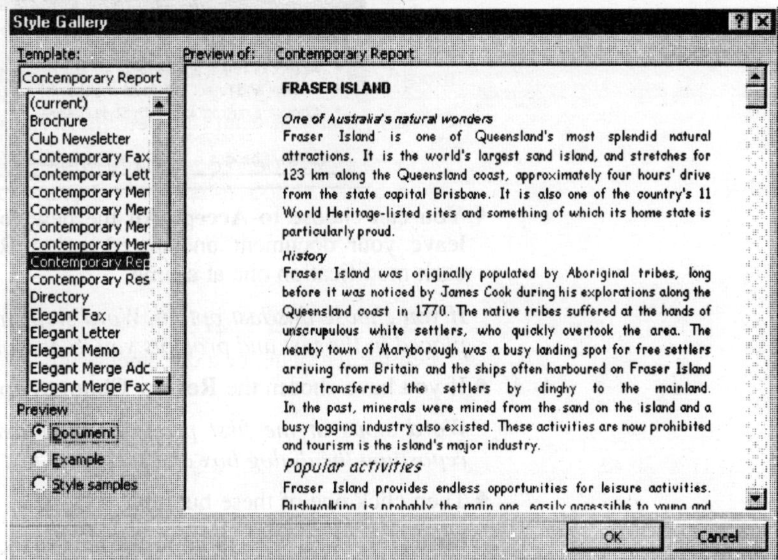

On the left of the dialog box you can see all the existing templates and, on the right, the active document, as it would look if you applied the styles from the ***Contemporary Report*** *template.*

♦ If you find a suitable template, click **OK** otherwise, click **Cancel**.

Using AutoFormat for your document

This technique allows you to make use of Word's capacities to improve your document's presentation.

♦ Open the document.

♦ **Format**
AutoFormat

♦ If necessary, click the **Options** button, customize the options on the **AutoFormat** tab, then click **OK**.

♦ Choose **AutoFormat now** if you want Word to go ahead and change the formatting, without giving you the chance to accept or reject the changes.

Choose **AutoFormat and review each change** if you want the change to approve or reject each of Word's proposed changes individually.

Click **OK**.

*If you choose **AutoFormat and review each change**, the AutoFormat dialog box appears:*

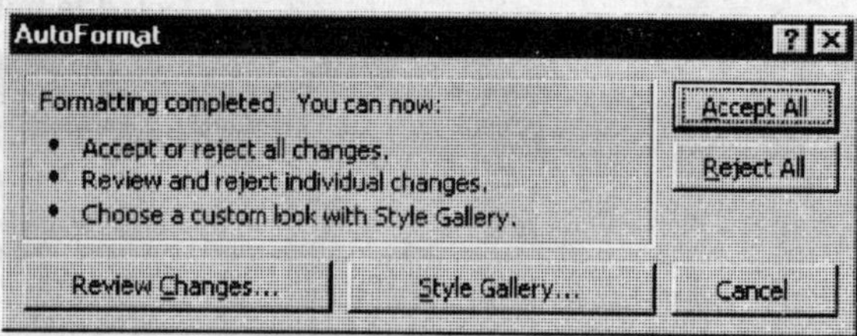

♦ You can choose to **Accept All** the new formatting, to **Reject All** and leave your document unchanged, or to **Review Changes** and check each modification one at a time.

If you choose this last option, Word stops at each of the revision marks placed in the text and prompts you to accept or reject the change.

♦ If you have chosen the **Review Changes** option, click **Find.**

Word stops at the first proposed modification. If you wish, you can reposition the dialog box and scroll the text using the scroll cursor.

♦ Then click one of these buttons:

Find	to go to the next mark.
Reject	to refuse the modification.
Undo	to reinstate a correction just cancelled.

When you reach the end of the document, Word proposes to review from the beginning.

♦ Click that dialog box's **Cancel** button.

♦ Click the **Cancel** button visible under the **Find** button on the **Review AutoFormat Changes** dialog box.

♦ Click **Accept All** to return to the document.

Creating an AutoText entry

An AutoText entry allows you to use an abbreviation to insert a text which you type repeatedly (such as an address or greeting).

♦ If you want to make the AutoText available for use in any document, open a document linked to Normal.dot or to any other template.
If the AutoText entry concerns a certain type of document created from a particular template, open a document based on that template.

♦ Enter the contents of the AutoText, not forgetting additional formatting and blank lines.

♦ Select the contents of the AutoText.

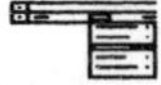

♦ **Insert**
AutoText
AutoText

♦ Open the **Look in** list then choose the template where you want to create the AutoText.

♦ Give a name for the AutoText in the **Enter AutoText entries here** text box.

♦ Click **Add**.

❑ *AutoText entries are added to the template definitively when it is saved. If the AutoText has been added to a template other than **Normal.dot**, you will be asked to save it when you save or close the document.*

❑ *Once you have stated where the AutoText entries are to be saved, you can create new entries with **Insert - AutoText - New** or Alt F3 or click the **New** button on the **AutoText** toolbar.*

Using an AutoText

♦ Move the insertion point to the place where you want to insert the text.

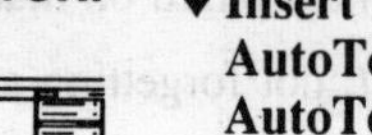

♦ **Insert**
AutoText
AutoText

♦ Choose the template, which contains the AutoText, from the **Look in** list.

♦ Click the name of the AutoText.

♦ Click the **Insert** button.

*When the template has been chosen in the **Look in** list, the AutoText entries linked to the active style are listed at the bottom of the **Insert - AutoText** menu or as a drop-down list on the second button of the **AutoText** toolbar. You can click them to insert the AutoText.*

First method

This method can only be used where the name of the AutoText contains at least four characters.

♦ Position the insertion point where you want the contents of the Auto-Text to appear.

♦ Type the first characters of the AutoText's name.

Word will use its AutoComplete function to supply the rest of the name in a ScreenTip.

♦ Press Enter to accept that entry.

*AutoComplete will only be used if the **Show AutoComplete suggestions** option is activated in the **AutoCorrect** dialog box (**Tools - AutoCorrect Options - AutoText** tab).*

Second method

♦ Place the insertion point where the contents of the AutoText should appear.

♦ Enter the name of the AutoText.

♦ Press F3.

Printing the AutoTexts

♦ If the AutoTexts are stored in a template, a document based on that template should be active.

♦ **File**
Print

♦ Ctrl P

♦ In the **Print what** list box, choose **AutoText entries.**

♦ Click **OK.**

❑ *First Word prints the AutoTexts belonging to the template, then those of Normal.dot. They appear in alphabetical order.*

Managing existing AutoTexts

Deleting an AutoText

♦ **Insert**
AutoText
AutoText

♦ In the **Look in** list, select the template containing the AutoText, if necessary.

♦ Click the name of the AutoText you wish to delete.

♦ Click the **Delete** button.

The name of the AutoText disappears immediately from the list.

♦ Close the dialog box by clicking **Close.**

Modifying the content of an AutoText

♦ Display the content of the AutoText entry and modify it as required.

♦ Select the new content.

♦ **Insert**
AutoText
AutoText

♦ Click the original AutoText name.

♦ Click the **Add** button.

♦ Confirm the changes to the content of the AutoText by clicking **Yes.**

❑ *When you modify or delete an AutoText, you modify the template. Remember to save it.*

Finding text

By its contents

♦ Position the insertion point where the search should begin, or select the text concerned.

♦ **Edit**
Find

♦ Ctrl F

*You can also click the **Find in this document** link on the **Basic Search** or **Advanced Search** task pane.*

♦ Enter the text you need to find in the **Find what** box.

*The **Find what** box will accept up to 255 characters.*

♦ If you want Word to select all the occurrences of the text, tick the **Highlight all items found in** option then if necessary open the attached list and select which part of the document should be searched (Main Document, Headers and Footers, Footnotes etc).

*If no text is selected, only the **Main Document** option appears.*

♦ Click the **More** button, if necessary, to specify how you want the search carried out. Activate:

Match case to find the text in question, written with the exact combination of upper and lower case letters entered in **Find what.**
For example, when searching for "lea"; if the option **Match case** is deactivated, Word will find "lea" of course, but also "Lea" and "LEA". To find only "lea", the option must be active.

Find whole words only if the character string you are looking for constitutes a word.
For example, the text "late": if this option is deactivated, Word will find "late" but also "lateness", "relate" or "lateral"; if the option is active, only "late" will be found.

Use wildcards to search for text from the **Find what** box using wildcard characters, symbols or special search operators. If the **Use wildcards** option is not active and the **Find what** box contains symbols, Word will consider those symbols as plain text and not as wildcards.

Sounds like (English)	this option is only available when English is the set language for editing. It looks for English words that have a similar pronunciation to the word entered in the **Find What** box.
Find all word forms (English)	looks for all the grammatical forms of the given word, for example, when you enter "sit", it will also look for "sat", "sitting"...

♦ In the **Search** box, in the **Search Options** frame, specify whether Word should search **Up** or **Down** from the position of the insertion point, or through **All** the document.

*The **Search** list is unavailable when the **Highlight all items found in** option is active.*

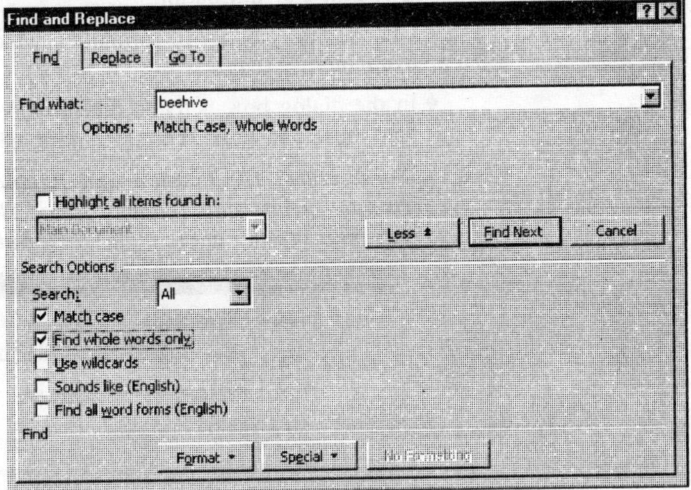

♦ Unless you have activated the **Highlight all items found in** option, start the search with the **Find Next** button or press Enter.

Almost immediately, the first occurrence of the text in the document is selected.

♦ If the **Highlight all items found in** option is active, click the **Find All** button.

All the corresponding text is highlighted in the document or in the selected text.

♦ If this first text is the one you are looking for, close the dialog box using **Cancel**; if it is not, continue by **Find Next**.

> Once the ***Find and Replace*** dialog box is closed, you can go on searching using ⇧ Shift F4.

By its format

♦ Place the insertion point where you wish to start searching, or select the text concerned.

♦ **Edit**
Find

♦ Delete any text appearing in the **Find what** text box.

♦ If necessary, click the **More** button to see further search options.

♦ Click the **Format** button.

♦ Choose the category of formatting which interests you from the options available.

♦ In the dialog box, activate the formats you are looking for and deactivate those you want Word to ignore. Click **OK**.

*Word returns to the **Find and Replace** dialog box because you may wish to specify additional criteria. The formats you selected appear with the **Format** option, under the **Find what** box.*

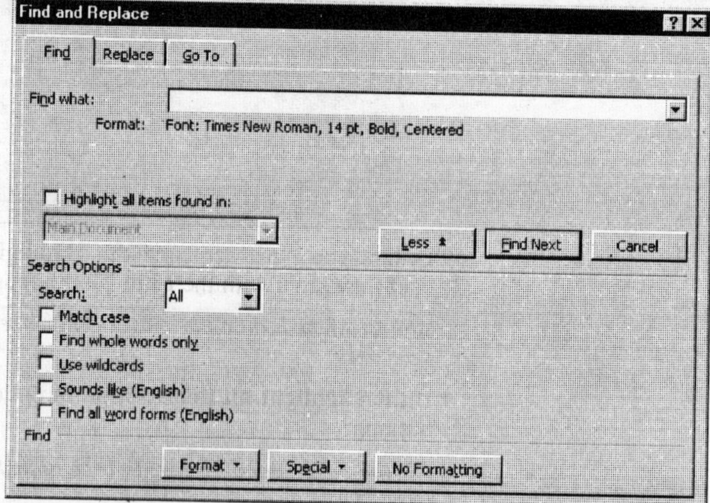

♦ Specify all the formats you wish to include in the search.

♦ If you want Word to select all the occurrences of the text, tick the **Highlight all items found in** option then if necessary open the attached list and select which part of the document should be searched.

♦ Start the search by clicking the **Find Next** button, or if the **Highlight all items found in** option is active, click the **Find All** button.

♦ If the first text found is the one you are looking for, close the dialog box with the **Cancel** button, otherwise click **Find Next** to continue.

Rather than clicking the ***Format*** *button to select the formats you want to find, you can press the appropriate shortcut keys (for example,* Ctrl ***B*** *if you are looking for bold type).*

Replacing one text by another

♦ Position the insertion point where you want Word to start looking for the text.

♦ **Edit**
Replace ♦ Ctrl H

♦ Enter the text you need to find in the **Find what** box, deleting old search criteria if necessary.

♦ Go into the **Replace with** box, delete its existing contents and enter the new text.

♦ If necessary, click **More** and specify how you want the replacement to be carried out (cf. Finding text).

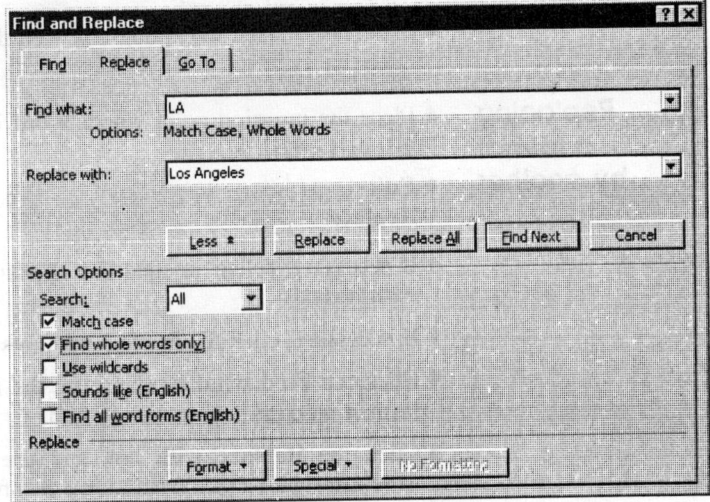

The ***Find whole words only*** *option is the same as the one in the* ***Find*** *dialog box.*
The ***Match case*** *option has considerable importance here. If you ask, for example, for BB to be replaced by Bluebird and the option is active, Word will only find occurrences of "BB" and will replace them by*

"Bluebird". If the option is not active, Word will find "BB" and replace it by "BLUEBIRD"; it will find "Bb" and replace it by "Bluebird"; it will find "bb" and replace it by "bluebird".

♦ Click **Find Next** to start the search.

Word selects the first string of characters it finds: if the dialog box hides the selection in the text, you can drag its title bar to move it.

♦ If you want to make the replacements one by one, use the **Replace** button to replace the selected string of characters and look for the next occurrence. If you click **Find Next**, you continue the search without making the replacement.
If you wish to make all the replacements at once, click the **Replace All** button.

The number of replacements made is displayed in a window:

♦ Click **OK**.

♦ If necessary, shut the dialog box with the **Close** button.

Replacing a format by another

♦ Place the insertion point where Word is to start its search or select the text concerned.

♦ **Edit**
Replace ♦ Ctrl H

♦ If necessary, delete any text that appears in the **Find what** and **Replace with** boxes.

♦ If necessary, click the **More** button to see further search options.

♦ Click the **Find what** box and use the **Format** button to choose which formatting criteria you wish to find.

♦ Click the **Replace with** box and use the **Format** button to choose which formatting you wish to use as a replacement.

♦ Click **Find Next** to start the search.

Word selects the first string of characters it finds: if the dialog box hides the selection in the text, you can drag its title bar to move it.

♦ If you want to make the replacements one by one, use the **Replace** button to replace the selected string of characters and look for the next occurrence. If you click **Find Next**, you continue the search without making the replacement.

If you wish to make all the replacements at once, click the **Replace All** button.

♦ Click **OK** on the message telling you how many replacements were made.

♦ Shut the dialog box by clicking **Close**.

Finding/replacing special characters

♦ Place the insertion point in the text where Word should start the search or select the text concerned.

♦ **Edit**
Find or **Replace**

♦ Ctrl **F** or Ctrl **H**

♦ Proceed as for any other replacement (or search) but use the **Special** button to choose the symbol, punctuation mark or cha-racter concerned.

The code representing the character appears.

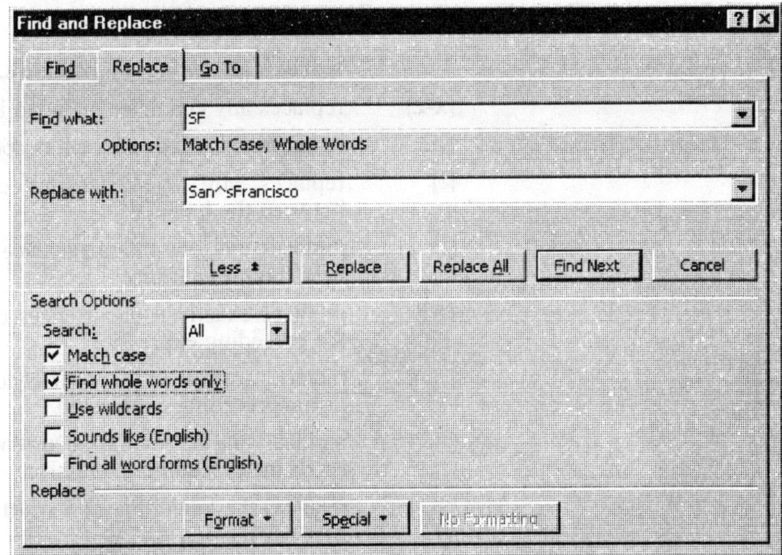

The ^s code corresponds to a nonbreaking space.

♦ Click the **Find Next** button.

Word selects the first string of characters it finds: if the dialog box hides the selection in the text, you can drag its title bar to move it.

♦ If you want to make the replacements one by one, use the **Replace** button to replace the selected string of characters and look for the next occurrence. If you click **Find Next**, you continue the search without making the replacement.

If you wish to make all the replacements at once, click the **Replace All** button.

♦ Click **OK** on the message telling you how many replacements were made.

♦ Shut the dialog box by clicking **Close**.

Using advanced search criteria

♦ Place the insertion point in the text where Word should start the search or select the text concerned.

♦ **Edit**
Find
or
Replace

♦ Ctrl F or Ctrl H

♦ Give the text you want to find, using the following operators:

?	replaces one character.
*	replaces any string of characters.
[x-z]	replaces any character included in the range defined.
[]	replaces one of the characters specified between the brackets.
[!]	replaces any one character except those which appear between the brackets.
[!x-z]	replaces any one character except those in the range quoted between the brackets.
{n}	replaces exactly n occurrences of the preceding character or the preceding expression.
{n,m}	replaces from n to m occurrences of the preceding character or the preceding expression.
@	replaces one or several occurrences of the preceding character or the preceding expression.
<	replaces the beginning of a word.
>	replaces the end of a word.

Example	can be used to find	but will not find
?aw	saw - law - raw	thaw
s*w	saw - sinew - somehow	jigsaw
drive[i-r]	driver - driven	drives
fo[uw]l	foul - fowl	foal
th[!i]n	than - then	thin
[!n-r]ole	dole - hole - sole	pole - role
fil{2}	fill - fillet - filly	file - filial
can{1,2}	cane - canary - canny	
co@	cocoa - cocoon	
<(in)	into - ink - investigate	drive-in
(re)>	centre	rewrite

- If necessary, give a replacement text in the **Replace with** text box.
- Click the **More** button (if necessary) and tick the **Use wildcards** option.
- Click the **Find Next** button.

Word selects the first string of characters it finds: if the dialog box hides the selection in the text, you can drag its title bar to move it.

- If you want to make the replacements one by one, use the **Replace** button to replace the selected string of characters and look for the next occurrence. If you click **Find Next**, you continue the search without making the replacement.

If you wish to make all the replacements at once, click the **Replace All** button.

Checking the grammar or spelling in a document

Starting a grammar/spelling check

♦ If the whole document is to be checked, position the insertion point at the top. If only a part of the text is concerned, select it.

When there is no selection, Word checks the entire document including footnotes, headers, footers and so on.

♦ **Tools**
Spelling and Grammar

♦ 

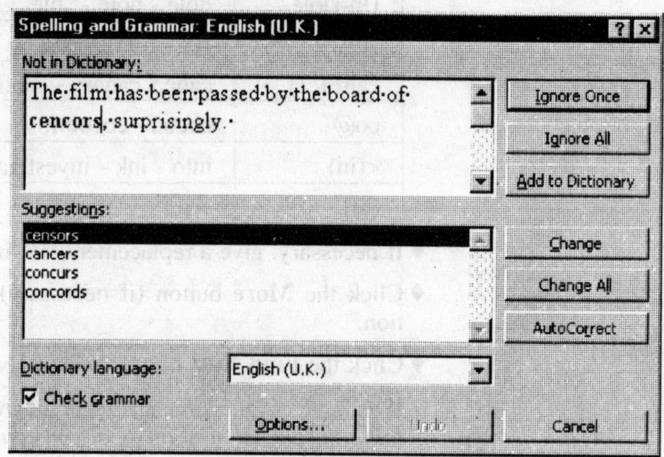

Words are queried for three main reasons: the word is unknown (does not occur in the application's dictionary), the word is repeated (example: I know that that is true), the word is entered with an unusual combination of upper and lower case letters (example: LEtter).

Spelling is checked against Word's main dictionary and as many custom dictionaries as you like (by default, there exists only one: CUSTOM.DIC).

♦ Select the dictionary you want to use for the spelling checks in the **Dictionary language** list box.

To use automatic language detection, your computer must first be configured for multi-lingual editing.

♦ Choose whether or not to look for grammar faults by activating or deactivating the **Check grammar** option.

Customising the spelling check

♦ Go into the **Spelling and Grammar** dialog box and click the **Options** button.

♦ Choose whether or not to **Ignore words in UPPERCASE** and/or **Ignore words with numbers.**

These options are useful if, for example, the document contains a list of proper nouns.

♦ Make sure that the **Always suggest corrections** option is active if you want Word to display potential corrections in the **Suggestions** list of the **Spelling and Grammar** dialog box.

♦ Tick the **Suggest from main dictionary only** option if you want Word to use only the main dictionary for the checks and not custom dictionaries.

♦ Activate or deactivate the **Ignore Internet and file addresses** option, depending on whether or not you want Word also to check Internet or email addresses or file paths.

Using a custom dictionary

When Word checks spelling, it uses the main dictionary and also the active custom dictionary (or dictionaries). Custom dictionaries contain special words that do not appear in the main dictionary, for example you could create a dictionary of medical terms, or, if such a file exists, load one. The default custom dictionary is called CUSTOM.DIC.

♦ **Tools**
Options

♦ Click the **Spelling and Grammar** tab.

♦ Click the **Custom Dictionaries** button.

♦ To create a new custom dictionary, click the **New** button, enter the **File name** for the new dictionary then click **Save.**

The new dictionary created appears in the list of existing dictionaries and is active automatically (to show this, a tick precedes its name).

♦ By default, when you click the **Add to Dictionary** button in the **Spelling and Grammar** dialog box, the word is added to the CUSTOM.DIC dictionary. If you want to add words to another custom dictionary, select it in the **Dictionary list** then click the **Change Default** button.

*The text **(default)** appears to the right of the chosen custom dictionary.*

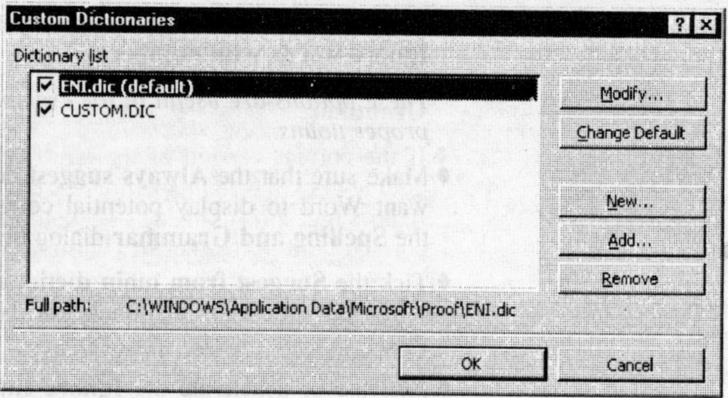

♦ To change a custom dictionary, click the **Add** button, select the drive then the folder containing the file and double-click the corresponding dictionary file name.

♦ To close an open dictionary, remove the tick next to its name.
Any dictionary that is not ticked is currently closed.

♦ Alternatively, to activate a dictionary, tick its checkbox.

♦ To modify the contents of a custom dictionary, select it in the list and click **Modify**.

♦ Click **OK** in the **Custom Dictionaries** dialog box.

♦ Click **OK** in the **Options** dialog box.

❑ *The **Remove** button in the **Custom Dictionaries** dialog box removes the selected dictionary from the **Dictionary list**. However, this does not delete the dictionary file (.DIC) from your computer.*

Managing correctly spelt words

♦ Go into the **Spelling and Grammar** dialog box (**Tools - Spelling and Grammar**).

♦ Click:

Ignore to leave the word as it is and continue the spelling check.

Ignore All to ignore the word each time it occurs during the check.

♦ To add the word to a custom dictionary so that Word will recognise it in future, click the **Options** button then the **Custom Dictionaries** button. Next, select the dictionary in the **Dictionary list** and click the **Modify** button. Click the **Add** button then click **OK** three times.

Correcting badly spelt words

♦ Go into the **Spelling and Grammar** dialog box (**Tools - Spelling and Grammar**).

♦ If the correct version of the word is proposed in the **Suggestions** list, double-click the right spelling (or click once then click **Change**).
If no suggestion is made and you know the correct spelling, enter the correct word in the **Not in Dictionary** text box and click **Change**.

❑ *Clicking the **AutoCorrect** button in the **Spelling and Grammar** dialog box adds the badly spelt word and its correction to the list of automatic corrections; the next time the mistake occurs, Word will correct it as you type.*

*If you enter by clicking the **Change All** button, then the same error is automatically corrected if it recurs in the document.*

Deleting duplicated words

♦ Go to the **Spelling and Grammar** dialog box.

♦ Click **Delete**.

Consulting/ modifying a custom dictionary

♦ **Tools**
Options
Spelling and Grammar tab

♦ Click the **Custom Dictionaries** button.

♦ In the **Dictionary list**, select the dictionary whose content you wish to see and/or modify and click the **Modify** button.

♦ To add a word to the custom dictionary, enter the word in the **Word** box and click the **Add** button.

♦ To delete a word from the custom dictionary, select the word you wish to delete in the **Dictionary** list and click **Delete**.

♦ To change the language of the custom dictionary, open the **Language** list and click the required language.

♦ Click **OK** three times.

*You can also consult and/or modify a custom dictionary by opening the dictionary file with **File - Open** and proceeding as usual (remember that it is not a Word document, but a file with a .DIC extension). To check where the custom dictionaries are saved, select the name of the dictionary concerned in the **Custom Dictionaries** dialog box (**Tools - Options - Spelling and Grammar** tab - **Custom Dictionaries** button) and check the **Full path**.*

Checking the grammar in a document

♦ **Tools Spelling and Grammar** ♦ F7

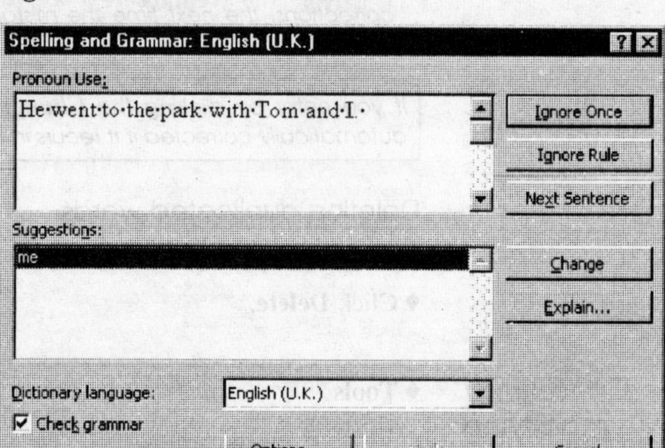

♦ To correct a mistake, double-click one of the **Suggestions** made or enter your correction in the text box where the grammar mistake appears in green (the name of this box depends on the type of mistake) then click the **Change** button.

♦ If you do not wish to correct the text, click:

Ignore or **Ignore Rule**	to leave the text unchanged and continue the check.
Next Sentence	to move the check on to the next sentence, even though the current one may contain further errors.

♦ Click **OK** on the dialog box that tells you the spelling and grammar check is finished.

❑ *If you want Word to **Explain** the grammar mistake you have made, click the corresponding button in the **Spelling and Grammar** dialog box.*

*The last corrections carried out can be undone by the **Undo** button in the **Spelling and Grammar** dialog box.*

Using AutoCorrect

Activating/deactivating AutoCorrect

If the AutoCorrect options are active, Word corrects common mistakes as you type (for instance, if you type "teh" Word will replace it with "the").

♦ **Tools**
AutoCorrect Options

♦ According to your requirements, activate or deactivate the options before the **Replace text as you type** box.

♦ Deactivate the **Replace text as you type** option if you do not want Word to correct common errors while you are typing.

By default, this option is active.

♦ Click **OK.**

❑ *The **Exceptions** button in the **AutoCorrect Options** dialog box (**Tools - AutoCorrect Options**) can be used to define text that you do not want Word to correct automatically.*

Defining the AutoCorrect entries

Word supplies you with a considerable default list of automatic corrections. You can add to this list your own words or abbreviations that Word will replace while you type.

♦ If the correctly spelt word exists in your document, select it.

If the selected text is formatted, Word gives you the opportunity to store that word with or without its formatting.

♦ **Tools**
AutoCorrect Options

♦ If necessary, tick the **Replace text as you type** option.

♦ Enter the badly spelt word or the abbreviation in the **Replace** box.

♦ If necessary, enter the correct spelling in the **With** box. If you already selected text in the document, it should appear automatically in this box.

♦ If required, activate the **Plain text** option to store the AutoCorrect entry without any formatting or the **Formatted text** option if you wish to conserve its current format.

These options are only available when you make a prior selection in the text.

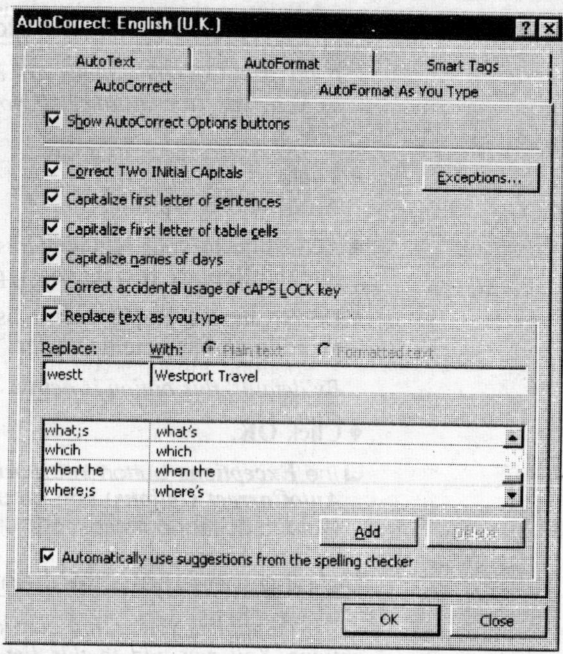

♦ Click the **Add** button.

♦ Add any mistakes you make frequently.

♦ If you want Word to replace automatically (as you type) spelling mistakes with suggestions made by the main and custom dictionary (or dictionaries), activate the **Automatically use suggestions from the spell checker** option.

This option is active by default.

♦ Click **OK.**

Using the AutoCorrect Options button

When a word is corrected automatically as you type, Word displays the AutoCorrect Options button so you can intervene on that correction if you wish.

♦ Make sure the **Show AutoCorrect Options button** option is active in the **AutoCorrect** dialog box (**Tools - AutoCorrect Options**).

This option is active by default.

♦ Point to the word that has been automatically corrected while you were typing.

A small blue rectangle appears under the first two letters of the word.

♦ Point to the blue rectangle to display the **AutoCorrect Options** button and click the button.

The Tynwald is made up of two chambers: the Legislative Council (upper house) and the House of Keys. The House of Keys has twenty four members and these are elected by the Manx Islanders themselves. These members represent each the island's fifteen constituencies

Change back to "constituensies"
Stop Automatically Correcting "constituensies"
Control AutoCorrect Options...

♦ To return to your initial spelling of the word, click the **Change back to** option. The **Redo AutoCorrect** option replaces the **Change back to** option, allowing you to retrieve the corrected version of the word if necessary.

♦ If the automatic correction puts a capital letter at the beginning of your sentence and you wish to **Stop Auto-capitalizing First Letter of Sentences**, click the corresponding option. When you choose this option, the **Capitalize first letter of sentences** option is deactivated in the **AutoCorrect Options** dialog box (**Tools - AutoCorrect Options**). You can tick this option again if you wish to return to the automatic placing of a capital letter at the start of each sentence.

♦ If you no longer want Word to correct that word automatically, click the **Stop Automatically Correcting** option; that word will now be included in the **Don't correct** list in the **AutoCorrect Exceptions** dialog box (**Tools - AutoCorrect Options, Exceptions** button, **Other Corrections** tab). If you want Word to resume correcting this word as you type, select it in the **Don't correct** list and click the **Delete** button.

♦ To open the **AutoCorrect Options** dialog box, click the **Control AutoCorrect Options** option.

Specifying the language used

The spelling, grammar, hyphens and so on are checked according to the language chosen.

♦ **Tools**
Language
Set Language

♦ Double-click the language used in the **Mark selected text as** list.

If all new documents are to be written in a particular language, click the language, click ***Default*** *and confirm.*

Counting words and other elements in a document

- Show the **Word Count** toolbar. To do this, use the **View - Toolbars - Word Count** command or right-click any toolbar and choose the **Word Count** option.
- If you wish to see the statistics for a certain part of the document, select that portion.
- Click the **Recount** button on the **Word Count** toolbar.
- Open the first list on the **Word Count** toolbar to see the statistics.

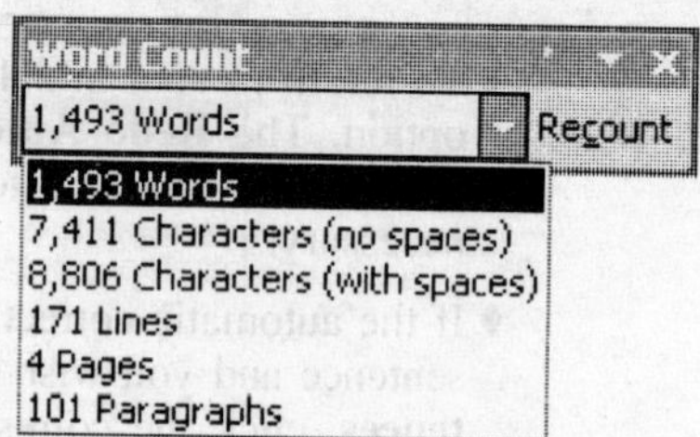

- To see the statistics for another part of the document, select that part and click **Recount**.
- If necessary, close the **Word Count** toolbar by clicking the [X] button.

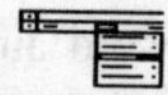

- If you wish to see the statistics for a certain part of the document, select that portion.
- **Tools**
  Word Count
- To **Include footnotes and endnotes** in the count, click the corresponding option.
- Consult the statistics then click **Close**.

❑ *The **Show Toolbar** button on the **Word Count** dialog box can be clicked to display the toolbar.*

Using the thesaurus

♦ Place the insertion point in the word whose synonym you are looking for, or just after it.

♦ **Tools**
Language
Thesaurus

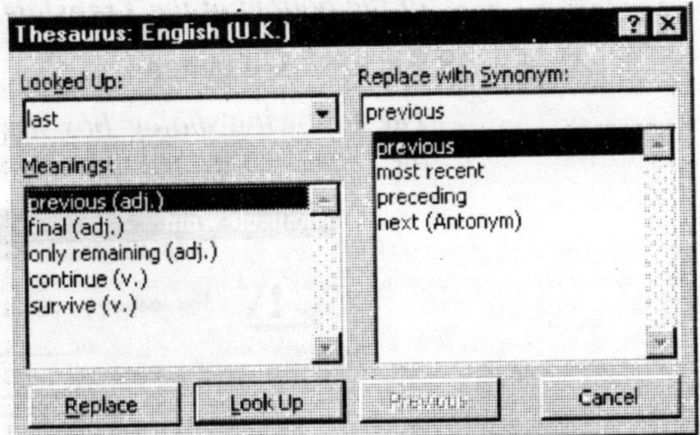

*Under **Meanings** on the left, the different meanings of the word are listed. On the right, all the synonyms of the selected meaning of the word appear.*

♦ In the **Meanings** list, click the appropriate meaning.

♦ To list synonyms of one of the synonyms, double-click it.

♦ Click **Previous** to return to the previous word looked up.

♦ If you wish to replace the word selected in the text with one of its synonyms, click the one in question, then click the **Replace** button; if you prefer to leave the original word, click **Cancel**.

❑ *To find current synonyms for a word while you are typing, right-click the word and select the **Synonyms** option. Click the word that you require from the list.*

Translating text

Word 2002 offers you a feature which can translate words or short texts into another language (for example, from English to French).

♦ **Tools**
Language
Translate

*The **Translate** task pane appears on the screen.*

♦ If the text you want to translate is already in the document, select it then activate the **Current selection** option. Otherwise, type it in the **Text** box.

♦ Open the **Dictionary** list in the **Look up in dictionary** frame and select the option that corresponds to the translation you require.

*The **Dictionary** list is unavailable when the **Entire document** choice is active under **Translate what?**. If you need to translate longer text, you should connect to the Web translation service (**Translate via the Web** at the bottom of the **Translate** task pane).*

♦ Click the **Go** button.

The following dialog box may appear if the necessary component for the requested translation is not installed:

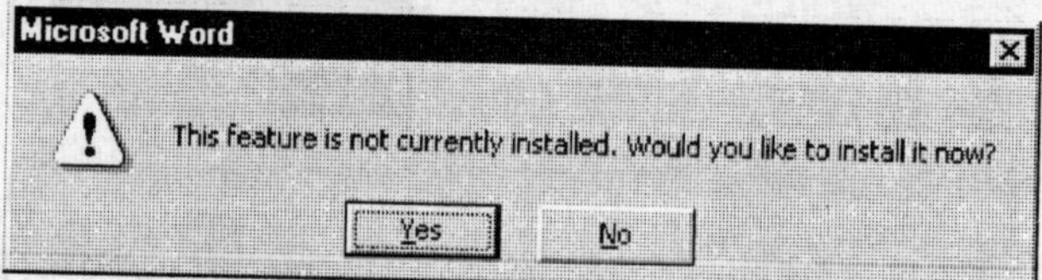

♦ If necessary, insert the Microsoft Office XP CD-ROM in the drive and click **Yes** to install the component. A window showing the installation progress appears briefly on the screen.

*The **Results** of the translation appear in the corresponding list in the **Translate** task pane.*

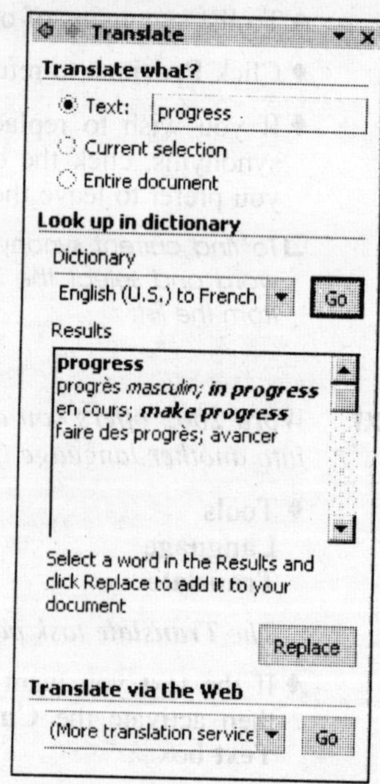

If Word does not find a translation, the text ***(No suggestions)*** *or* ***(No suggestions. Try looking up a single word at a time, or use Translate via the Web.)*** *appears in the* ***Results*** *list.*

♦ To replace the selected text by the translation, select the translated text in the **Results** list and click the **Replace** button.

♦ If required, close the **Translate** task pane by clicking the ☒ button in the top right corner of the pane.

Hyphenating words

Breaking words up and hyphenating them smoothes irregularities along the margin, or, in justified alignment, reduces the space left between each word.

Automatic hyphenation

Word hyphenates the document without asking for confirmation. If you add text to the document at a later stage, the hyphenation will be adjusted as you type.

♦ Place the insertion point at the beginning of the document.

♦ **Tools**
Language
Hyphenation

♦ Tick the **Automatically hyphenate document** option.

♦ Determine how hyphenation is to be carried out:

Hyphenate words in CAPS — If this choice is deactivated, Word will not hyphenate words with capital letters.

Hyphenation zone — If the space available on a line is superior to the value of this zone, Word tries to break up the first word of the following line. Unless you modify it, the value proposed is 0.63 cm.

Limit consecutive hyphens to — Indicate here the maximum number of consecutive lines that can end in hyphens. The usual value is three.

♦ Click **OK**.

An error message may appear if the hyphenation component is not installed.

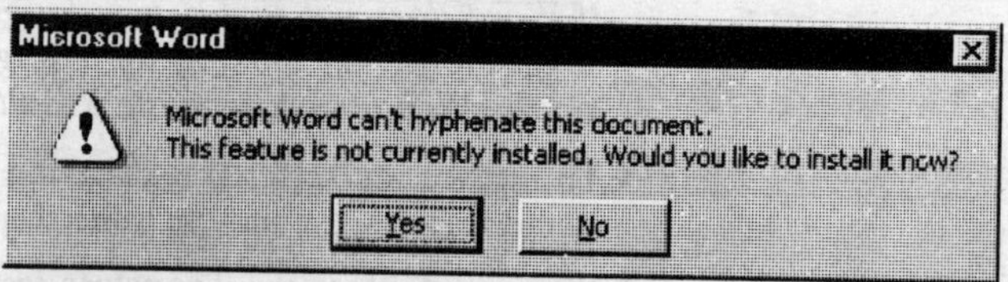

- If this happens, insert the Microsoft Office XP or Word 2002 CD-ROM in the drive and click **Yes** to install the component. A window showing the installation progress appears briefly on the screen.

Word inserts hyphens into the document automatically wherever necessary.

❑ *If you do not want words to be hyphenated in a certain portion of text, select that part of the document and tick the **Don't hyphenate** option in the **Paragraph** dialog box (**Format - Paragraph - Line and Page Breaks** tab) before proceeding with the automatic hyphenation.*

*To remove the existing automatic hyphens from the document, deactivate the **Automatically hyphenate document** option in the **Hyphenation** dialog box (**Tools - Language - Hyphenation**).*

Manual hyphenation

When you use manual hyphenation, Word will ask your permission before hyphenating any words.

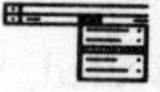

- If you wish to hyphenate the whole document, place the insertion point at the beginning of the document. Otherwise, select the portion of text concerned.
- **Tools**
  Language
  Hyphenation
- Define the hyphenation options as for automatic hyphenation (cf. the section above): **Hyphenate words in CAPS**, **Hyphenation zone** and **Limit consecutive hyphens to.**
- Click the **Manual** button.

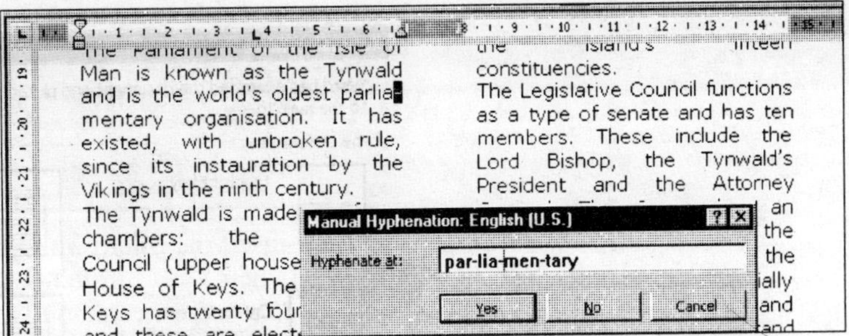

A black rectangle flashes on the proposed hyphenation: all the text preceding it plus the hyphen will move up to the previous line, if you accept. The small grey vertical line corresponds to the end of the line. Other hyphens may appear showing other hyphenation possibilities within the same word.

♦ To accept the hyphenation, click the **Yes** button, to reject the hyphenation, click **No** and to move the hyphen, use the → or ← arrows and click **Yes**.

♦ Click **OK** on the message that tells you the hyphenation is complete.

♦ Place the insertion point where you wish to hyphenate a word.

♦ Insert an optional hyphen with Ctrl -.

❑ *You must use an optional hyphen when working with the keyboard. It ensures that, if ever you modify your text and the hyphenated word is no longer at the end of a line, the hyphen will not appear.*

Creating a summary of a document

♦ Open the document concerned.

♦ **Tools**
AutoSummarize

Word takes a few seconds to produce the summary dialog box.

♦ Choose the **Type of summary** you require.

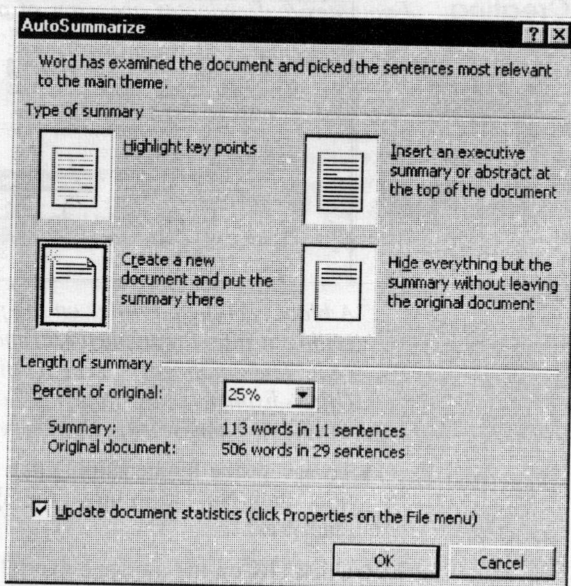

- ♦ If you wish, change the size attributed to the summary using the **Percent of original** option.
- ♦ Click **OK**.

  The summary appears on the screen.
- ♦ If you chose to **Hide everything but the summary without leaving the original document** or **Highlight key points**, click the **Close** button on the **AutoSummarize** toolbar to return to your document.

Creating footnotes and endnotes

Footnotes and endnotes are ways of adding explanations, comments and references relative to the main text of your document.

♦ Position the insertion point where you wish to insert the note reference.

♦ **Insert**
Reference
Footnote

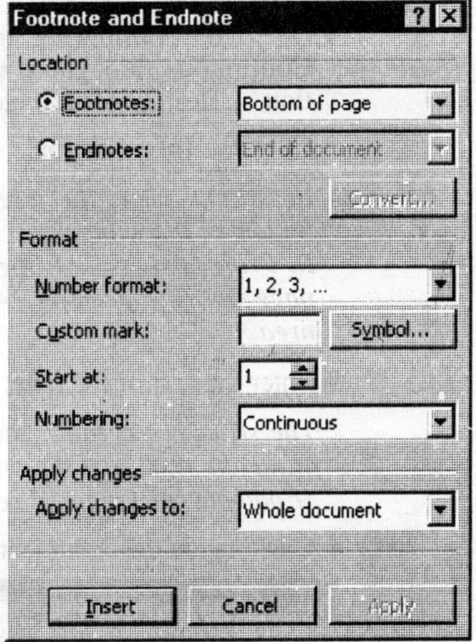

♦ Specify what sort of note you are creating by choosing **Footnotes** or **Endnotes** in the **Location** frame.

♦ Indicate where the note should be printed, using the drop-down list on **Footnotes** or **Endnotes**, whichever is active:

	Place at	Position on page
For footnotes	**Bottom of page** **Below text**	in the bottom margin just under the last line of text
For endnotes	**End of section** **End of document**	at the end of a section at the end of the document

♦ If you want the notes to be numbered automatically, use the **Number format** list to change the way numbers look.

When automatic numbering is in place, Word updates the numbers when you add, move or delete notes.

♦ If you want to create your own note reference, click the text box on the **Custom mark** option and enter the note reference (up to 10 characters) or click the **Symbol** button to choose a symbol as the reference.

*The **Number format** and **Start at** options become unavailable when you create a custom reference.*

♦ When automatic numbering is in place, you can enter a new number or character by which to start numbering in the **Start at** box.

♦ Open the **Numbering** list to specify whether numbering should be **Continuous** throughout the document, or should it **Restart each section** or **Restart each page**.

♦ Click the **Insert** button.

In Normal view, the insertion point appears in the notes pane at the bottom of the window.

In Print Layout view, the insertion point appears at the bottom of the page above the footer. A line separates the text area from the note area.

♦ Enter the text of the note.

The styles reserved for the text of a note are called "Footnote text" and "Endnote text" and the one for the marks referring to the note is called "Footnote (or Endnote) reference".

♦ Click inside the document or press F6 if you are in Normal view.

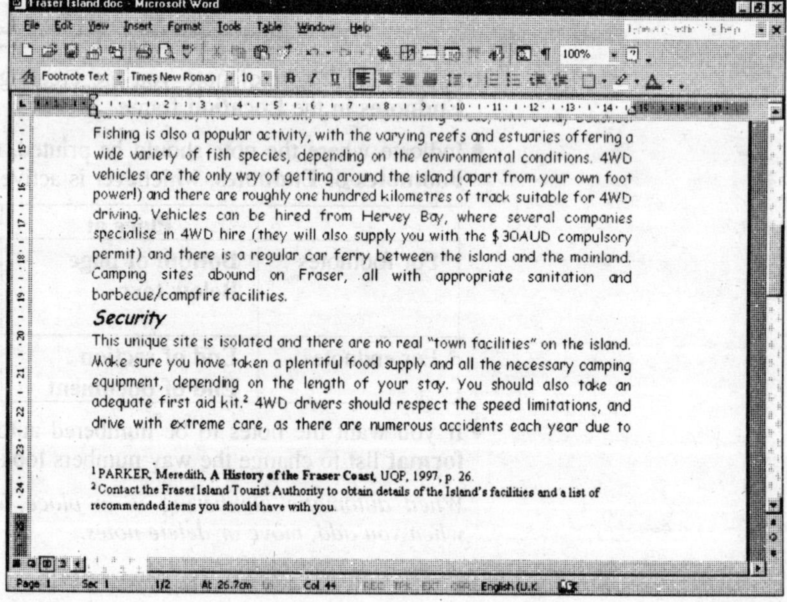

♦ To see the content of a note, point to its reference (without clicking) or, if you are in Normal view, use the note pane (cf. Using the note pane).

*When you point to a reference, the content of the note appears in a ScreenTip, providing the **ScreenTips** option is active in **Tools - Options**, **View** tab.*

❑ *The **Convert** button on the **Footnote and Endnote** dialog box (**Insert - Reference - Footnote**) converts a footnote into an endnote and vice versa.*
Word keeps space at the end of the page so that footnote contents are always printed on the same page as their reference.

*To move from note to note, click the **Select Browse Object** ( ) button on the vertical scroll bar then the button or the button to browse endnotes and footnotes respectively.*

Using the note pane

♦ **View**
Normal

♦ To open the note pane, while in Normal view, activate the **Footnotes** option in the **View** menu, or double-click the note reference.

♦ To alter the height of the note pane, drag the top edge of the pane.

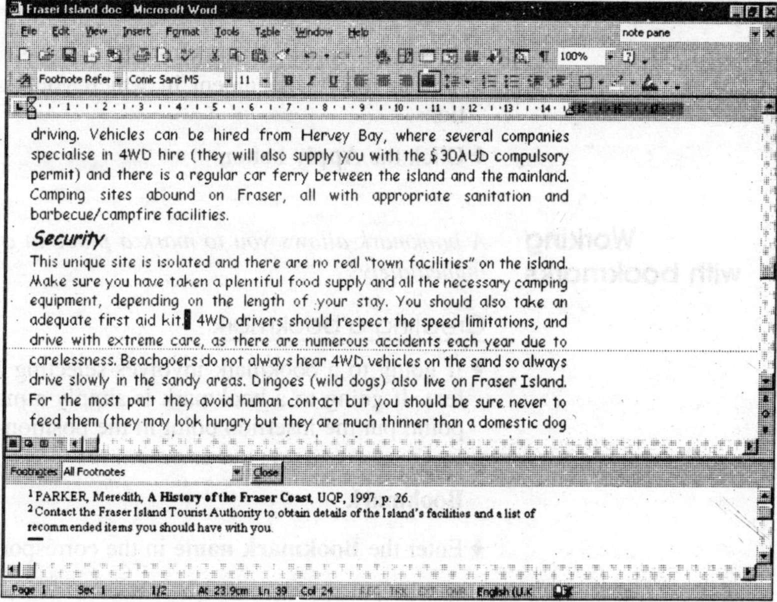

♦ To reach a note reference quickly, click the text of the corresponding footnote or endnote, then click the reference in the text.

♦ To close the note pane, deactivate the **Footnotes** option in the **View** menu, or click the **Close** button on the note pane.

Managing notes

To manage notes, you need to work on the note reference and not the text of the note.

♦ To change a note's contents while in **Print Layout** view, double-click the note reference and make your changes.

♦ To delete a note, select the note reference and press Del.

♦ To move a note, move the note reference as you would a normal piece of text.

❑ *The notes are then automatically re-numbered (when automatic numbering is active).*

Modifying the format of notes

♦ Place the mouse pointer anywhere in the document.

♦ **Insert**
Reference
Footnote

♦ Make your changes in the **Format** frame.

♦ Open the **Apply changes to** list and click the option corresponding to the part of the document in which you want to apply your modifications.

♦ Click the **Apply** button.

Working with bookmarks

A bookmark allows you to mark a place in a text, so that you can find it immediately.

Creating a bookmark

♦ If going to a bookmark involves selecting a passage of text, select that text. If going to a bookmark is simply a matter of moving the insertion point, put the insertion point in the position required.

♦ **Insert**
Bookmark

♦ Ctrl Shift F5

♦ Enter the **Bookmark name** in the corresponding box.

A bookmark name can contain up to 40 characters; it must start with a letter and must not contain any spaces.

♦ Click the **Add** button.

Deleting a bookmark

♦ **Insert Bookmark** ♦ Ctrl Shift F5

♦ In the **Bookmark name** list box, select the bookmark to delete.

♦ Click the **Delete** button, then click **Close.**

Using a bookmark

♦ **Insert Bookmark** ♦ Ctrl Shift F5

♦ If required, in **Sort by**, choose to sort the bookmark list by the **Location** of the bookmark in the document, or by its **Name**.

♦ Double-click the bookmark you want to reach, or select it and click the **Go to** button.

♦ Shut the dialog box using the **Close** button.

Bookmarks can also be reached via ***Edit - Go To*** *or* Ctrl ***G****.*

Creating an outline using preset styles

♦ Activate **Outline** view:

View
Outline

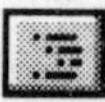

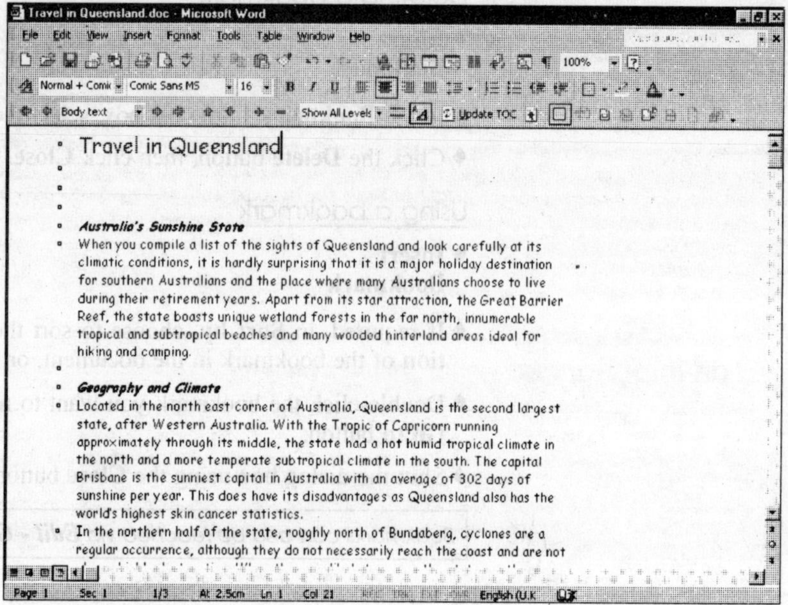

*The **Outline** toolbar replaces the ruler and each paragraph is preceded by a hollow square.*

♦ To enter a heading into the outline use the **Style** list on the **Formatting** toolbar to apply one of the following styles, depending on the importance of the heading:

Heading 1	main headings
Heading 2	subheadings
Heading 3	sub-subheadings.

*Nine predefined styles are available but only three can be seen in the **Style** list. To see all of them, display the **Styles and Formatting** task pane and click the **All styles** option in the **Show** list.*

*You can also apply preset styles in views other than Outline view. Applying the styles **Heading 1**, **Heading 2**, **Heading 3** (and so on) obviously cancels any existing formatting of your own. You can however re-apply your own formatting subsequently. You can also customise the predefined styles. A cross to the left of the text indicates that this is an outline heading.*

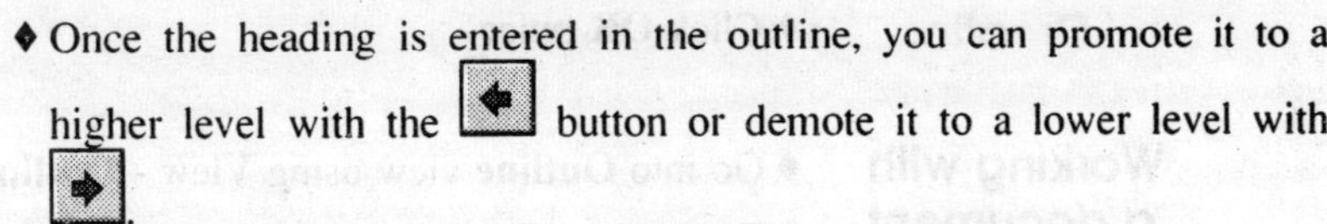

♦ Once the heading is entered in the outline, you can promote it to a higher level with the button or demote it to a lower level with .

❑ *If a normal paragraph has been defined as a heading by mistake, return to it and give it another style (not **Heading 1**, **Heading 2** or any of the other heading styles).*

❑ *Leave Outline view by activating another view.*

❑ *If certain paragraphs of your text are formatted in custom styles that you do not wish to replace by preset styles, you must give an importance level to each style before you can usefully include the paragraphs in an outline (cf. below).*

Assigning an importance level

If you want to create a table of contents or automatically number headings while keeping the styles created in the document (these would be custom styles, not preset ones), you must assign an importance level to each paragraph (or to each paragraph style).

To a paragraph

♦ Place the insertion point in the paragraph concerned or select the paragraph.

♦ **Format**
Paragraph
Indents and Spacing tab

♦ In the **Outline level** list, choose a level for the heading (from 1 to 9).

♦ Click **OK**.

♦ Assign an importance level for each paragraph in the same way.

To a paragraph style

♦ Show the **Styles and Formatting** task pane by clicking the tool button on the **Formatting** toolbar.

♦ In the **Pick formatting to apply** list, point to the style to which you wish to attribute an outline level, click the button and choose **Modify**.

♦ Click the **Format** button then the **Paragraph** option.

♦ In the **Outline level** list, choose a level for the paragraph style (from 1 to 9).

♦ Click **OK** twice.

Working with a document outline

♦ Go into **Outline** view using **View - Outline**.

♦ To display the headings of a particular level and above, open the **Show Level** list [Show Level 4 ▾] on the **Outlining** toolbar and click the appropriate option for the required level. For example, if you click **Show Level 4** you will see all the Level 4 headings as well as those for levels 1, 2 and 3.

You can also select a level by holding down [Alt] and [⇧Shift] and typing the level's number on the alphanumerical keyboard.

- Travel in Queensland
  - *Australia's Sunshine State*
  - *Geography and Climate*
  - *History*
    - *First landings*
    - *First towns*
    - *Industry and agriculture*
    - *Growth and change*
  - *Main Tourist Sites*
    - *South-East Queensland*
    - *Brisbane - The State Capital*
      - *Modest beginnings*
      - *Small town in the big city*
      - *A growing sophistication*
    - *Gold Coast and Hinterland*
      - *A surfer's paradise*
      - *Forests of a delicate beauty*

♦ To view the whole document (headings and text), open the **Show Level** list [Show Level 4 ▾] and click the **Show All Levels** option.

♦ To hide the text linked to the active heading, double-click the cross that precedes the heading or click the [−] tool button or press the - (minus) key on the number pad.

♦ To show the text linked to the active heading, double-click the cross that precedes the heading or click the [+] tool button or press the + (plus) key on the number pad.

♦ To promote a heading up one level, place the insertion point in the heading concerned, then click the [⇦] tool button or press [Alt] [⇧Shift] [←].

♦ To demote a heading down one level, place the insertion point in the heading concerned, then click the tool button or press Alt Shift →.

♦ To move a heading with any associated text or subheadings, point to the cross that precedes the heading then drag it to its new position or click the title then the or tool button.

♦ To print a document outline, show only the headings then start printing.

The print preview shows the whole document, but only the outline's headings will actually be printed.

Numbering headings

Numbering headings created using Heading styles

♦ Any view you like can be active; place the insertion point anywhere in the text.

♦ **Format**
Bullets and Numbering

♦ Activate the **Outline Numbered** tab.

♦ Choose one of the options where the word **Heading** appears.

♦ Click **OK.**

The numbers are applied immediately. The format of each number depends on the option you chose and the level of the paragraph.

Numbering paragraphs presented with styles

♦ Go into **Normal** or **Print Layout** view.

♦ If only part of the document is to be numbered, select that part, otherwise click anywhere in the document.

♦ **Format**
Bullets and Numbering

♦ Click the **Outline Numbered** tab.

♦ Choose a list numbering format that does not include the word Heading.

♦ Click the **Customize** button.

♦ For each style level you wish to define:

– Select the **Level** in the corresponding list.

– Click the **More** button if you need to expand the dialog box.

– Choose the style you want to associate with a level using the **Link level to style** list.

♦ If you wish, modify the numbering format options (cf. title below).

♦ Click **OK**.

❑ *To remove numbering in a document, select the whole document, use the* ***Format - Bullets and Numbering*** *command, click the* ***None*** *presentation and click* ***OK****. If you wish to remove numbering on only part of the document, select the portion of text concerned and proceed as described above. In this case Word will automatically renumber the document.*

Customising numbering on outline headings

♦ Any view you like can be active (Normal, Outline or Print Layout).

♦ **Format**
Bullets and Numbering

♦ Click the model that comes closest to the numbering you want to create.

If the document is already numbered, Word selects the current numbering model.

♦ Click the **Customize** button and, if the dialog box is not fully expanded, click **More**.

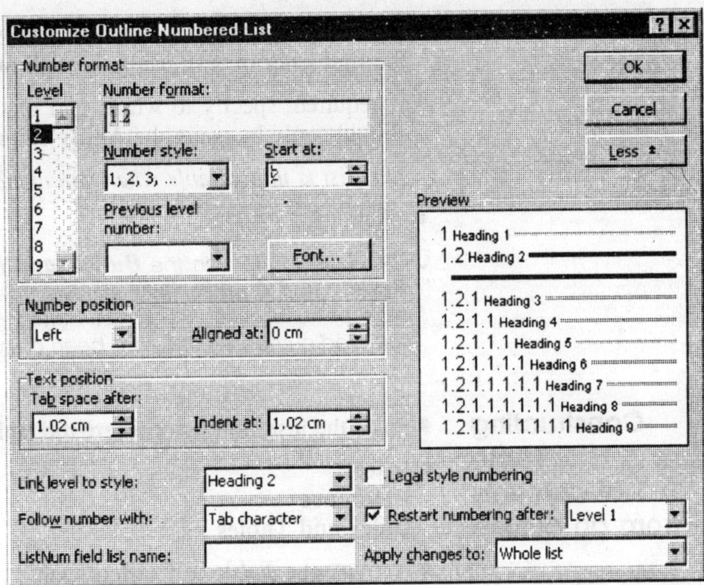

♦ Select the **Level** you wish to modify in the **Number format** frame.

♦ If necessary, choose the style that you wish to associate with the selected level using the **Link level to style** list.

♦ Select the numbering style in the **Number style** list then if necessary, enter a new starting number in the **Start at** box.

♦ Customize the text used for the numbers in the **Number format** text box.

♦ If necessary, tick the **Legal style numbering** option if you want to replace the numbers shown in the **Number format** with the corresponding Arabic numerals (for example replace Section V by Section 5).

♦ Using the **Number position** options, choose where the numbers should be placed and how they will be aligned.

♦ In the **Tab space after** text box, enter the distance that should separate the end of the number and the beginning of the first line of text.

This text box is only available when the ***Tab character*** *option is active in the* ***Follow number with*** *list.*

♦ Enter in the **Indent at** box the indent distance that should be applied to all the lines of text except the first one.

To line up all the lines of text, make sure the ***Tab space after*** *value is equal to the value in the* ***Indent at*** *box.*

♦ If necessary, modify the character that should separate the number from the first letter of text, using the **Follow number with** options.

♦ If required, specify to which part of the document your customisations should apply by using the **Apply changes to** list.

This list is unavailable when you number a document for the first time.

♦ Click **OK**.

❑ *The **Reset** button on the **Bullets and Numbering** dialog box (**Format - Bullets and Numbering**) retrieves the default settings for the selected type of numbering. The **Reset** button only becomes available when the selected numbering style has been customised.*

Constructing a table of contents from an outline

♦ Place the insertion point where the table is to be inserted.

♦ **Insert**
Reference
Index and Tables

♦ Activate the **Table of Contents** tab.

♦ In the **Formats** list in the **General** frame, choose the format you prefer. You can check the result in the **Print Preview** frame.

You can also see a Web Preview of your table of contents, showing how it would appear in a Web browser.

♦ If you wish, indicate the items to display and how to display them: do you wish to **Show page numbers**? If so, do you want to **Right align page numbers**?

♦ For all the formats except **Simple** and **Modern**, indicate whether you wish to add a **Tab leader** (a dotted line) between the headings and the page numbers.

♦ Using the **Show levels** list, give the number of heading levels that should appear in the table of contents.

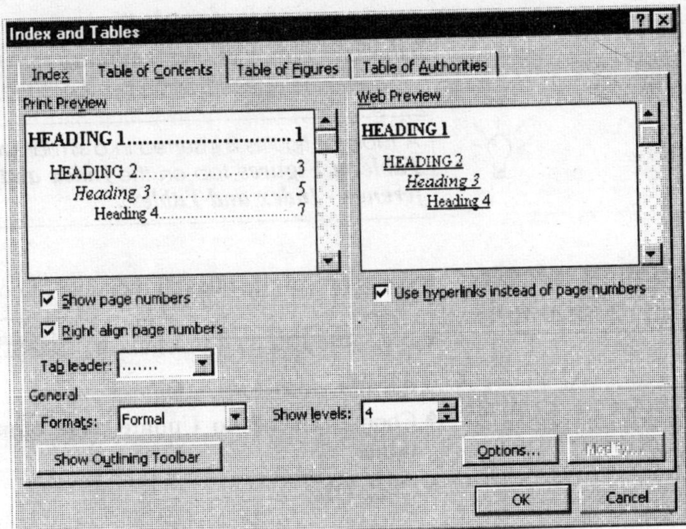

♦ If you intend to display your table of contents in a Web browser and you want a hyperlink to be created for each heading, make sure the **Use hyperlinks instead of page numbers** option is active.

When this option is active, hyperlinks are created for each title in the table of contents inserted in the document, without removing the page numbers.

♦ If you want to see the **Outlining** toolbar in the document, click the **Show Outlining Toolbar** button.

♦ Click **OK**.

♦ If required, use Alt F9 to hide the code corresponding to the table of contents and view the entries it contains.

For each heading in the table, a hyperlink is created.

♦ To go to a heading in the document, hold down Ctrl and click the corresponding title in the table of contents.

❑ *When you select the table of contents, it appears with a grey background. You can choose to display this background permanently (or never to display it at all) using the* ***Field shading*** *option in the* ***Options*** *dialog box (****Tools - Options - View*** *tab).*

❑ *To change how the table of contents is presented, select another* ***Format*** *in the* ***Table of Contents*** *tab in the* ***Index and Tables*** *dialog box (****Insert - Index and Tables****). After you have confirmed your choice, the new presentation will replace the old one.*

❑ *The* [button] *button on the* ***Outlining*** *toolbar selects the table of contents no matter where the insertion point is in the document.*

A table of figures is inserted in a similar way to a table of contents; use the ***Table of Figures*** *tab on the* ***Index and Tables*** *dialog box (****Insert - Reference - Index and Tables****).*

Updating a table of contents

♦ Click one of the titles in the table of contents to activate it.

♦ Press the F9 key or click the Update TOC button on the **Outlining** toolbar.

♦ Choose whether to **Update page numbers only** or to **Update entire table.**

♦ Click **OK.**

Making an index

Here is an example of the type of index you might draw up:

Defining an entry for the index

♦ If the entry you want in the index is already entered, select it, otherwise place the insertion point where the subject to be indexed is discussed.

♦ **Insert**
Reference
Index and Tables
Index tab
Mark Entry button

♦ Alt Shift X

♦ Type the **Main entry**, if necessary.

♦ If required, access the **Subentry** box and type in the secondary entry.

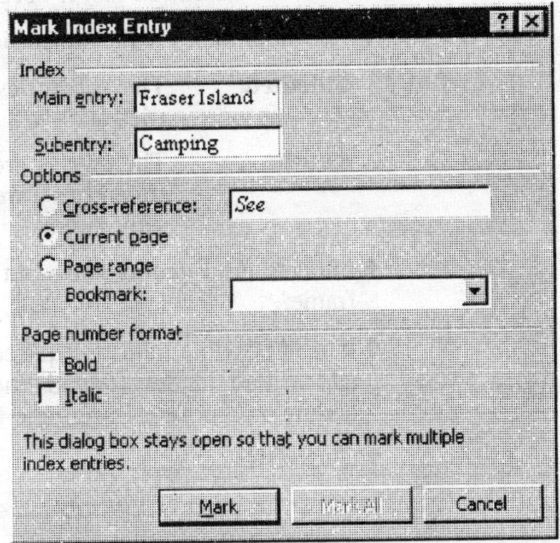

♦ If you want to create other levels of entries, type a colon (:) before continuing to enter the text in the **Subentry** box.

♦ Use the **Cross-reference** option to add a reference to another index entry instead of a page number.

♦ Use the **Current page** option to display the page number corresponding to the selected index entry.

This option is active by default.

♦ Use the **Page Range** option to select in the **Bookmark** list the bookmark that indicates the group of pages to be included in the entry.

♦ If you wish to apply **Bold** or **Italic** type to the page numbers given to that index entry, tick the corresponding **Page number format** option.

♦ If required, use shortcut keys to format the characters entered.

♦ Confirm by clicking **Mark** then click **Close**.

If the nonprinting characters are visible, you will be able to see the inserted field {XE...}.

Inserting the index

- ♦ Place the insertion point where you want to put the index.
- ♦ **Insert**
  Reference
  Index and Tables
- ♦ Activate the **Index** tab, if necessary.
- ♦ Choose a look for the subentries under **Type**:

Indented The subentries are indented in relation to the main entries and they are one underneath the other.

Run-in The entries are listed one underneath the other, but the subentries are listed side by side, separated by semi-colons.

- ♦ Indicate the **Format** you want and check its appearance in the **Preview** frame.
- ♦ If it is possible, and if required, choose to **Right align page numbers**, add a **Tab leader** (dotted line), place the index in two or more **Columns** or choose a **Language** for the index.
- ♦ Click **OK**.

❑ *The styles used in the table are called **Index 1**, **Index 2**... They can, of course, be modified.*

❑ *When you select an index, as with a table of contents, it appears with a grey background. You can choose to display this background permanently (or never at all) using the **Field shading** option in the **Options** dialog box (**Tools - Options - View** tab).*

Updating an index

- ♦ Click inside the index table.
- ♦ Press F9.

Creating a master document

A master document brings together a group of associated documents called subdocuments. A long document can sometimes be managed more easily by splitting it into several subdocuments.

- Create a new document using the template common to all the sub-documents.
- **View**
  Outline

  *Word displays the **Outlining** toolbar (this can be moved if not all its tools are showing).*
- If necessary, click the tool to activate the **Master Document** mode and the corresponding tools.
- To insert a sub-document, click the tool, select the document you wish to insert and click the **Open** button.

  The sub-document outline appears in a grey border.
- To show only the outline of the subdocument, open the Show Level 4 list on the **Outlining** toolbar then click the required level depending on which headings you wish to see.
- Save the master document then close it.

Using a master document

- Open the master document that contains the subdocuments.

  When you open a master document, it is condensed, with each subdocument appearing as a hyperlink. You can Ctrl-click the hyperlink to open the subdocument. When the nonprinting characters are on display, you can see that subdocuments are separated by section breaks.
- Click the tool button to expand the subdocuments.
- Choose what you wish to see using the tools on the **Outlining** toolbar.
- To open a sub-document, double-click the sub-document's icon in the top left corner of the frame. When you have finished working on it, close the sub-document before coming back to the master document.

  If you do not close it, the sub-document will be locked in the master document (you will see a padlock symbol appear above the icon) and you will not be able to make any changes to it.

♦ To lock a sub-document to prevent any changes being made, click in the sub-document concerned then click the tool button. To unlock, click the tool button again.

♦ To reorganise the contents of the master document, select within the subdocument the heading(s) you wish to move then use the or tool button. Alternatively, point to the cross preceding the heading and drag it to its new position.

To move items you can also drag them with the mouse or use the and tools.

♦ To divide a sub-document, position the insertion point at the place where you wish to break up the sub-document and click .

The tool will only be available if the insertion point is located at the beginning of a paragraph.

♦ To merge sub-documents, select them then click the tool button.

The tool will only be available if no paragraph (not even a blank paragraph) is selected outside the frames of the sub- documents being merged.

♦ To delete a sub-document, select the sub-document by clicking its icon then press the Del key.

When this is done, the sub-document will no longer be part of the master document. You can however continue to use it as a normal Word document.

♦ To insert or delete page or section breaks in a master document, you should show the hidden characters then proceed as you would for a document in **Normal** or **Print Layout** view.

♦ If you wish to number the headings or pages, or insert a table of contents or an index or create headers and footers and so on, proceed as you would on any other document.

♦ To print all the subdocuments, print the master document.

Inserting a table

♦ Position the insertion point where you want to insert the table.

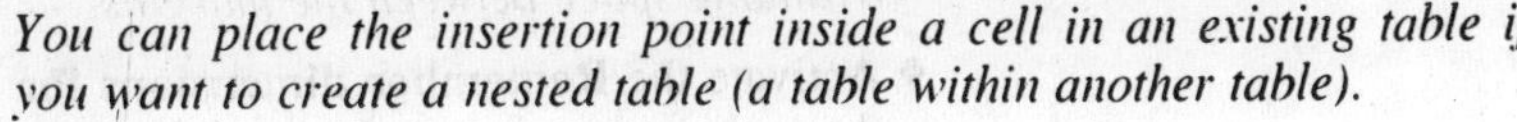

You can place the insertion point inside a cell in an existing table if you want to create a nested table (a table within another table).

♦ **Table**
Insert
Table

♦ Specify the **Number of columns** and the **Number of rows.**

The columns in Word tables correspond to columns of text (or numbers, drawings, etc) and the rows to rows correspond of cells and not to lines of text.

♦ In the **AutoFit behaviour** frame, click one of the three options:

Fixed column width	The width of each column is not automatically adjusted as you enter data. In the text box, either choose **Auto** to let Word choose the width of the columns or specify a width of your own.
AutoFit to contents	The table is inserted with columns of minimum width. As you enter data, the column width is automatically adjusted to fit the contents. Note that if you have already manually adjusted the width of a column, AutoFit will no longer work.
AutoFit to window	The table is inserted between the margins of your document; when the margins change, the table is adjusted automatically.

Whatever option is chosen, if an object or picture is inserted into the table, the column width is automatically adjusted to the size of that object or picture.

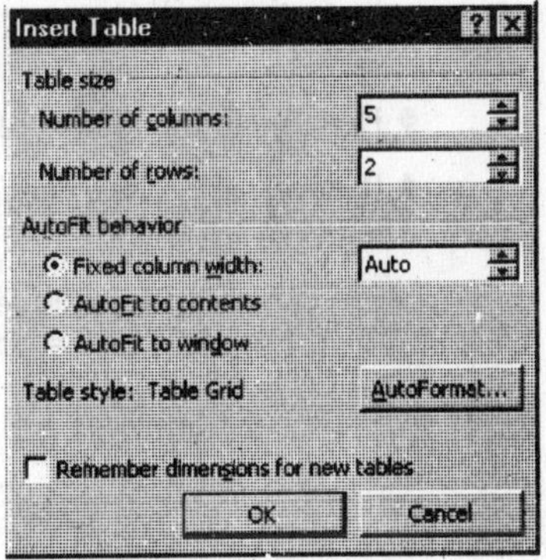
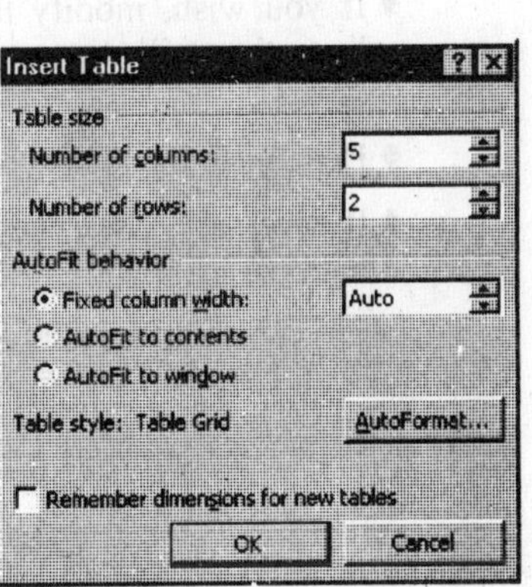

*The **Auto** choice spreads the required number of columns over the available space between the margins.*

♦ Activate the **Remember dimensions for new tables** option if you want these chosen settings to be used for any new table you create.

♦ Click **OK**.

A table is instantly inserted. On the ruler, a grid-patterned rectangle shows the width of each column. When the table is first inserted, the first cell (in the top left corner) is active.

♦ Next, fill in your table. To do this, click the required cell and enter the contents as you would a normal paragraph.

The cells in a table can also be formatted like any other paragraph.

❑ *A table can contain a maximum of 63 columns.*

❑ *A table can also be inserted using the button on the **Standard** toolbar.*

♦ If necessary, show the **Tables and Borders** toolbar by clicking the  tool button.

*Clicking the tool button activates **Print Layout** view.*

♦ If necessary, activate the tool.

The mouse pointer takes the shape of a pencil.

♦ Using the , ½ and tools, choose the style, thickness and colour for the outline of the table.

♦ Drag to draw the table's outline.

♦ If you wish, modify the line thickness, style or colour then draw the lines that will separate the rows then those that will separate the columns.

♦ Deactivate the tool.

♦ If necessary, close the **Tables and Borders** toolbar by clicking the button.

❑ *The advantage of this technique is that you can decide the height of the rows, the width of the columns and the type of lines used.*

Moving around a table

♦ With the mouse, use the normal pointing and clicking techniques.

♦ With the keyboard, use the following keys:

Keys	Action
Tab / Shift Tab	the cell to the right/left.
↓ / ↑	the cell below/above.
Alt Home / Alt End	the first/last cell of the active row.
Alt Pg Up / Alt Pg Dn	the first/last cell of the active column.

Selecting in a table

♦ Depending on what you are selecting, use one of the following techniques:

Mouse	Menu
To select a CELL	
Position the mouse pointer inside the cell at the left (it adopts the form of an arrow pointing top right) and click.	activate the cell concerned then use **Table - Select - Cell.**
To select a COLUMN	
Position the mouse pointer above the column (it adopts the form of a black arrow pointing down) and click.	activate a cell from the column then use **Table - Select - column.**
To select a ROW	
Position the mouse pointer at the left of the row (it adopts the form of an arrow pointing top right) and click.	activate a cell from the row then use **Table - Select - Row.**
To select the TABLE	
Drag over the table or Shift-click the first and last cells.	click inside the table then use **Table - Select - Table.**

♦ To cancel the selection, click outside it.

❑ *You can also select the table by clicking in the table then pressing* Alt ***5*** *(with num lock off).*

Placing and using tabs in a table

♦ Position your tab stops as for a paragraph of text.

♦ For any tab other than a decimal one, press Ctrl Tab; in the case of a decimal tab, the value you enter is automatically aligned with the tab stop.

Inserting columns

♦ Select the column before or after which you want to insert a new column. To insert several columns, select as many existing columns as you want to insert new ones.

♦ **Table**
Insert
Columns to the Left or **to the Right**

If you use the tool, the new columns are inserted to the left of the selection.
The new column(s) appear(s) and each cell in it takes on the format of the cell located to its right.

Inserting rows

♦ Select the row next to the place where you want to insert the new row.

♦ **Table**
Insert
Rows Above or **Below**

If you use the tool, the new rows are inserted above the selection.
New rows adopt the presentation of the row which was active when the insertion was made.

If you want to insert a new row at the end of a table, activate the last cell in the table and press Tab.

Inserting cells

♦ Select an appropriate group of cells: the new cells will be inserted before them.

♦ **Table**
Insert
Cells

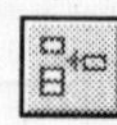

Word proposes two different ways of moving the selected cells to make room for the insertion. You also have the option of inserting a row or a column.

♦ Decide what you want to do with the selected cells:

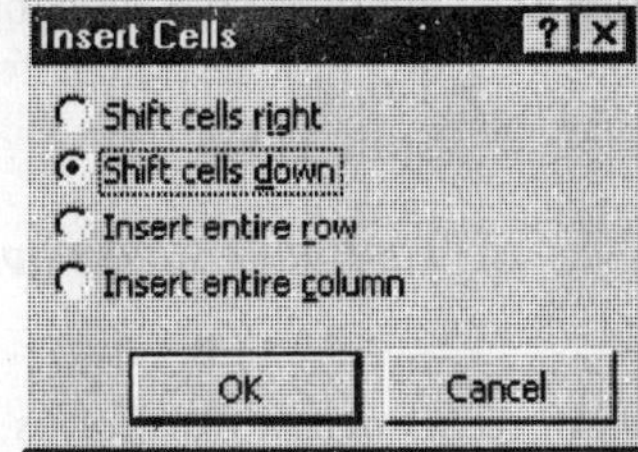

♦ Click **OK**.

The new cell takes on the presentation of the cell that was active at the time of insertion.

Deleting rows/ columns/cells

Rows and/or columns

♦ Select the rows/columns you want deleted.

♦ **Table**
Delete
Rows or **Columns**

Cells

♦ Select the cells to be deleted.

♦ **Table**
Delete
Cells

♦ Decide what should happen to the remaining cells:

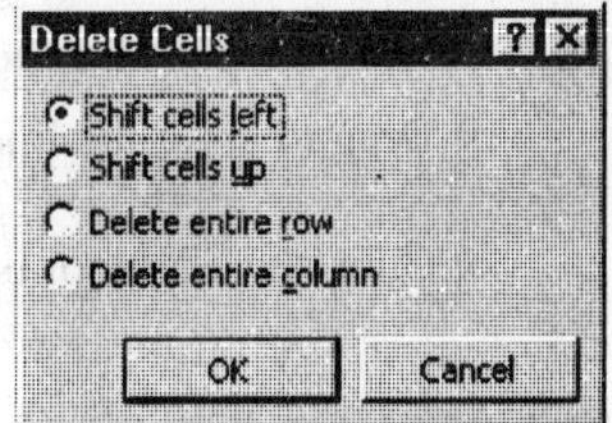

You can also choose to delete the whole row or column.

♦ Click **OK**.

Splitting a table in two

♦ Place the insertion point in the row below the point where you are going to split the table.

♦ **Table**
Split Table

♦ Ctrl Shift Enter

Your table splits into two tables separated by a paragraph.

Merging cells

This action transforms several cells into a single cell. For example:

these cells have been merged

		1st Quarter			2nd Quarter		
		Jan	Feb	Mar	Apr	May	June
Category A	Juniors	15	10	5	14	9	12
	Seniors	12	9	6	11	5	13
Category B	Juniors	8	9	2	7	8	6
	Seniors	12	10	3	11	7	10

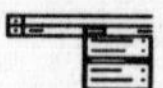

♦ Select the cells you want to merge.

♦ **Table**
Merge Cells

You can also click the button on the ***Tables and Borders*** *toolbar.*

♦ If necessary, display the **Tables and Borders** toolbar by clicking the tool button.

♦ Click the tool button.

The pointer takes the form of an eraser.

♦ Drag to erase the line separating the cells you want to merge.

♦ Click the tool button again to deactivate this tool.

Splitting cells

This technique, the opposite of merging, allows you to divide one cell into several cells.

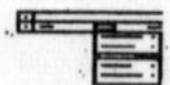

♦ Select the cells you want to split.

♦ **Table**
Split Cells

You can also click the button on the ***Tables and Borders*** *toolbar.*

♦ Specify the **Number of columns** and/or **Number of rows** that you want to create.

♦ If you want to merge all the selected cells into one before splitting divide the resulting cell into rows and columns, click the **Merge cells before split** option. If this option is not active, each cell in the selection will be divided into the stated number of rows or columns.

♦ Click **OK** to confirm your entry.

♦ Click the button in the **Tables and Borders** toolbar.

The pointer takes the form of a pencil.

♦ Drag the pointer (pencil) horizontally or vertically to create new cell divisions.

♦ When you having finished splitting the cells, click the button again to deactivate this tool.

Sorting a table

♦ Select all the elements of the table that need sorting. If the whole table is to be sorted, you do not have to select it, just click inside the table.

♦ **Table**
Sort

Note that you can sort the table by up to three different criteria.

♦ If the first row in the column contains a title and should not be included in the sort, click the **Header row** option in the **My list has** frame.

♦ Select in the **Sort by** list box the number or heading of the column containing the data by which to sort the table.

♦ In the **Type** list box, choose what sort of data you are sorting: **Text, Number** and **Date** (for data showing at least the day and month or the month and year).

♦ Specify if the sort is to be done in **Ascending** or **Descending** order.

♦ If several cells of the column used for the sort contain the same information, choose a secondary sort column in the **Then by** list box.

♦ If necessary, choose a third sort column in the last **Then by** list box.

♦ When all the criteria have been defined, click **OK** to validate.

❑ *If you are not satisfied with the new order of the data, use the button to restore the original order.*

❑ *You can also use the* ***Table - Sort*** *command to sort a list (a series of paragraphs containing text presented in columns, separated by tabs or commas).*

*You can also use the [A↓Z] or [Z↓A] tools on the **Tables and Borders** toolbar to sort the contents of the active column in ascending or descending order.*

Sorting one column of a table

♦ Select the column to be sorted.

♦ **Table**
Sort

♦ Specify the **Type** of contents in the column.

♦ Click the **Options** button.

♦ Activate **Sort column only** in the **Sort options** frame.

♦ Click **OK** then click it again to start sorting.

Converting text into a table

You can transform columns of text separated by tabs or commas into a table.

♦ Select the text.

♦ **Table**
Convert
Text To Table

♦ If necessary, enter the **Number of columns** the table should contain.

♦ Select one of the three options in the **AutoFit behaviour** frame to define how the width of the columns should be determined.

You can see further details of this function in the "Inserting a table" section.

♦ In the **Separate text at** text box, select the character you wish to use as a column indicator.

♦ Click **OK**.

A new column is produced at each tab character [⇄]. A new row is produced at each end of paragraph [Enter] or line break [⇧Shift][Enter] character.

Copying/ moving cells in a table

♦ To copy cells or to move them elsewhere, proceed as for text, using the **Copy**, **Cut** and **Paste** commands from the **Edit** menu (or the corresponding tool buttons and shortcut keys).

To insert the copied item, you do not have to select the destination cell: just place the insertion point inside it.

Fixing column headings

If the table takes up several pages, this technique allows the column headings to be printed at the top of each page.

♦ Select the rows containing the headings you want to fix.

The selection must contain the first row of the table and be continuous, if fixing more than one row.

♦ **Table**
Heading Rows Repeat

❑ *To unfix the headings, select the rows concerned and use the* ***Table - Heading Rows Repeat*** *command again.*

Modifying column width/row height

One column/row

♦ Place the insertion point in the table.

♦ To change a column's width, point to the vertical line at the right of the column you wish to modify.

The mouse pointer takes this shape: [⟛].

♦ Next, drag:

with just the mouse	to modify the width of the particular column and compensate by changing the width of the column on the right (the total width is unchanged).
with Shift	to modify the width of the particular column without adjusting any others: the overall width of the table is affected.
with Ctrl Shift	to modify the width of the particular column and adjust all the columns to the right, to preserve the overall width of the table.

♦ To change the height of a row, go into **Print Layout** view, if necessary then point to the horizontal line beneath the row concerned: the pointer takes this shape [⇳]. Drag the line as required.

❑ *Double-clicking the vertical line to the right of the active column will adjust the column width to its contents.*

❑ *If you hold down the* Alt *key as you drag, the dimensions of the column/row appear on the ruler.*

Several columns

♦ Select the columns: they will all be given the same new width.

♦ **Table**
Table Properties — Double-click one of the column indicators ( )shown on the ruler

♦ Activate the **Column** tab.

Word displays which columns are to be modified. When the selected columns are all the same width, their size appears in the first text box. If this is not the case, the width of the first column selected will appear in grey in this box.

♦ If necessary, activate the **Preferred width** option. Select a unit of measurement for the width in the **Measure in** list and enter the new column width in the **Preferred width** text box.

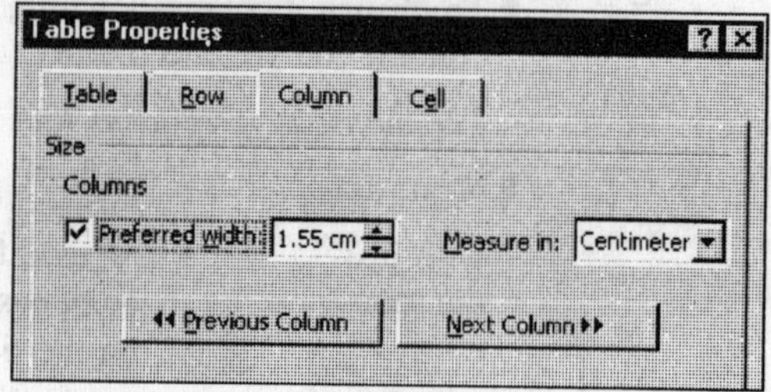

♦ If the **Next Column** or **Previous Column** also needs modifying, click the appropriate button to continue the process. When you have finished all modifications, click **OK**.

Several rows

♦ Select each row concerned.

♦ **Table**
Table Properties — Double-click one of the column indicators ( ) shown on the ruler

♦ If necessary, click the **Row** tab.

♦ In the **Size** frame, activate the **Specify height** option.

♦ In the **Row height is** list, choose between:

At least	to define a minimum height.
Exactly	to define a fixed height.

♦ After having chosen **At least** or **Exactly**, enter the new minimum or exact height in the **Specify height** text box.

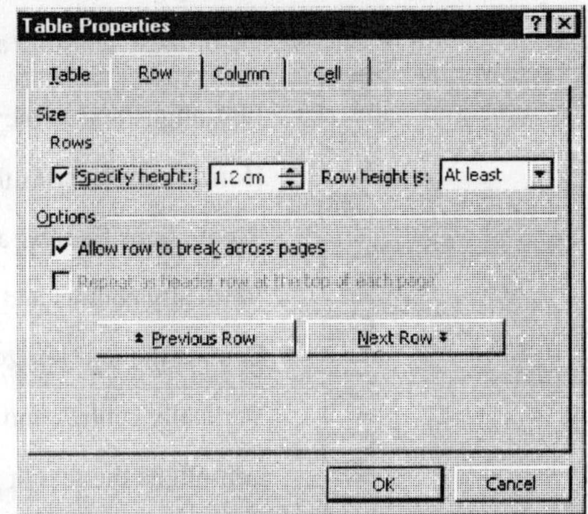

♦ If the **Next Row** or **Previous Row** also have to be modified, click the appropriate button to continue the process. When you have finished all modifications, click **OK**.

Standardising column widths/ row heights

♦ Select the rows or columns, which should be of the same height or width.

♦ To standardise the height of rows, choose:

Table
AutoFit
Distribute Rows Evenly

♦ To standardise the width of columns, choose:

Table
AutoFit
Distribute Columns Evenly

Changing horizontal or vertical alignment in a cell

♦ Select the cell or cells concerned.

♦ If necessary, display the **Tables and Borders** toolbar.

♦ Open the list on the tool button by clicking the arrow on this button.

♦ Choose one of these possible alignments:

Left-aligns text at the top of the cell.

Horizontally centres the text at the top of the cell.

Right-aligns the text at the top of the cell.

Vertically centres and left-aligns the text.

Centres the text horizontally and vertically in the cell.

Vertically centres and right-aligns the text.

Left-aligns the text at the bottom of the cell

Horizontally centres the text at the bottom of the cell.

Right-aligns the text at the bottom of the cell.

❑ *To change how text is oriented with a cell, click the cell(s) concerned and use the **Format - Text Direction** command. Click the required **Orientation** and click **OK**.*

Applying an AutoFormat to a table

You can apply a predefined style to the active table; this can be a custom style that you create or a style existing in Word.

♦ Click inside the table you wish to format.

♦ **Table**
Table AutoFormat

♦ In the **Category** list, choose which type of style you wish to see in the list.

♦ Choose one of the **Table styles** listed, depending on your needs. An example of the format appears in the **Preview** box.

♦ If the table style does not exactly meet your needs, you can click the **Modify** button to change the formatting elements used in the table.
*Be careful: the changes you make will be carried over to all the tables to which you apply this style in the rest of your document and to all the tables in the document that currently use this style. If the **Add to template** option is ticked when you modify a style, the changes you make will be added to the template associated with the current document and will thus apply to all new documents made with that template.*

♦ Activate or deactivate the **Apply special formats to** options depending on which elements in the table should adopt the chosen formatting.

♦ Click the **Default** button to make the selected style the default style for all tables created in documents based on the current template.

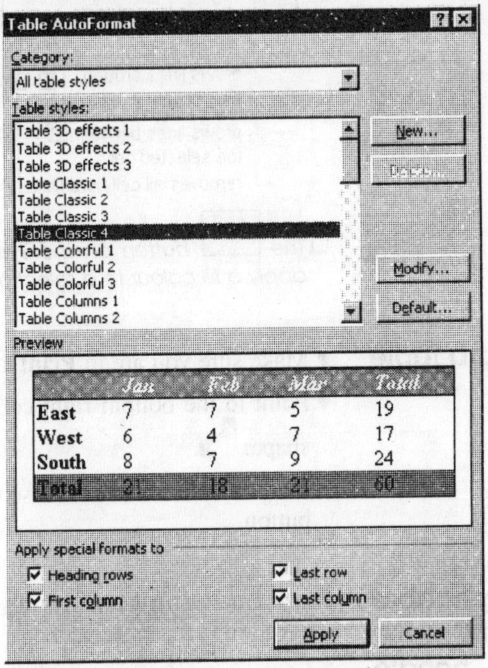

♦ Click **OK**.

*The **New** button on the **Table AutoFormat** dialog box (**Table - AutoFormat Table**) can be used to create a new table style, while the **Delete** button removes the selected style. You can only delete styles that you have created yourself or Word styles that you have modified.*

Modifying borders in a table

♦ Select the cells concerned, or the whole table.

♦ If necessary, display the **Tables and Borders** toolbar by clicking the tool button.

♦ Open the list on the tool and choose a line style.

♦ Open the list on the ½ tool and choose a line width.

♦ Open the list on the tool button then choose the colour you want to apply to the border.

♦ Open the list on the tool button and choose the type of border.

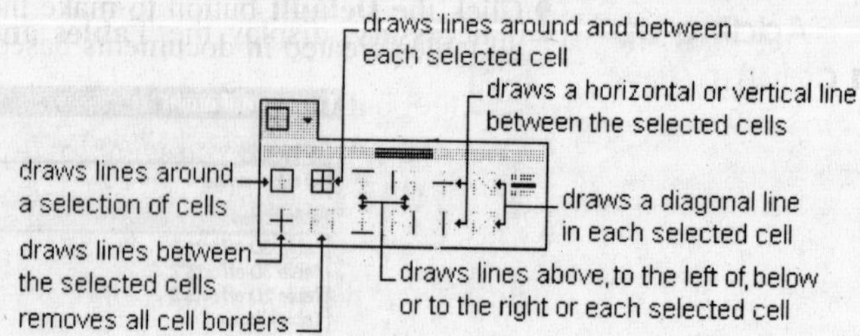

❑ *The* button *on the* ***Tables and Borders*** *toolbar can be used to apply a fill colour to a selection of cells.*

Resizing a table

♦ Make sure you are in **Print Layout** view.

♦ Point to the bottom right corner of the table until the pointer takes this shape: ↘.

♦ Drag to increase or decrease the size of the table then release the mouse button.

Moving a table by its move handle

Tables are considered as objects and can be moved anywhere on the page.

♦ Make sure you are in **Print Layout** view.

♦ Point to the upper left corner of the table until the pointer takes this shape: ✥.

♦ Drag the table into its new position then release the mouse button.

❑ *If the* ***Around*** *option in the* ***Text Wrapping*** *frame of the* ***Table Properties*** *dialog box (in* ***Table - Properties - Table*** *tab) is active, the text will wrap itself around the table, as it would with a picture.*

Positioning a table across a page

♦ Place the insertion point in the table.

♦ **Table**
Table Properties

♦ If necessary, click the **Table** tab.

♦ In the **Alignment** frame, click the required position for the table.

♦ If you choose a **Left** alignment, give an **Indent from left** value, if required, to place the table in relation to the left margin.

♦ Click **OK**.

Adding up a column/row

♦ If necessary, display the **Tables and Borders** toolbar by clicking the tool button.

♦ Click the cell where you want to display the result.

♦ Click Σ.

By default, Word first adds the cells above the result cell.

Managing a table as a spreadsheet

Basic principles

♦ Each column is identified by a letter (the first column is A, the second column is B...) and each row by a number (the first row is 1, the second row is 2...).
The cell reference is the association of its column letter with its row number (A2, B5...).

♦ To refer to consecutive cells, give the reference of the first cell, type a colon (:) and the reference of the last cell (e.g. C2:C4).
To refer to non-consecutive cells, use the comma as the separator (e.g. B5,D5).

Entering a calculation formula

♦ Activate the result cell.

♦ **Table**
Formula

♦ In the **Formula** box, enter your formula after the = sign, using the cell references and the following mathematical operators:

-	subtraction
/	division
*	multiplication
%	percentage calculation
^	raise to the power of ...
+	addition

♦ If required, choose a **Number format** and click **OK**.

Using an integrated function in a table

♦ Activate the cell in which you want to display the result.

♦ **Table**
Formula

♦ If there is anything showing in the **Formula** box, delete it, except for the = sign.

♦ In the **Paste function** list, choose the function that corresponds to the calculation you want to make.

♦ In the **Formula** box, indicate to which elements the formula should apply by inserting between the brackets one of the following definitions:

ABOVE	All cells above
BELOW	All cells below
LEFT	All cells to the left
RIGHT	All cells to the right
cell ref: cell ref	For consecutive cells
cell ref, cell ref	For non-consecutive cells

♦ If you wish, choose the **Number format** for the result.

♦ Click **OK**.

Formatting a calculation result

♦ **Table**
Formula

♦ Enter your calculation formula.

♦ Open the **Number format** list and chose a style. Here are some examples of styles using the number -3637.54:

# ##0	-3 638
# ##0.00	-3 637.54
£# ##0.00;(£# ##0.00)	(£3 637.54)
0	-3638
0%	-3638%
0.00	-3637.54
0.00%	-3637.54%

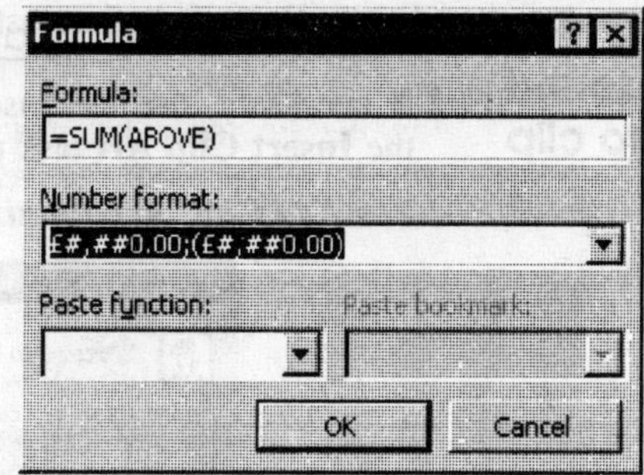

♦ Click **OK** to insert the formula into the table.

❑ *Every calculation result is in fact the result of a **FIELD**.*

❑ *The values appear if you are viewing results and not if you are viewing field codes.*

Displaying/hiding field codes

♦ To display or hide the field codes for a whole document, press Alt F9.

To display or hide a particular field code, place the insertion point in the field and press Shift F9.

Starting Point	Arrival Point	Distance in kilometres
Miami	Key West	250
Key West	Naples	350
Naples	Sarasota	170
Sarasota	Orlando	230
Orlando	Cape Canaveral	100
Cape Canaveral	Miami	350
Distance covered	**In kilometres**	**{ =SUM(ABOVE) }**
	In miles (1 mile = 1.609 km)	**{ =C8*0.621 \# "0.00" }**

The formulas entered appear between braces. The formulas are the true cell contents so if an associated cell value changes, the results can be updated.

Updating a field

♦ Place the insertion point in the field concerned.

♦ Press F9.

*An alternative way of updating a field is to right-click it and choose the **Update Field** option.*

Inserting a picture, a sound or a video clip

Finding and inserting a picture, a sound or a video clip

♦ If necessary, use the **Insert - Picture - Clip Art** command to display the **Insert Clip Art** task pane.

*The **Add Clips to Organizer** dialog box may appear on the screen:*

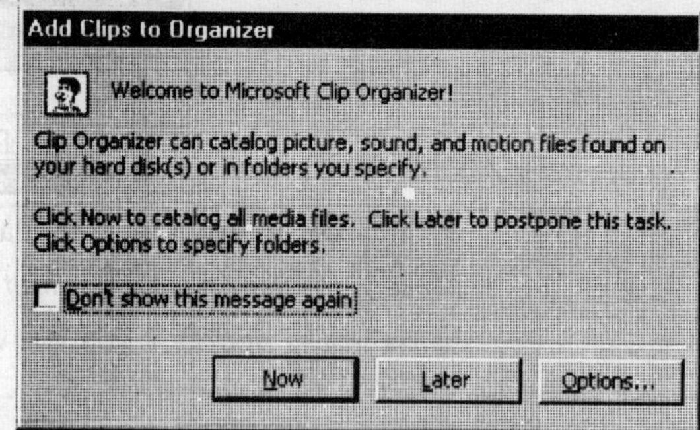

♦ Click the **Now** button if you want to add the image, audio and video files from your hard disk into the Clip Organizer. If you do not want to do that just yet, click the **Later** button.

♦ Enter one or more words in the **Search text** box.

♦ To define where the search should be carried out, open the **Search in** list and make a choice, following these guidelines: the plus (+) sign expands the hierarchy while the minus (-) sign collapses it. Click a check box to select (or deselect) the corresponding category: double-clicking selects (or deselects) that category and all its subcategories.

*The **Office Collections** category and its subcategories correspond to the image, sound and video elements installed with Office. The **Web Collections** category provides you with elements found on the Web (or more precisely on the Microsoft site). Word will only take this category into account if you have an open Internet connection.*

♦ To limit the type of items being searched for (**Clip Art, Photographs, Movies** or **Sounds**), open the **Results should be** list and deselect any elements that should be excluded from the search. You can also limit the search to certain file types. To do this, click the plus (+) sign on the type of element concerned and deselect any file types that should not be included in the search.

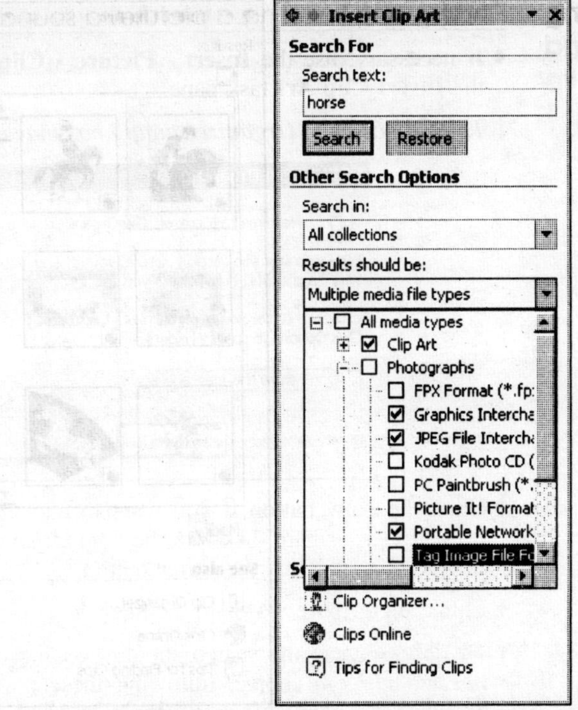

♦ Click outside the list box to close it then click the **Search** button to start searching.

If you want to interrupt the search, click the ***Stop*** *button that appears near the bottom of the pane.*

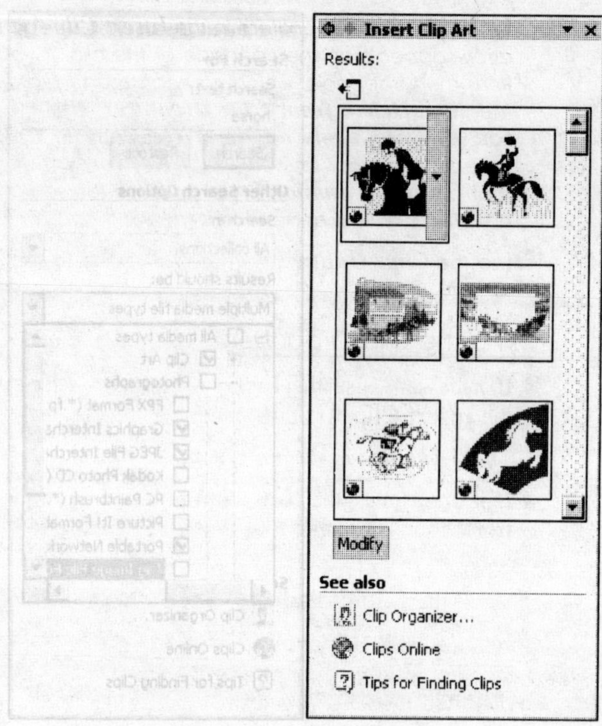

*If you have included a Web search in your search, by activating **Web Collections** in the **Search in** list and if your Internet connection is open, the [icon] icon at the bottom left of an item indicates that it was found on the Web.*

♦ When the search is finished or if you click the **Stop** button, the **Modify** button appears, which you can use to set up a new search.

♦ To insert one of the items found into your active document, place the insertion point where you wish to put the item then click the clip in the **Insert Clip Art** task pane.

*The item appears where the insertion point was and is considered as a character, since the default wrapping style is **In line with text**. Any changes to the text change the position of the object and the object cannot be moved freely. If you want the item to be considered as a drawing object, and not as a character, you should change its wrapping style (cf. **Changing an object's wrapping** in the MANAGING OBJECTS chapter).*

♦ If necessary, close the task pane by clicking its [X] button.

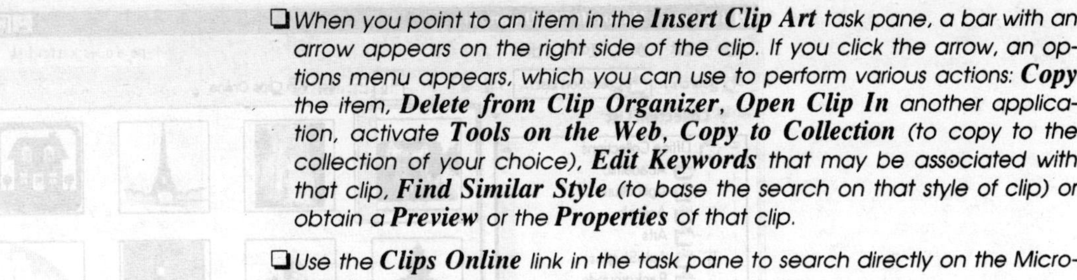

❑ *When you point to an item in the* ***Insert Clip Art*** *task pane, a bar with an arrow appears on the right side of the clip. If you click the arrow, an options menu appears, which you can use to perform various actions:* ***Copy*** *the item,* ***Delete from Clip Organizer***, ***Open Clip In*** *another application, activate* ***Tools on the Web***, ***Copy to Collection*** *(to copy to the collection of your choice),* ***Edit Keywords*** *that may be associated with that clip,* ***Find Similar Style*** *(to base the search on that style of clip) or obtain a* ***Preview*** *or the* ***Properties*** *of that clip.*

❑ *Use the* ***Clips Online*** *link in the task pane to search directly on the Microsoft site.*

Using the Clip Organizer

♦ If necessary, use the **Insert - Picture - Clip Art** command to display the **Insert Clip Art** task pane.

The ***Add Clips to Organizer*** *dialog box may appear on the screen:*

♦ If it does, click the **Now** button to add the image, audio and video files from your hard disk into the Clip Organizer. If you do not want to do that just yet, click the **Later** button.

♦ Click the **Clip Organizer** link at the bottom of the task pane.

♦ If the **Add Clips to Organizer** dialog box appears again, choose whether or not to add the image, audio and video files from your hard disk into the Clip Organizer by clicking **Now** or **Later**.

♦ To browse the collections of image sound or video items available in Office, expand the **Office Collections** hierarchy (click the + sign) then click the subcategory of your choice to display its contents in the right side of the window.

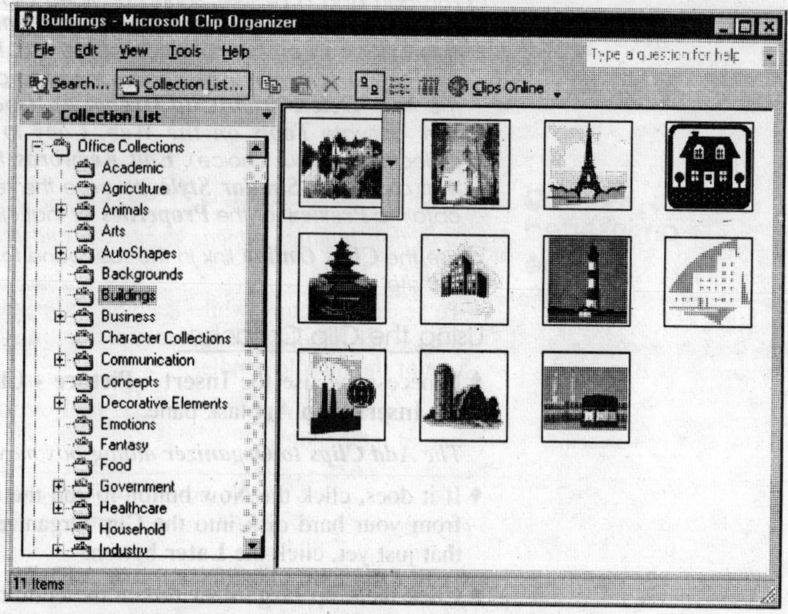

♦ In the **My Collections** collection, you can create and manage your own custom subcollections:

– To create a new collection within **My Collections**, select **My Collections** then use the **File - New Collection** command and enter the new collection's **Name**. Decide where to store this new collection then click **OK**.

– To copy a picture, sound or video clip into a subcollection of **My Collections**, look for the item in the **Office Collections** or **Web Collections** (if you are connected to the Internet) then drag the item from the right pane into the required subcollection in the left pane.

– To change the name of a subcollection created in **My Collections**, select the subcollection in question, then use the **Edit - Rename Collection** command. Type in the new name and press Enter.

– To delete one of the subcollections created in **My Collections**, select the subcollection concerned and press the Del button. Click **Yes** to confirm the deletion.

When you point to an item in the right pane of the Clip Organizer, an arrow appears on the right of it: clicking this arrow displays the list of options described in the section above.

♦ Close the **Clip Organizer** by clicking the ☒ button on its window and if necessary, close the task pane by clicking its ☒ button.

❑ *You can add a picture, sound or video clip to your document from the **Microsoft Clip Organizer** window. To do this, drag the item from the right pane of the Clip Organizer window onto the active document. The Clip Organizer window disappears but is still open in the background; you can reactivate it by clicking its link on the task pane.*

Resizing an inserted picture

♦ Click the inserted picture to select it.

*Selection handles appear around it and the **Picture** toolbar comes up on the screen.*

♦ To resize a picture while keeping its original proportions, drag one of the corner handles. To resize a picture, distorting it in the process, drag one of the middle handles.

♦ To crop a picture, click the tool on the **Picture** toolbar then drag one of the handles.

*You can use the **Format Picture** dialog box (**Format - Picture - Size** tab) to define the exact size for an inserted picture. The **Reset** button on this dialog box will restore the picture's original size.*

Drawing a shape

Any drawn shape is a drawing object.

Drawing a simple shape

♦ If necessary, show the **Drawing** toolbar using **View - Toolbars - Drawing** or .

♦ Place the insertion point where you want the drawing canvas to appear.

♦ Click the tool corresponding to the object you wish to draw:

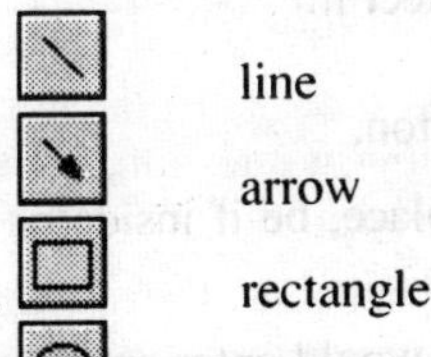

Word inserts a drawing area called the drawing canvas at the insertion point; you can create your drawing within that area. The drawing canvas is especially useful when you are drawing several objects. The objects you create there can be organised in the document more easily and their alignment and/or spacing can be defined in relation to the drawing canvas.

♦ To draw an object within the drawing canvas, position the mouse pointer within that area: if you do not wish to use the drawing canvas, place the pointer outside it.

♦ Drag to draw your shape and (if you have used it) click outside the drawing canvas to deactivate it.

If you start to draw outside the drawing canvas, it disappears automatically.

❑ *To create a new object on an existing drawing canvas, select one of the objects already in that canvas then activate the re-quired drawing tool.*

❑ *As the drawing canvas is inserted at the insertion point, it is considered as a character. Any modification to your text changes the position of the drawing canvas. Furthermore, the canvas cannot be moved freely. If you want the drawing canvas to be considered as a drawing object, and not as text, you should change the text wrapping for that area, which, by default, is* ***In line with text*** *(cf.* ***Changing an object's wrapping*** *in the MANAGING OBJECTS chapter).*

To obtain a square or circle, use the rectangle or oval tool and hold down ⇧Shift *as you draw. To draw a rectangle/square or oval/circle from its centre (and not from one side), hold down* Ctrl *as you draw.*

Creating a text box

Creating a text box allows you to position text anywhere on the page, or to put paragraphs side by side.

♦ If necessary, display the **Drawing** toolbar then put the insertion point at the place where you want the text box to appear.

♦ If you want to create the text box inside an existing drawing canvas, click that canvas to select it.

♦ Click the tool button.

♦ Drag in the required place, be it inside or outside a drawing canvas, to create the text box.

♦ Enter your text as you would enter an ordinary paragraph.

♦ Click outside the box to end.

♦ If you have used one, click outside the drawing canvas to deactivate it.

❑ *Text in a text box can be formatted using the usual commands.*

❑ *If the text is too long to fit in the text box, you will not be able to see all of it.*

> *To add text inside an object (a simple shape or AutoShape), right-click the object concerned and click the* ***Add Text*** *option.*

Drawing an AutoShape

♦ If necessary, display the **Drawing** toolbar then put the insertion point at the place where you want the AutoShape to appear.

♦ If you want to create the AutoShape inside an existing drawing canvas, click that canvas to select it.

♦ Open the **AutoShapes** drop-down list.

♦ Activate the category which contains the required shape and select the shape.

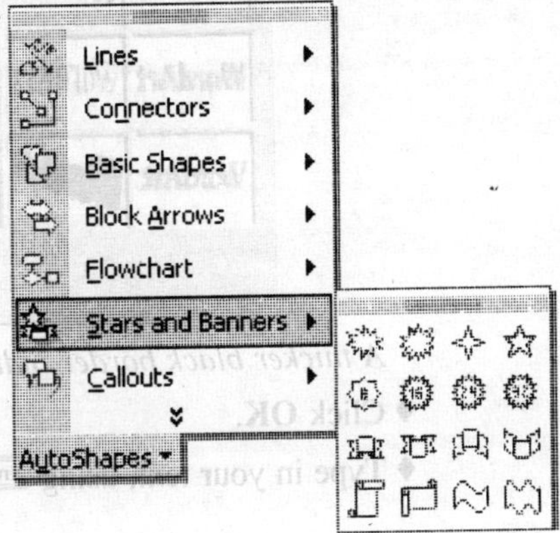

♦ Drag at the required place, be it inside or outside a drawing canvas, to create the AutoShape.

♦ If you have used one, click outside the drawing canvas to deactivate it.

Creating a WordArt object

Word Art enables you to apply special typographic effects to your text.

♦ If necessary, display the **Drawing** toolbar.

♦ If you want to create the WordArt object inside an existing drawing canvas, click that canvas to select it. Otherwise, place the insertion point where the WordArt object should appear in the document.

♦ Click the tool button.

♦ Choose the effect you wish to apply.

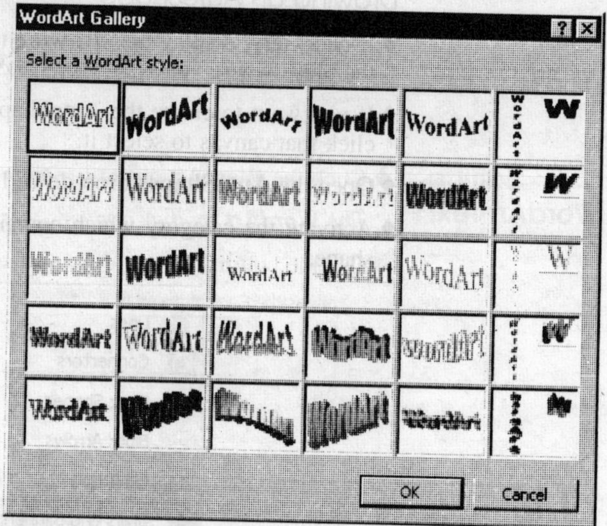

A thicker black border indicates the selected effect.

♦ Click **OK**.

♦ Type in your text, using Enter to change lines.

♦ If you wish, format your text using the **Font** and **Size** lists and the B and I tool buttons.

♦ Click **OK**.

♦ If you have used one, click outside the drawing canvas to deactivate it.

If the WordArt object is not entered in a drawing canvas, it appears at the insertion point and is considered as a character. Any modification to your text changes the position of the WordArt object. Furthermore, the object cannot be moved freely. If you want the WordArt object to be considered as a drawing object, and not as text, you should change the text wrapping for that object, which, by default, is ***In line with text*** *(cf.* ***Changing an object's wrapping*** *in the MANAGING OBJECTS chapter).*

Editing WordArt text

♦ Click the WordArt object to select it, if necessary.

The ***WordArt*** *toolbar appears on the screen.*

♦ Use the buttons on the **WordArt** toolbar to edit it.

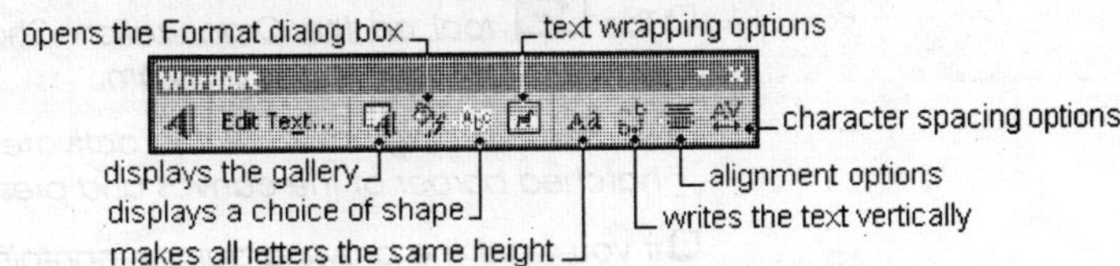

Clicking the ***Edit Text*** *button displays the dialog box used for entering text.*

Inserting a diagram

Here is an example of an organization chart type of diagram:

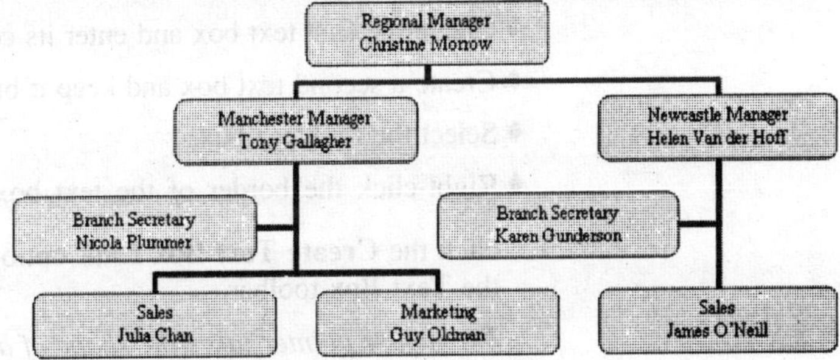

♦ Put the insertion point where the drawing canvas should appear in the document.

♦ Click the tool button on the **Drawing** toolbar or use the **Insert - Diagram** command.

♦ Select the type of diagram you wish to use then click **OK**.

*The chosen type of diagram appears in a drawing canvas and the **Organization Chart** toolbar appears (if you choose that type of diagram): if you choose another type, the **Diagram** toolbar appears.*

- ♦ Enter your text in the **Click to add text** boxes.
- ♦ To add another shape to an **Organization Chart**, choose the shape to which you wish to add a new one then open the **Insert Shape** list on the **Organization Chart** toolbar and select the type of shape you wish to add. For other types of diagram, click the **Insert Shape** button on the **Diagram** toolbar.
- ♦ To delete a shape from a diagram, click the edge of the shape to select it, then press Del.

❑ *The tool on the Organization Chart or Diagram toolbar applies an automatic format to the diagram.*

❑ *To delete a diagram, click it to activate the drawing canvas then click the hatched border of the canvas and press Del.*

❑ *If you want the drawing canvas containing the diagram to be considered as a drawing object, and not as text, you should change the text wrapping for that canvas, which is **In line with text** by default.*

Linking two text boxes

When you link text boxes, excess text will flow over from the first text box into the second.

- ♦ Create the first text box and enter its contents.
- ♦ Create a second text box and keep it blank.
- ♦ Select the first text box.
- ♦ Right-click the border of the text box to open its shortcut menu then click the **Create Text Box Link** option or click the tool button on the **Text Box** toolbar.

  The mouse pointer takes the shape of a jug .
- ♦ Click the blank text box.

  The excess text from the first text box overflows into the second one.

❑ *You can remove the link between two text boxes. To do this select the first text box then click the tool button on the **Text Box** toolbar.*

The and tool buttons can be used when several text boxes are linked, to go to the previous or next text box.

Selecting objects

♦ Point to the object you wish to select; if the object is a text box, point to one of its edges.

♦ When the mouse pointer appears as a four-headed arrow, click.

♦ To select several objects, click to select the first one then hold down Shift as you click the other objects you wish to select.

You can also activate the button on the **Drawing** toolbar and drag a selection rectangle around all the objects you wish to select. As you do this, take care to enclose each object in its entirety.

❑ *To cancel the selection, click an empty space outside it.*

Sizing objects

♦ To change an object's size, select it (the small circles surrounding the object are called **handles**), then drag one of the selection handles.

♦ To resize several objects at once, select them using Shift-clicks then drag one of the selection handles.

♦ To resize all the objects on a drawing canvas simultaneously, activate the drawing canvas in question. If the **Drawing Canvas** toolbar does not appear automatically, right-click the canvas and click the **Show Drawing Canvas Toolbar** option. Click the **Scale Drawing** button on the **Drawing Canvas** toolbar and drag one of the handles that appear on the canvas' hatched border. Click the **Scale Drawing** button to deactivate it.

♦ To resize the drawing canvas without changing the size of the objects it contains, activate the drawing canvas in question, then drag one of the thick black lines that appear just inside the hatched border.

*You can also enlarge a drawing canvas by clicking the **Expand** button on the **Drawing Canvas** toolbar. Click once or several times depending on the required size.*

♦ To make a drawing canvas fit its contents, activate the drawing canvas then click the **Fit** button on the **Drawing Canvas** toolbar.

This button only becomes available when the drawing canvas contains two or more items.

❑ *To give an object an exact size, use the **Format** dialog box (to access the dialog box, choose the last option in the **Format** menu and select the **Size** tab).*

If you want to change an object's size without distorting its proportions, hold down Shift as you resize it.

Moving objects

- To move an object, point to it (or if it is a text box, point to its edge) and when the pointer becomes a four-headed arrow, drag the object to its new position.
- To move several objects, select them with Shift-clicks then point to one of the selected objects: when the pointer becomes a four-headed arrow, drag the group of objects to its new position.
- To move all the objects on a drawing canvas, activate the drawing canvas concerned, point to one of the edges of the frame surrounding it and when the pointer becomes a four-headed arrow, drag the drawing canvas to its new position.

❑ *If the **Snap objects to grid** option is active in the **Drawing Grid** dialog box (open the **Draw** list on the **Drawing** toolbar and take the **Grid** option), selected objects are attracted towards invisible gridlines on the page as you move them.*

Positioning an object

Created in a drawing canvas

This action defines the object's position in the drawing canvas.

- Select the object concerned in the drawing canvas.
- Click the last option in the **Format** menu.

*The name of this option changes depending on the object selected (**AutoShape**, **Text Box**, **Drawing Canvas**, **Picture**).*

- Click the **Layout** tab.
- Give the **Horizontal** and/or **Vertical** positions of the selected object then use the **From** lists associated with each of these options to set the point from which the object should be positioned on the drawing canvas.
- Click **OK**.

Created outside a drawing canvas

- Select the object concerned. If you have selected a picture with a view to changing its position, make sure that its wrapping style is not **In line with text**.
- Click the last option in the **Format** menu.
- Click the **Layout** tab.
- Click the **Advanced** button then the **Picture Position** tab.

♦ In the **Horizontal** frame, click the required type of horizontal alignment then use the corresponding lists to define exactly how the object should be positioned. Choose from the following options:

Alignment Aligns the object to the left of, centred in or to the right of the element selected in the **relative to** list box.

Book layout Lines up the object in relation to the inside or outside of the page or page margins (this is useful if you need to take book binding into account).

Absolute position Aligns the object horizontally: the distance given in the text box is the space left between the left side of the object and the left side of the element selected in the **to the right of** list.

♦ In the **Vertical** frame, click the required type of vertical alignment then use the corresponding lists to define exactly how the object should be positioned. You have the choice of these two options:

Alignment choose an element in the **relative to** list box. The object will be aligned relative to the top, centre, bottom, inside or outside edge of the element selected.

Absolute position select an element in the **below** list: this can be a paragraph, a margin etc. The object will be vertically aligned with the chosen element and the amount of space specified in the text box will be left between the top of the object and the top of the element.

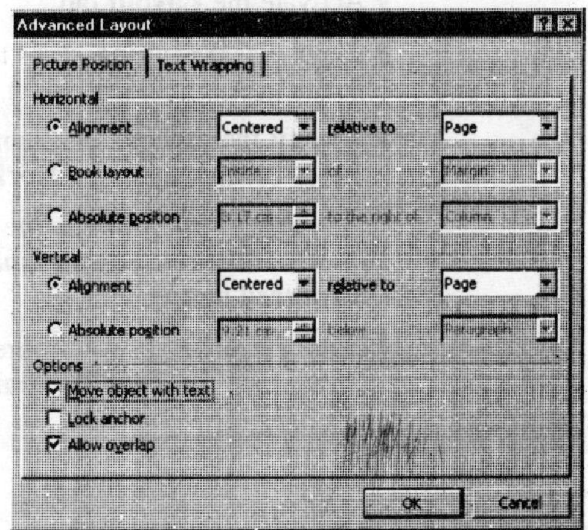

- Set the attachment **Options** for the object:

Move object with text	if this option is active, the object will move up or down with the text to which it is anchored.
Lock anchor	activate this option to maintain the object's position in relation to the same paragraph; a padlock icon appears, indicating that the anchor position will remain the same even if the object is moved elsewhere.
Allow overlap	if this option is active, objects that have the same wrapping style can be overlapped.

- Click **OK** twice.

Deleting an object

- To delete one or more objects, select them then press the Del key.
- To delete all of the objects on a drawing canvas, click one of the hatched edges of the canvas in question then press the Del key.

Changing an object's wrapping

- Select the object concerned.

You cannot change the wrapping of an object within a drawing canvas. However, the drawing canvas is itself considered as an object so its wrapping can be changed.

- Choose the last option in the **Format** menu.

*The name of this option depends on the selected object (**Picture**, **Text Box**, **AutoShape** or **Drawing Canvas**).*

- Activate the **Layout** tab.
- Choose a **Wrapping style** to define how the surrounding text will be positioned around the object.
- Specify the object's horizontal alignment in relation to the margins by using the options in the **Horizontal alignment** frame.

*The **Other** option aligns the object in accordance with what is defined in the **Advanced Layout** dialog box, which appears when you click the **Advanced** button.*

- You can make an even more precise choice by clicking the **Advanced** button then the **Text Wrapping** tab.

♦ If you wish, choose another **Wrapping style**.

In the **Wrap text** frame, indicate how the text should be distributed in relation to the object: on **Both sides**, on the **Left only**, on the **Right only** or **Largest only** (to place the text around the side of the object where there is most space).

*These options are only available for the **Square**, **Tight** and **Through** wrapping styles.*

♦ If necessary, use the **Distance from text** options to modify the distance separating the text from the sides of the object.

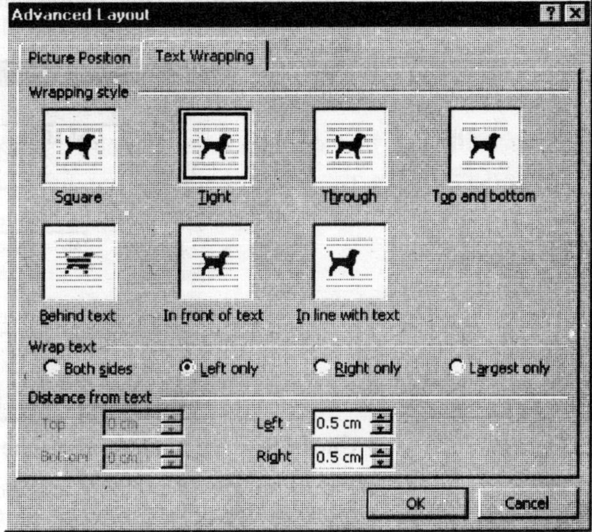

♦ Click **OK**.

*You return to the **Format** dialog box.*

♦ Click **OK** again.

*The button on the **Picture** and **Drawing Canvas** toolbars can also be used to change the wrapping style.*

Attaching a caption to an object

♦ Select the object concerned (picture, chart, table, etc.).

♦ **Insert**
Reference
Caption

- In the **Label** list choose a suitable caption for the type of object: **Equation, Figure** or **Table.** Alternatively click the **New Label** button to write your own caption.

  *If you choose this last option, the new text is displayed immediately in the **Caption** box.*

- If necessary, use the **Caption** box to add to the text display.
- In the **Position** list, choose where the caption should go: **Above** or **Below selected item.**
- Click the **Numbering** button, and use the **Format** list box to specify the format of the numbers then click **OK.**

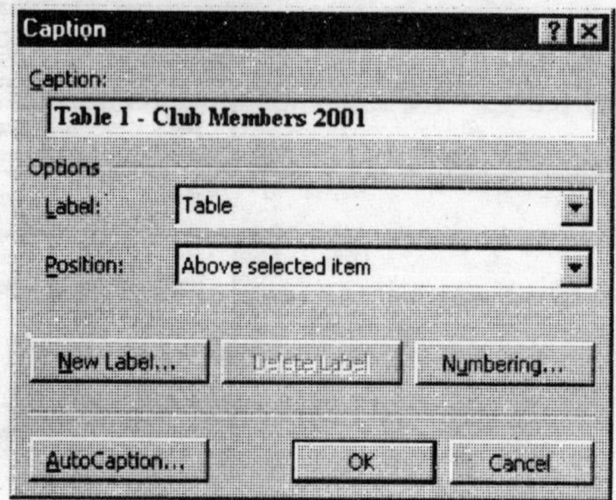

- Click **OK** once more to insert the caption.

❑ *The **AutoCaption** button in this dialog box is used to add captions automatically, as objects of a given type are inserted. This choice must be made when you create the document, before the first object has been inserted.*

Aligning/spacing objects

You can select a group of objects and define how they are aligned and how they are spaced out.

- Select the objects you wish to align or space.
- Open the **Draw** list on the **Drawing** toolbar and point to the **Align or Distribute** option.
- Choose the type of alignment you require.
- To align or space objects in relation to the page or to the drawing canvas and not in relation to each other, open the **Draw** list on the **Drawing** toolbar, point to the **Align or Distribute option** and choose **Relative to Page** or **Relative to Canvas** as appropriate.

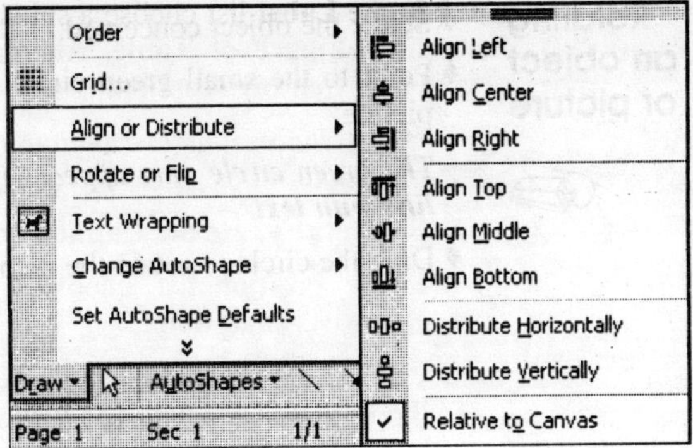

Changing the stacking order of objects

♦ Select the object concerned.

♦ Open the **Draw** list on the **Drawing** toolbar and point to the **Order** option.

♦ Click one of the options given:

Bring to Front/ Send to Back	To make the object the first/last of all.
Bring Forward/ Send Backward	To move the object forward/backward one place.

Grouping/ ungrouping objects

You can group several objects (so that they can be moved all at once, for example), or separate a group of objects.

♦ Select the objects you wish to group or ungroup.

♦ Open the **Draw** list on the **Drawing** toolbar.

♦ Activate **Group** or **Ungroup.**

*The **Regroup** option regroups objects which have been ungrouped.*

Replacing one AutoShape with another

♦ Select the shape concerned.

♦ Open the **Draw** list on the **Drawing** toolbar.

♦ Activate the **Change AutoShape** option.

♦ Select the category containing the new shape.

♦ Activate the desired shape.

Rotating an object or picture

♦ Select the object concerned.

♦ Point to the small green circle that appears at the top of the object or picture.

The green circle only appears if the picture's wrapping style is not ***In line with text****.*

♦ Drag the circle to rotate the item.

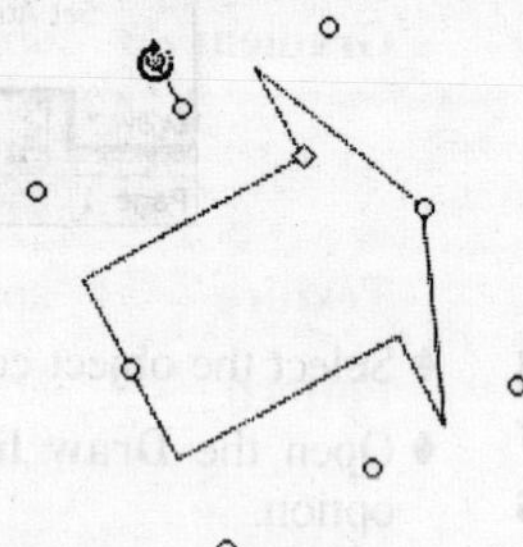

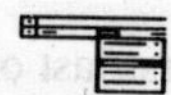

♦ Select the object.

♦ Open the **Draw** list and activate **Rotate or Flip**.

♦ Choose **Free Rotate, Rotate Left, Rotate Right, Flip Horizontal** or **Flip Vertical**.

Modifying the outline of an object

♦ Select the object.

♦ Click one of the following buttons on the **Drawing** toolbar:

to change the colour of the outline, or to choose a repeated pattern to replace the line.

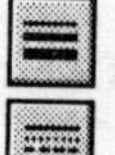

to change the line style (the thickness in particular).

to change the type of line.

Changing an object's fill

Applying a colour

♦ Select the object.

♦ Open the list on the button on the **Drawing** toolbar then click the colour you wish to apply to the object.

The ***More Fill Colours*** *option can be used to select another colour or to create your own custom colours.*

Applying a pattern or texture

♦ Select the object.

♦ Open the [fill colour button] list on the **Drawing** toolbar.

♦ Click the **Fill Effects** option.

♦ Use one of the following tabs:

Gradient	applies **One color** or **Two colors** or **Preset** gradients which may run in these directions: **Horizontal, Vertical, Diagonal up, Diagonal down, From corner** or **From center.**
Texture	applies a special textured fill effect.
Pattern	applies a **Pattern** using a **Foreground** and a **Background** colour.
Picture	fills the object with a picture.

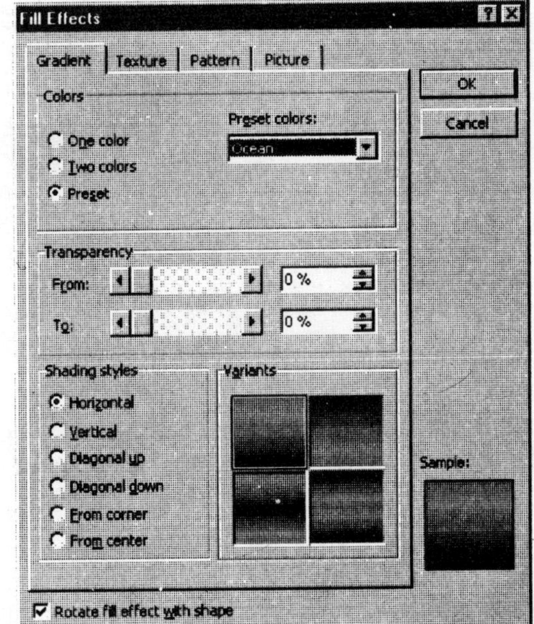

♦ Click **OK.**

❑ *To remove an object's fill colour, open the* [fill colour button] *list then click the* ***No Fill*** *option.*

Giving a shadow to an object

♦ Select the object.

♦ Click the button on the **Drawing** toolbar.

♦ Choose the shadow effect you require.

*The **Shadow Settings** option allows you to customise the shadow (for example, you can change its colour).*

Applying a 3D effect

♦ Select the object.

♦ Click on the **Drawing** toolbar.

♦ Choose the 3D effect you require.

*The **No 3-D** option returns the object to the original shape: the **3-D Settings** option allows you to customise your effect.*

.... Personal notes ....

Creating a chart

Starting Microsoft Graph

♦ If the data you are going to represent are already entered in a document, copy them into the clipboard.

♦ Place the insertion point where you want to put the chart.

♦ **Insert**
Object

♦ Double-click **Microsoft Graph Chart.**

*After a few seconds the **Microsoft Graph** application opens: you see a window called **Datasheet** containing the data to be represented by a chart, and the chart itself, which appears with a hatched border. The data shown is only sample data for the moment.*

♦ It is a good idea to re-organise the screen by moving the **Datasheet** window so that the chart is also visible.

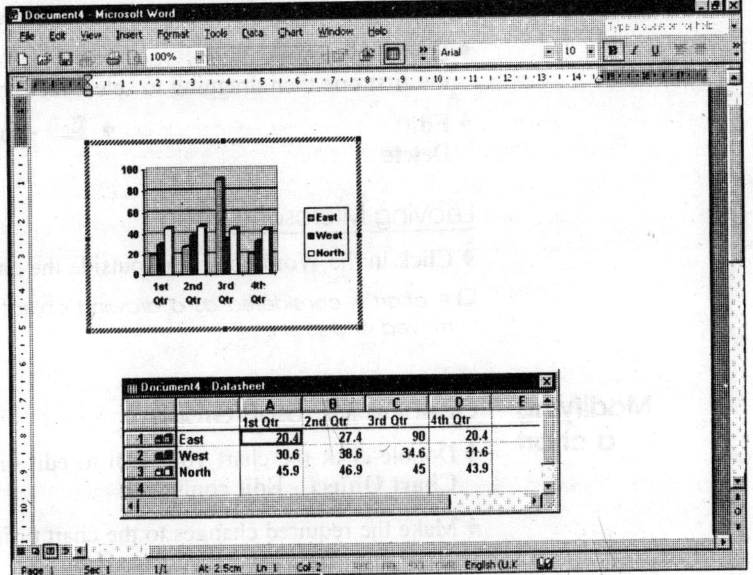

♦ Enter the data you want to use into the datasheet then define the chart settings (cf. below).

Clearing the contents of cells

♦ Select the cells to be cleared.

♦ **Edit**
Clear

You can delete the cells' contents or their format or both.

♦ Choose what you want to clear: the **Contents** or both the contents and the format (**All**).

The numerical data are no longer represented on the chart. However, Microsoft Graph considers that the 3 rows and 4 columns of sample data still exist.

Entering data into the datasheet

♦ Click the first cell in which you want to enter data or the first destination cell for copied data.

♦ Enter your data or use the **Edit - Paste** command to copy in the contents of the clipboard.

Enter data as for a Word table: pasted data is copied as with any Windows application. Changes appear simultaneously on the chart.

Deleting rows/columns in the datasheet

♦ Select the rows/columns you want to delete by clicking the header of the first one then dragging to select the others.

♦ **Edit**
Delete

♦ Ctrl - (on the number pad)

Leaving Microsoft Graph

♦ Click in the Word document outside the chart.

❑ *A chart is considered as a drawing object and as such can be resized, moved and so on.*

Modifying a chart

Opening Microsoft Graph

♦ Double-click the chart you wish to edit or select it and use the **Edit - Chart Object - Edit** command.

♦ Make the required changes to the chart or in the datasheet.

Specifying whether data series are in rows or columns

♦ **Data**
Series in Rows or **Series in Columns**

Changing the type of chart

♦ **Chart**
Chart Type

A list of all the main chart types appears.

♦ Choose a type from the **Chart type** list.

♦ Double-click the format you prefer in the **Chart sub-type** frame.

Managing the legend

♦ **Chart**
Chart Options
Legend tab

♦ Choose whether or not to display the legend by activating or deactivating the **Show Legend** option.

♦ Use the options under **Placement** to position the legend.

♦ Click **OK**.

Adding a chart/axis title

♦ **Chart**
Chart Options
Titles tab

♦ Click the text box corresponding to the sort of title you want to insert.

♦ Click **OK**.

Formatting chart objects

♦ Click the object to select it. For example, to select an axis, click the axis label.

Handles appear on any selected object. Black handles indicate that the object can be resized and/or moved.

♦ Open the **Format** menu then click the first option on this menu which corresponds to the object's name. You can also double-click the object you wish to modify.

♦ Click the tab that refers to the attributes you are editing.

*The **Format** dialog box contains different tabs according to the item that is selected.*

♦ Change the format options as required.

♦ Click **OK**.

Creating a form

A form is a document containing permanent text and spaces for filling in variable data. Here is an example:

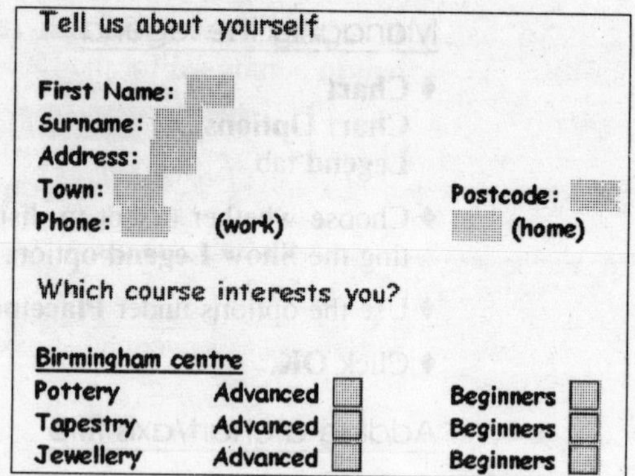
Tell us about yourself

First Name:
Surname:
Address:
Town: Postcode:
Phone: (work) (home)

Which course interests you?

Birmingham centre

Pottery	Advanced	Beginners
Tapestry	Advanced	Beginners
Jewellery	Advanced	Beginners

- Create or modify a document template.
- Enter the permanent text.
- At each place you wish to enter variable data, insert a form field using the **Forms** toolbar (cf. below).
- When you have completed the form, protect it (cf. Protecting a form) and save it.

Inserting form fields

A ***form field*** *can be presented as a text box, a drop-down list or a check box.*

- Display the **Forms** toolbar with the **View - Toolbars - Forms** command.
- Place the insertion point where the field should appear.
- Click the abl tool button to insert a text field, the tool button for a check box or the tool button for a drop-down list.

  A greyed-out form field appears in the document.

- Define the options depending on which form field you have chosen (see below).

❑ *If field codes are displayed (Shift F9), the form fields appear as follows: {FORMTEXT} for a text field, {FORMCHECKBOX} for a check box field and {FORMDROPDOWN} for a dropdown list field.*

❑ *These three form fields can only be used if the document is protected as a form.*

Defining text field options

- Click the text field concerned then click the button on the **Forms** toolbar.
- Define what **Type** of text field it is.
- If required, set a **Default text** to appear in the field, a **Maximum length** authorised for the field as well and **Text format**.

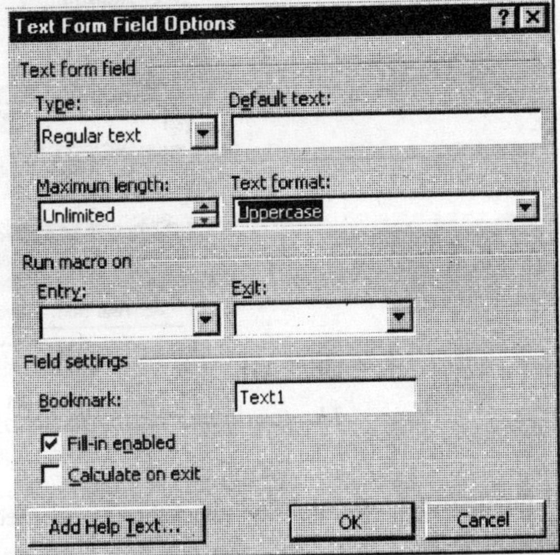

- If you want a brief message to appear on the status bar, click the **Add Help Text** button and enter the text in the **Type your own** text box then click **OK**.
- Click **OK** to close the dialog box.

Defining drop-down list field options

- Click the drop-down list, then click .
- For each item you want to have in the list, enter it in the **Drop-down item** text box then click **Add**.
- If you want to remove an item, select it in the **Items in drop-down list** list then click **Remove**.
- If required, reorganise the list using the **Move** buttons.
- Click **Add Help Text** to write a message which will appear when the insertion point is in the field.

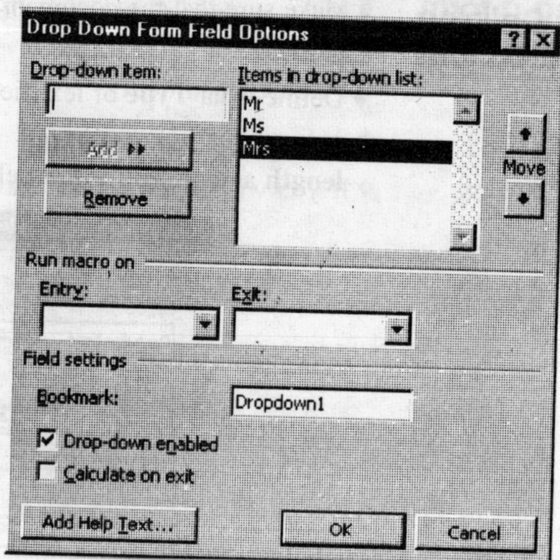

♦ Click **OK**.

The first name on the list is always displayed by default.

Defining check box field options

♦ Click the check box concerned then click .

♦ Specify how you want the check box to look using the options in the **Check box size** and **Default value** frames.

♦ If you wish, click **Add Help Text** and write your help message.

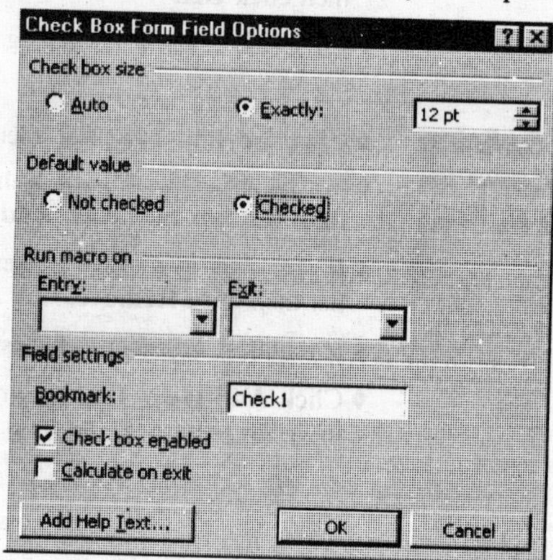

♦ Click **OK**.

Protecting a form

♦ Make sure that the document is completely finished.

♦ **Tools**
Protect Document

♦ Activate the **Forms** option.

♦ If you wish, enter a **Password** with a maximum of 15 characters.

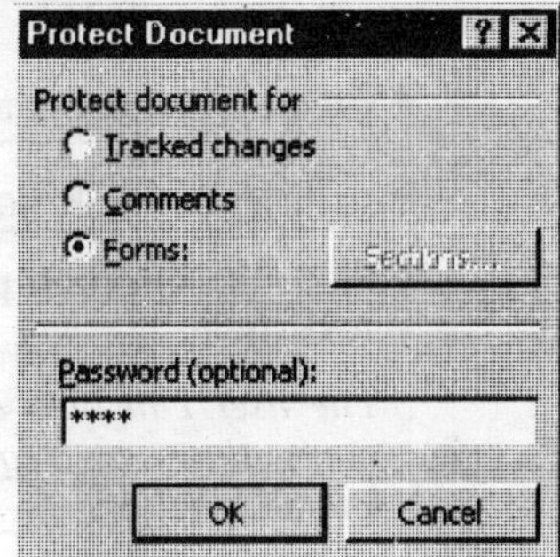

On the screen, the characters of the password are always replaced by asterisks (*). Be careful about the case of the letters you use.

♦ Click **OK**.

To ensure against mistakes, you must enter the password again.

♦ Enter the password and click **OK**.

♦ Save the form and close it.

❑ *To remove the protection, use **Tools - Unprotect Document** and enter the password used to protect the document (if these is one) then click **OK**. Remember to use the same uppercase or lowercase characters.*

*The button on the **Forms** toolbar allows you to protect/unprotect a form without setting a password.*

Using a form

♦ Create a new document based on a form template.

The first form field is selected and its help text is displayed on the status bar.

Because the document is protected as a form, access is authorised to form fields only.

♦ Move from field to field using Tab and Shift Tab, and fill in the data.

Using ASK and FILLIN fields

When you insert these types of field, your document is similar to a form but it contains variable data supplied by the user; it can be saved or printed.

An ASK field prompts the user to enter information in a custom field and that information can be repeated as many times as necessary in the document. A FILLIN field requires the user to enter a specific text directly in the field.

♦ Create a document and enter the permanent items of text.

Inserting an ASK field

♦ Place the insertion point at the beginning of the document to insert the ASK field.

The user can then define a "custom field" which can be called up as many times as required within the body of the document (see the example below).

Once you have filled in it in, an ASK field's message and its syntax will not be printed with the document.

♦ Press Ctrl F9 to insert the field.

♦ Enter the following syntax between the braces:

ASK space **Name_of_your_field** space **"Prompt_message"**

Name_of_your_field *corresponds to the variable piece of information. This can have up to 20 characters, must start with a letter and not contain any spaces.*

The ***Prompt message*** *(entered between quotation marks) is the text that appears next to the text box so you know what information is required.*

♦ To confirm what you have entered in an ASK field, use the arrow keys.

♦ Place the insertion point where the contents of the ASK field should appear and press Ctrl F9.

Enter the **Name_of_your_field** between the braces.

♦ Place your custom field in the text as many times as necessary.

{ ASK entrant_name "Enter customer's name" }

{ entrant_name }, you have been selected to participate in our Grand Prize draw! There are hundreds of prizes to be won, including a new car!

To take part, you must be present for the draw, which takes place at 7pm on **Friday August 12** at Barton's Home Centre, Booth Road, Salisbury.

We look forward to seeing you, { entrant _name } and hope that you will be one of the lucky winners.

Maureen Stockton
Store Manager

♦ Save the document.

Inserting a FILLIN field

♦ Place the insertion point where the variable data should appear and press Ctrl F9 to insert the FILLIN field.

♦ Enter the following syntax: **FILLIN** space **"Prompt_message".**

*The **Prompt message** (entered between quotation marks) is the text that appears next to the text box so you know what information is required.*

♦ To confirm what you have entered in an ASK field, use the arrow keys.

♦ Place your FILLIN field in the text in as many places as you want to insert one-off pieces of data.

{ ASK entrant_name "Enter customer's name" }

{ entrant_name }, you have been selected to participate in our Grand Prize draw! There are hundreds of prizes to be won, including a new car!

To take part, you must be present for the draw, which takes place at 7pm on { FILLIN "Enter date" } at Barton's Home Centre, Booth Road, Salisbury. You must also present your Lucky Number, which is { FILLIN "Enter lucky number" }

We look forward to seeing you, { entrant _name } and hope that you will be one of the lucky winners.

Maureen Stockton
Store Manager

♦ Save the document.

Entering data in ASK and FILLIN fields

♦ Open the document concerned.

♦ Select the entire document with Ctrl **A** then press F9.

Word displays a window for each ASK and FILLIN field that needs to be filled in.

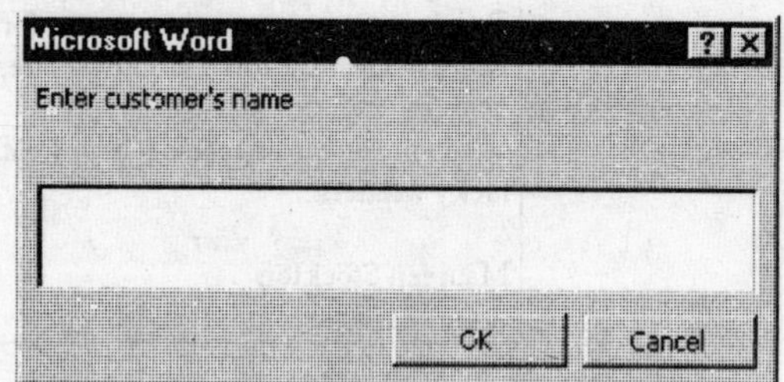

♦ Answer each question, using Enter to change lines, if necessary and click **OK** after each response.

♦ Enter all the information in the same way.

♦ Print your document.

♦ Close the document but do not save it unless you want to save the answers you provided.

❑ *To show or hide the ASK and FILLIN field codes in a document, press* Alt F9.

*You can also fill in these types of fields once you have started printing. If the **Update fields option** is active in the **Print** tab of the **Tools - Options** dialog box, Word will display each message as it prints.*

Planning a mail merge

*Word's **mail merge** function (also called a mailshot or mailout) can produce a number of copies of a document and link them to names, addresses or references contained in a separate data file.*

♦ Two files are used in this technique:

– a **data source** file containing the variable information.

– a **main document** containing the permanent text and the fields which act as links to the data source file.

♦ If it does not already exist, create the data source file: this should be made up of **fields** and **records**. For example:

First Name	Surname
Fiona	Blackburn
William	Ross

Each line of information, concerning for example Fiona Blackburn or William Ross, is a record. Each record is numbered according to the order in which it was entered or according to a sort order.

♦ If necessary, create the main document.

♦ Link the data file to the main document.

♦ Insert the fields from the data file at the appropriate places in the main document.

♦ Start the mail merge.

Creating a mail merge

To create a mail merge, you need to follow all the steps in the Mail Merge Wizard.

♦ You can use an existing document or template for your main document or you can create a new blank document (**File - New**) and enter the permanent text.

♦ **Tools**
Letters and Mailings
Mail Merge Wizard

The Mail Merge task pane appears on the screen:

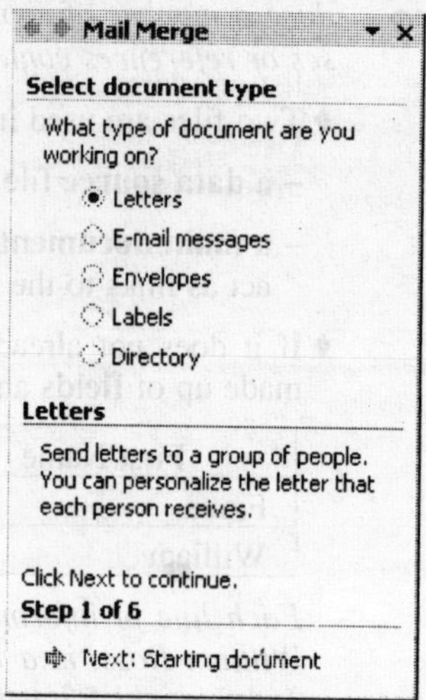

♦ Activate the **Letters** option in the **Select document type** section.

♦ Click the **Next: Starting document** link at the bottom of the task pane.

♦ In the **Select starting document** section, select the option that describes what you wish to use as your main document:

Use the current document	The mail merge's main document is the active document.
Start from a template	The mail merge's main document is a ready to use mail merge template that you can customise if you wish. To choose a template, click the **Select template** link that appears in the **Start from a template** frame then double-click the name of the template you wish to use.
Start from existing document	The main document is based on an existing document. This could be an ordinary document or a main document used in a previous mail merge. If it can be seen in the **Start from existing** list box, select its name then click the **Open** button. Otherwise double-click the **(More Files...)** option, select the required document then click the **Open** button. A new document based on the existing document appears on the screen.

♦ Click the **Next: Select recipients** link to go to the next step.

*The **Previous: Select document type** link takes you back to the last step.*

♦ Activate one of the options in the **Select recipients** section to select the list of addressees:

Use an existing list	You can select a file or database containing the list of recipients. To do this, click the **Browse** link under **Use an existing list** and select the file or database that contains the list of contacts. If required, modify the contents of the list then click **OK.** If the selected list is not what you were looking for, click the **Select a different list** link.

If your selected list of data is an Excel workbook (.xls) or an Access database, Word opens a dialog box when it opens the file so you can choose which worksheet in the workbook or which table in the database you want to use for the mailshot.

Select from Outlook contacts	you can select the list of recipients from your Outlook contacts folder. Click the **Choose Contacts folder** link in the **Select from Outlook contacts** section then double-click the name of the contacts folder that contains the required information. Modify the list of contacts if necessary then click **OK.**
Type a new list	enter the contents of a new recipients list (cf. **Creating a list of data** in this chapter).

♦ Click the **Next: Write your letter** link to go to the next step.

♦ Enter or modify as necessary the contents of the main document (the part of the text that remains the same).

♦ Insert the fields (the information referring to each recipient) into the main document. For each field you are inserting, follow this procedure:

– Place the insertion point where the field's contents should print.

– Click the **More items** link on the task pane, select the required field then click the **Insert** button and **Close.**

*The **Address block** link takes you to the **Insert Address Block** dialog box which contains options for inserting recipient addresses in various forms [AddressBlock field]. The **Greeting line** link opens a dialog box which you can use to insert greeting phrases to start your letter [GreetingLine].*

♦ Click the **Next: Preview your letters** link to go to the next step.

In the main document you can see a preview of the letter containing the information from the first record in the data list.

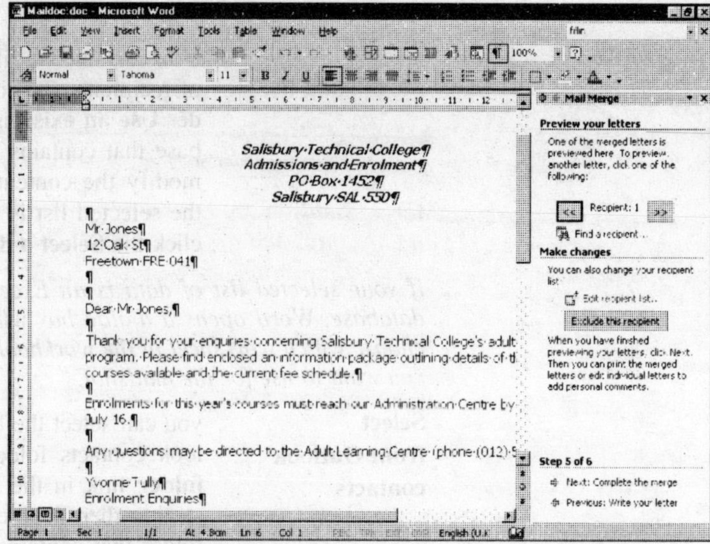

♦ Use the << and >> button in the **Preview your letters** section to see a preview of the letter containing the information from the previous or next record.

*To **Find a recipient** in the list of data, click this link (cf. **Managing records in a list of data** in this chapter).*

♦ To exclude the active record from the mail merge, click the **Exclude this recipient** button in the **Make changes** frame.

♦ Click the **Next: Complete the merge** link to go to the next step.

♦ Click the **Print** link to merge to the printer and print the mailout letters or click the **Edit individual letters** link to create the merged letters in a new document.

♦ Specify which records should be merged. To merge all the records selected in the list of data, activate the **All** option. To merge the active record, click **Current record** (you cannot merge the current record if the records have been filtered). To merge using a group of records selected in the list of data, enter the number of the first record in the **From** text box then the last record in the **To** box.

♦ If you merge to a new document, make the required changes, print and/or save the document and close it.

♦ Save the main document and close it.

If changes have been made to the list of data, Word prompts you to save them.

♦ If necessary, click **Yes** to save any changes made to the data list.

❑ *The* ***Edit recipients list*** *link that appears in steps 3 and 5 of the Mail Merge Wizard opens the* ***Mail Merge Recipients*** *dialog box so you can modify the contents of the data list.*

You can also insert a field into the main document by clicking the ***Insert Merge Fields*** *( ) button on the* ***Mail Merge*** *toolbar* ***(Tools - Letters and Mailings - Show Mail Merge Toolbar).***

You can use the ***Merge to New Document*** *( ) or* ***Merge to Printer*** *( ) button on the* ***Mail Merge*** *toolbar to run the mail merge to a new document or to the printer.*

Creating a list of data

♦ If the main document already exists, open it, otherwise create a new document in which you enter the fixed text for the mailshot.

♦ **Tools**
Letters and Mailings
Mail Merge Wizard

♦ Click the **Next** link at the bottom of the task pane twice, until you reach step 3 of the **Mail Merge Wizard.**

♦ Activate the **Type a new list** option in the **Select recipients** section and click the **Create** link.

The ***New Address List*** *dialog box appears on the screen, displaying a list of predefined fields.*

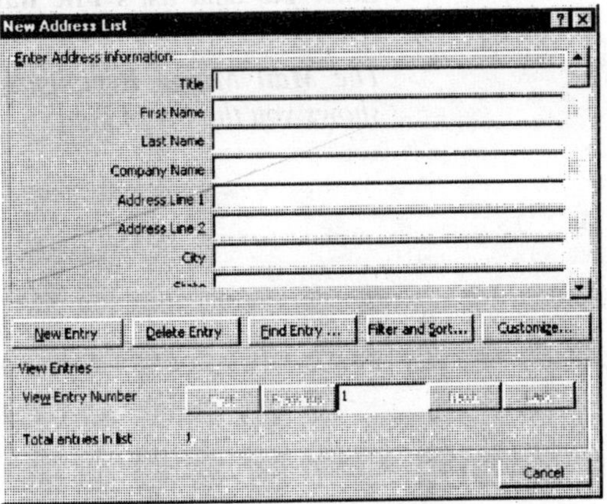

♦ Click the **Customize** button to define the fields in the new list then follow these instructions:

– To delete a field, select it in the list, click the **Delete** button and click **Yes** to confirm the deletion.

– To add a new custom field, click the **Add** button, **Type a name for your field** in the corresponding text box and click **OK**.

The customised field is added under the selected field.

– To rename a field, select it in the list, click the **Rename** button, enter the new name in the text box and click **OK**.

– To move a field, select it in the list then click the **Move Up** or **Move Down** button.

Ideally, the fields should appear in the order in which you will be entering the data.

♦ When the structure of the data file is satisfactory, click **OK**.

The data entry grid, containing the previously defined fields, reappears on the screen.

♦ Click the text box of the first field.

♦ For each record:

– Enter the data, using [Tab] to go to the next text box or [Shift] [Tab] to return to the previous text box.

– After you have filled in the last field, press [Enter] twice or click the **New Entry** button to create a new record.

♦ When you have finished entering all the records, click the **Close** button.

*The **Save Address List** dialog box appears on the screen.*

♦ Enter the data list's **File name** in the corresponding text box and if required choose the folder where it must be saved. Click **OK**.

*The **Mail Merge Recipients** dialog box appears on the screen and shows you the list of data.*

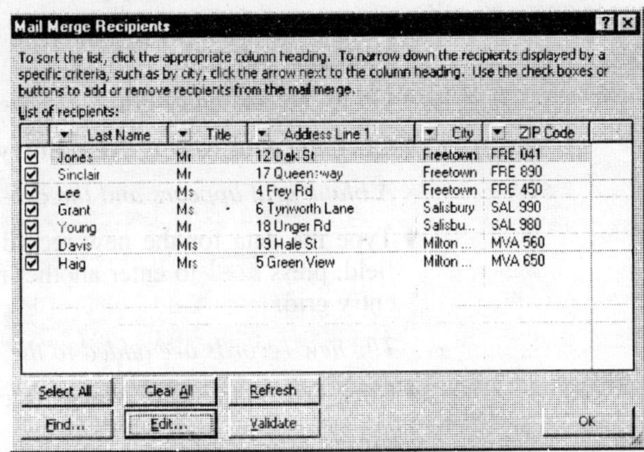

♦ Click **OK**.

You return to the main document. The ***Mail Merge*** *toolbar may appear on the screen. This provides tools relevant to the mail merge feature.*

Managing the records in a data list

You can only use the data entry grid to manage a data list created during the mail merge setup or an existing list in a Word document (.doc). If you are using a list contained in an Excel worksheet (.xls) or a table in an Access database (.mdb), you will have to work on the list of records by opening the relevant file in its own application.

Going to the data entry grid

♦ Open the main document.

♦ If necessary, display the **Mail Merge** toolbar, using the **View - Toolbars - Mail Merge** command or with **Tools - Letters and Mailings - Show Mail Merge Toolbar**.

♦ Click the **Mail Merge Recipients** ( ) button on the **Mail Merge** toolbar.

♦ Click the **Edit** button.

The grid opens and you can see the first record.

The look and titles of the buttons in the entry grid dialog box differ depending on the file type of the data list (which may be a Word file (.doc) or a Microsoft Office Address List (*.mdb), for example.*

♦ Use the buttons in the **View Entries** frame at the bottom of the entry grid to scroll through the records.

Adding a record

♦ Go to the data entry grid.

♦ Click the **Add New** or **New Entry** button (whichever is shown).

*A blank grid appears and the current **Entry Number** changes.*

♦ Type the data for the new record and when you have entered the last field, press [Enter] to enter another new record or click **Close** to close the entry grid.

The new records are added to the end of the list.

♦ Click **OK** on the **Mail Merge Recipients** dialog box.

Finding a record

♦ Go to the entry grid.

♦ Go to the first record by clicking the [|◄] button or the **First** button, whichever appears.

♦ Click either **Find** or **Find Entry**.

♦ In the **Find** or **Find What** box, enter the value you are looking for.

♦ In the **In field** or **This field** box (whichever appears), select the name of the field that you want to search for the value.

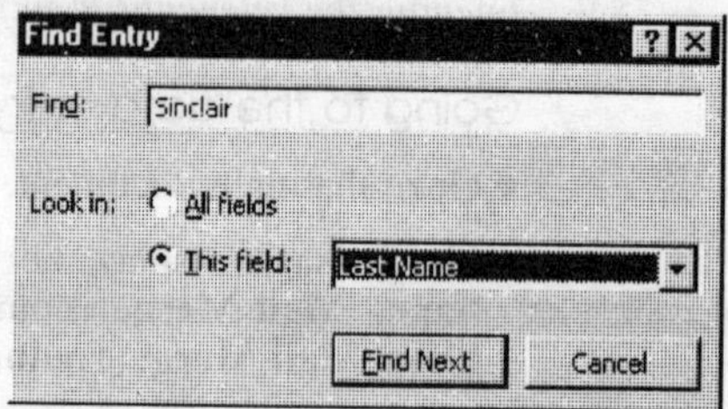

*The **All fields** option is only available when the list of data was entered during the mail merge process and carries out the search in all the fields in the list.*

♦ Start the search by clicking **Find First** (or **Find Next**) then click **Find Next** as many times as necessary until you reach the required record.

♦ Click the **Close** button when you have finished searching. A **Cancel** button may appear instead of close, in which case, click **Cancel**.

♦ Click **Close** (or **Cancel**) to close the entry grid.

*You can also look for a record by clicking the **Find Entry** ( ) button on the **Mail Merge** toolbar.*

Deleting a record

♦ Go to the entry grid.

♦ Go to the record you wish to delete.

♦ Click the **Delete** or **Delete Entry** button.

♦ If necessary, click the **Yes** button to confirm the deletion.

♦ Click the **Close** button then click **OK**.

Editing a record

♦ Go to the entry grid.

♦ Go to the record you wish to modify.

♦ Make your changes.

♦ If you notice a mistake, click the **Restore** button (if it is available) to retrieve the original data.

♦ Click **Close** then **OK**.

To modify the structure of a data list, open the corresponding data file as a document (the records appear in a table). Make your changes as required and save the document.

Setting criteria on a mail merge

Filtering on a value in one or more fields

Each field is in fact a list that you can open by clicking the arrowhead that appears at the right of the field name.

♦ Open the main document and if it is not on the screen, display the **Mail Merge** toolbar.

♦ Click the  button on the **Mail Merge** toolbar.

♦ For each field you wish to filter:

– Open the list on the field concerned.

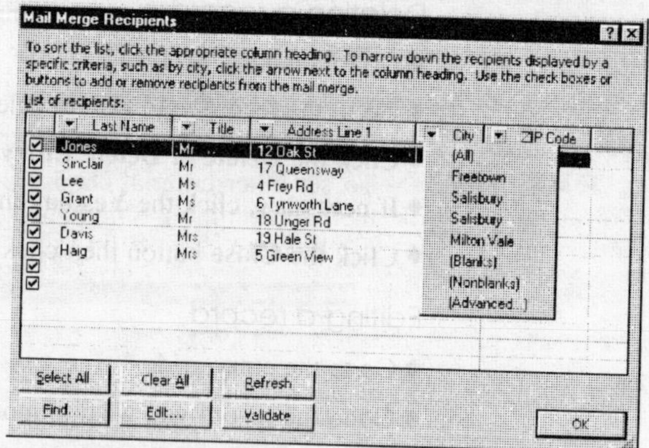

*Each list contains all the values in that field and the **(All)**, **(Blanks)**, **(Nonblanks)** and **(Advanced)** options.*

– Click the value you require. The **(Blanks)** option show all the records which do not have a value in that field and inversely the **(Nonblanks)** option shows all the records that do have a value in the field.

Only the records that meet your filter criterion are displayed. The arrow on the field names appears in blue when that field is filtered.

♦ To remove the filter from a field and show all its records again, open the field list and choose the **(All)** option.

❏ *A checkbox appears to the left of each recipients name in the **Mail Merge Recipients** dialog box (which you open by clicking). Tick the box to select or remove the tick to deselect that record for the mail merge. The **Select All** button will select all records once again and the **Clear All** button will deselect all the records.*

Filtering on several values from one or more fields

♦ Open the main document and, if it is not on the screen, display the **Mail Merge** toolbar.

♦ Click the buttonl on the **Mail Merge** toolbar.

♦ Open the list associated with one of the fields then click the **(Advanced)** option.

♦ If necessary, click the **Filter Records** tab.

♦ For each criterion you wish to set:

– Select the name of the field in the **Field** list.

*The **(none)** option can be used to clear that particular criteria row.*

– If necessary, modify the **Comparison** operator using the corresponding list.

– Click the **Compare to** box and enter the value you require.

– If you do not want to set any other criteria, click **OK**.

– To set other criteria, choose the linking operator: select **And** to test the two conditions simultaneously or **Or** if one or the other condition can be met.

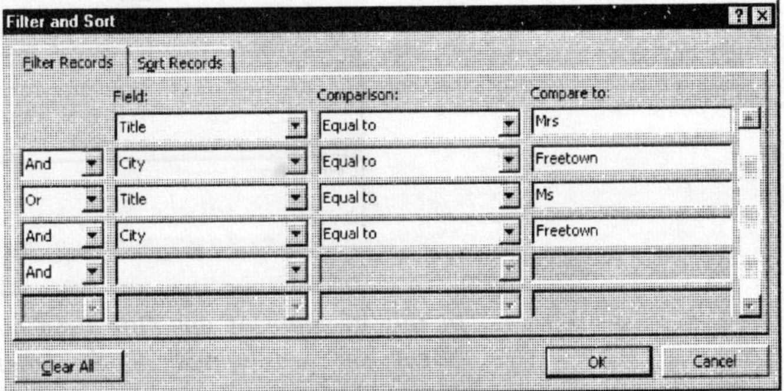

♦ Click **OK**.

*The filtered list appears in the **Mail Merge Recipients** dialog box.*

♦ Click **OK**.

The set criteria are saved within the main document.

*To delete all set criteria, click the **Clear All** button on the **Query Options** or **Filter and Sort** dialog box (this name depends on whether or not the address list is a Word document (.doc)).*

Setting conditions for printing a text

You can set a condition so this text or that text will be displayed depending on the outcome.

♦ Open the main document and if it is hidden, show the **Mail Merge** toolbar.

♦ Place the insertion point where the text is to appear in the main document.

♦ Click the **Insert Word Field** button then the **If ... Then ... Else** option.

♦ Enter your condition using the **Field name**, **Comparison** and **Compare to** lists.

♦ In the **Insert this text** box, enter the text which will be printed if the condition is satisfied.

♦ Then use the **Otherwise insert this text** box to enter a text which will be printed if the condition is not satisfied.

*You cannot format the text entered in the **Insert this text** or **Otherwise insert this text** boxes: this must be performed in the main document.*

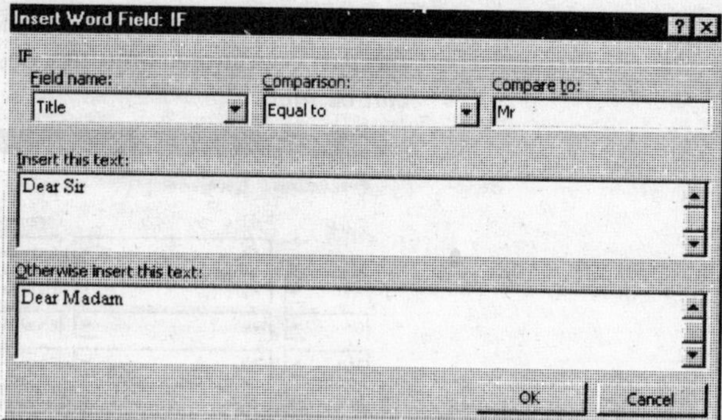

In this example, if the Title field contains the mention "Mr", the text "Dear Sir" will appear in the letter and if it contains another title, "Dear Madam" will appear.

♦ Finish by clicking the **OK** button.

If the field code display is no longer active, display the codes by pressing Alt F9 *to read what you have just created.*
Example: {IF{MERGEFIELD TITLE} = "Mr" "Dear Sir" "Dear Madam"}

♦ Save the main document and close it.

Setting conditions for the insertion of another document

♦ Open the main document and if it is hidden, show the **Mail Merge** toolbar.

♦ Place the insertion point in the main document where you want the inserted document to appear.

♦ If necessary, press Alt F9 to display the field codes.

♦ Insert an **IF** field by clicking the **Insert Word Field** button on the **Mail Merge** toolbar and choosing the **If_Then_Else** option (cf. above).

♦ Using the **Field name, Comparison** and **Compare to** boxes, enter your condition.

♦ Click the **Insert this text** box and press Ctrl F9 to insert braces.

The insertion point flashes between the two braces.

Enter the INCLUDETEXT field with the following syntax: **INCLUDE-TEXT** [space] **File_name.**

Give the complete file path if the document you want to insert is not in the same folder as the main document.

♦ Click the **Otherwise insert this text** box and press [Ctrl][F9] to insert braces.

The insertion point flashes between the two braces.

Enter the INCLUDETEXT field with the following syntax: **INCLUDE-TEXT** [space] **File_name.**

Give the complete file path if the document you want to insert is not in the same folder as the main document.

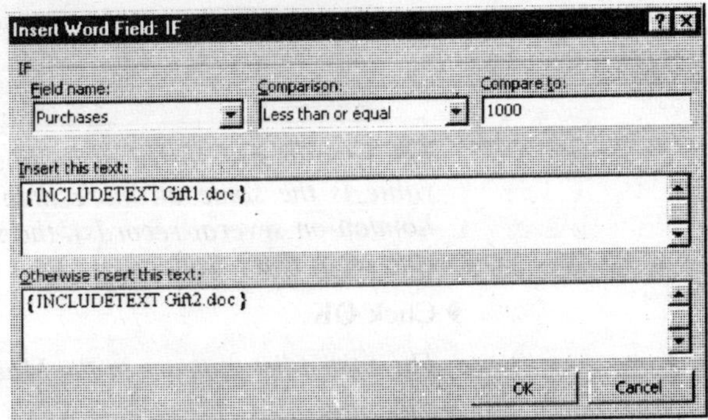

In this example, if the amount of ***Purchases*** *is equal to or less than 1000, the* ***Gift1.doc*** *file will be inserted. If the amount is higher, the* ***Gift2.doc*** *document will be inserted.*

In the document, the set condition will have this syntax:
{IF{MERGEFIELD Purchases} <= "1000" "{INCLUDETEXT Gift1.doc}" "{INCLUDETEXT Gift2.doc}"

♦ Save the main document and close it.

Sorting a list of data

♦ Open the main document and, if it is hidden, show the **Mail Merge** toolbar.

♦ Click the button on the **Mail Merge** toolbar.

♦ Open the list associated with one of the fields then click the **(Advanced)** option.

♦ If necessary, click the **Sort Records** tab.

When the dialog box opens, you can see that you can sort by up to three fields.

♦ Open the **Sort by** list, click the name of the field and specify whether the records should be sorted in **Ascending** or **Descending** order.

♦ If several records are likely to have the same value, use the **Then by** lists to indicate a second and even a third field to sort by.

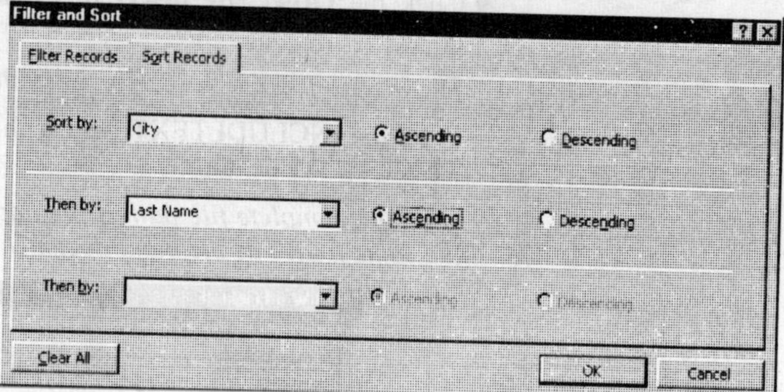

The records are sorted according to the first sort criterion. When this value is the same on more than one record (for example, the city is London on several records), the second sort criterion comes into effect (the records for London are then sorted by name) and so on.

♦ Click **OK**.

*The sorted list appears in the **Mail Merge Recipients** dialog box.*

♦ Click **OK**.

*You can set a single sort order for the list in the **Mail Merge Recipients** dialog box (click the tool button to open it): click the name of the field by which you want to sort and it will be sorted in ascending order. Click again to sort in descending order.*

Creating mailing labels

♦ For the main document, you can use an existing mailing labels document from a previous merge or you can create a new blank document.

Whichever of these options you intend to take, start by clicking the button on the **Standard** toolbar.

♦ **Tools**
Letters and Mailings
Mail Merge Wizard

♦ Activate the **Labels** option in the **Select document type** frame.

♦ Click the **Next: Starting document** link at the bottom of the task pane.

♦ In the **Select starting document** frame, select the option that corresponds to how you wish to make up your mailing labels:

Change document layout The main document for the mail merge labels is the current document, in which you define the size of the mailing labels. To choose the size of the labels, click the **Label Options** link in the **Change document layout** frame and double-click the required **Product number** then click **OK**.

*The **Details** button in the **Label Options** dialog box can be used to customize the options of the selected label and the **New Label** button leads you to create a new custom label that will be added to the **Product number** list.*

Start from existing document The main document for the mailing labels is based on an existing mail merge document (already containing mailing labels). If this document's name appears in the **Start from existing** list, select its name and click the **Open** button, otherwise double-click the **[More files...]** option, select the file in the **Open** dialog box and click **Open. A new DocumentX** based on the selected mail merge document appears on the screen.

♦ Click the **Next: Select recipients** link to go to the next step.

*The **Previous: Select document type** link takes you back to the step before.*

♦ Activate one of the options in the **Select recipients** frame to choose a list of addressees:

Use an existing list use to select a file or database containing the list of recipients. Click the **Browse** link in the **Use existing list** frame to select the file or database containing the names and addresses. If necessary, modify the contents of the file and click **OK**. If the selected list is no longer suitable, **Select a different list** by clicking this link.

If your data list is an Excel workbook (.xls) or an Access database (.mdb), Word will show you a dialog box when the file opens so you can choose the workbook sheet or the database table containing the data you need to use for the mailing labels.

Select from Outlook contacts use to select the recipient list from an Outlook contacts folder. To do this, click the **Choose Contacts Folder** link in the **Select from Outlook contacts** frame, double-click the contacts folder containing the recipients' names, modify the list if necessary then click **OK**.

Type a new list	to enter the contents of a new mailing list (cf. Creating a list of data).

♦ Click the **Next: Arrange your labels** link to go to the next step.

♦ Define how to set out the contents of the labels in the first label on the page. For each field you wish to insert, follow this procedure:

– Place the insertion point where the contents of the label should print.

– Click the **More items** link on the task pane, select the field concerned and click the **Insert** button. Click **Close.**

*The **Address block** link opens the **Insert Address Block** dialog box, where you can choose predefined formats for the name and address (these insert an **AddressBlock** field). The **Greeting line** link provides a dialog box with options for inserting an initial greeting in your letter (a **GreetingLine** field).*

♦ If necessary, apply formatting to the label's contents.

♦ Copy the layout of the first label onto the other labels on the page by clicking the **Update all labels** button in the **Replicate labels** frame.

♦ Click the **Next: Preview your labels** link to go to the next step.

In the main document, you see a preview of the first page of labels.

♦ To display the field codes instead of the data and vice versa, press Alt F9.

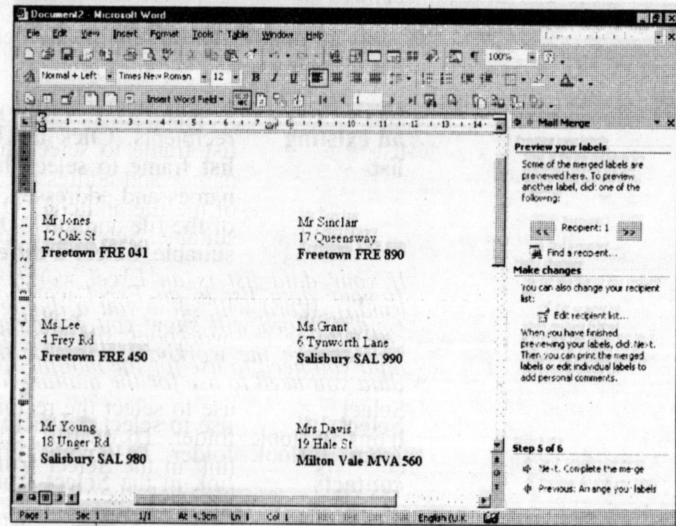

♦ Use the << and >> buttons in the **Preview your labels** frame to show the label for the previous or next record.

♦ Click the **Next: Complete the merge** link to go to the last step of the wizard.

♦ Click the **Print** link to merge to the printer and print your mailing labels or the **Edit individual labels** link to create the merged labels in a new document called **Labels** followed by a number.

♦ If you have chosen to **Edit individual labels**, specify which labels should be merged. To merge all the selected records in the list of data, activate the **All** option. To merge the records corresponding to the first page of labels, activate the **Current record** option. To limit the merge to certain selected records in the list of data, give the number of the first label required in the **From** box and the last in the **To** box. However, even if you do this, Word will always print a complete page of labels and may print records you did not request. For example, if you request records 5 to 15 and there are eight records to a page, records 5 to 12 will print on one page but 13 to 20 will print on the next as Word will complete the page it has started, so as to leave no blank labels.

If you merge to a new document, make the required changes, print and/or save the document and close it.

♦ Save the main document and close it.

If changes have been made to the list of data, Word prompts you to save them.

♦ If necessary, click **Yes** to save any changes made to the data list.

Creating a macro

A macro saves a series of commands as a single command in order to automate your work in Word. A macro is written in the Visual Basic programming language. Macros are stored in the document or in a document template.

♦ If you wish to save the macro in a particular document or template, open that document (for a template you can open a document based on that template). If no document is open, the macro will be saved in the Normal.dot template.

♦ **Tools**
Macro
Record New Macro

♦ Enter the **Macro name** in the appropriate text box.

♦ In the **Store macro in** list, give the name of the document or template in which the macro should be saved.

*Macros can be saved in the standard template (**All Documents (Normal.dot)**), in the active document or in the template on which the active document is based.*

♦ If you wish, enter a **Description**.

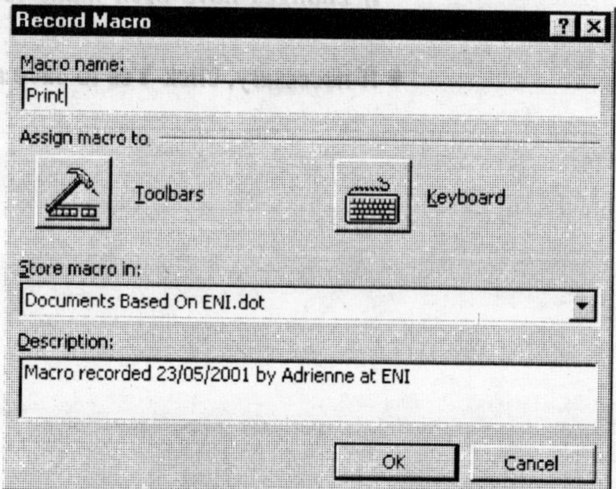

♦ To run your macro quickly and easily, you can associate it with a tool button or a keyboard shortcut by clicking one of these buttons:

Toolbars	using the **Commands** frame on the **Commands** tab, drag the macro icon onto the appropriate toolbar, creating a button associated with the macro.
Keyboard	give a keyboard shortcut to your macro.

♦ Click **OK**.

*The macro **Stop Recording** toolbar appears and the letters **REC** appear in bold on the status bar.*

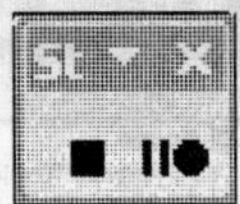

♦ Make all the actions you wish the macro to record.

♦ If you want to perform an action that should not be recorded, pause the recording by clicking the button on the **Stop Recording** toolbar. Click this button again to resume recording.

♦ When you have performed all the necessary actions, click the button on the **Stop Recording** toolbar.

The letters REC appear once again in grey on the status bar.

Running a macro

♦ **Tools**
Macro
Macros

♦ Alt F8

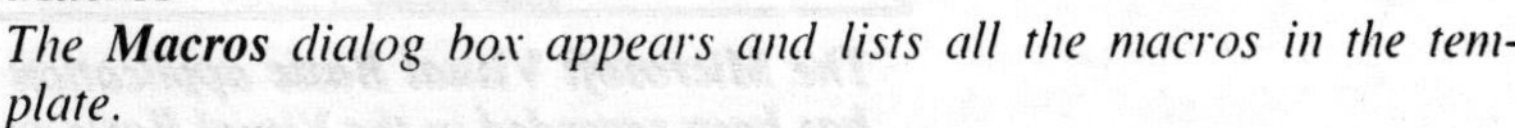

*The **Macros** dialog box appears and lists all the macros in the template.*

♦ If required, open the **Macros in** list to select the document or template containing the macro you wish to run.

♦ Double-click the **Macro name** you want to run or select the name and click the **Run** button.

If you associated a tool button or shortcut key to the macro, you can run it by clicking its tool button or pressing the shortcut key.

Modifying a macro

♦ **Tools**
Macro
Macros

♦ 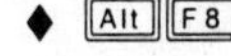

♦ Select the **Macro name** you wish to modify.

♦ Click the **Edit** button.

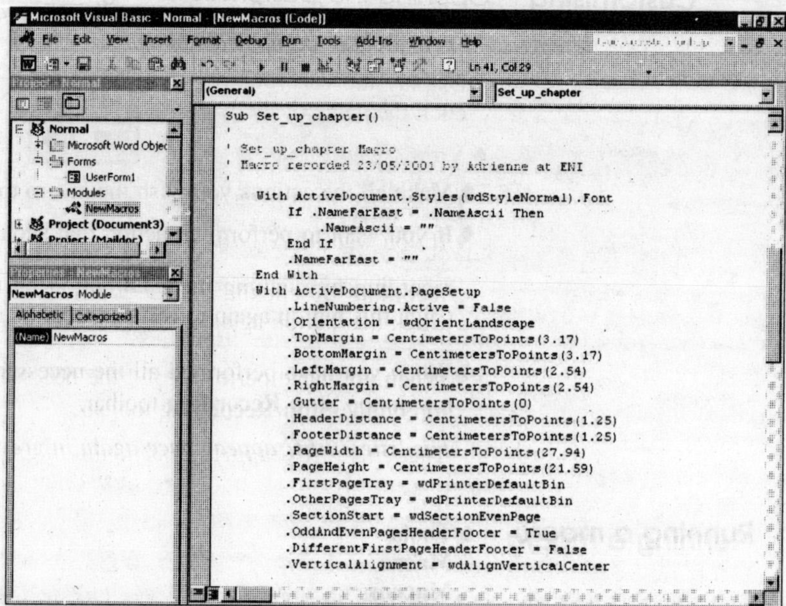

*The **Microsoft Visual Basic** application window shows how the macro has been recorded in the Visual Basic programming language.*

♦ Make any required changes.

♦ Leave the **Microsoft Visual Basic** application with **File - Close and Return to Microsoft Word** or Alt Q.

Deleting a macro

♦ **Tools**
Macro
Macros

♦ If required, open the **Macros in** list to select the document or template containing the macro you wish to delete.

♦ Select the **Macro name** you want to delete.

♦ Click the **Delete** button and confirm the deletion by clicking **Yes**.

♦ Click the **Close** button.

Customising a toolbar

Opening the Customize dialog box

♦ Go into the template concerned.

♦ Display the bar you wish to customise (go into **View - Toolbars** and click the name of the bar).

♦ **View**
Toolbars
Customize

❑ *You can also access this dialog box with the* ***Tools - Customize*** *command or by right-clicking any toolbar and choosing the* ***Customize*** *option.*

Removing a tool button

♦ Make sure that the bar from which you want to delete a tool button is displayed.

♦ Open the **Customize** dialog box.

♦ If necessary, click the **Commands** tab and open the **Save in** list to choose the document or template containing the tool you want to delete.

♦ On the toolbar itself, point to the tool button you want to remove, and drag it off the bar.

As soon as you release the mouse button, the tool button disappears.

♦ Click the **Close** button on the **Customize** dialog box.

Adding a tool button

♦ Open the **Customize** dialog box.

♦ Click the **Commands** tab.

♦ In the **Save in** list, choose the document or template in which you want to add the tool button to the bar.

♦ Select the category of the tool in the **Categories** box.

♦ In the **Commands** list, click the row of the command you wish to add.

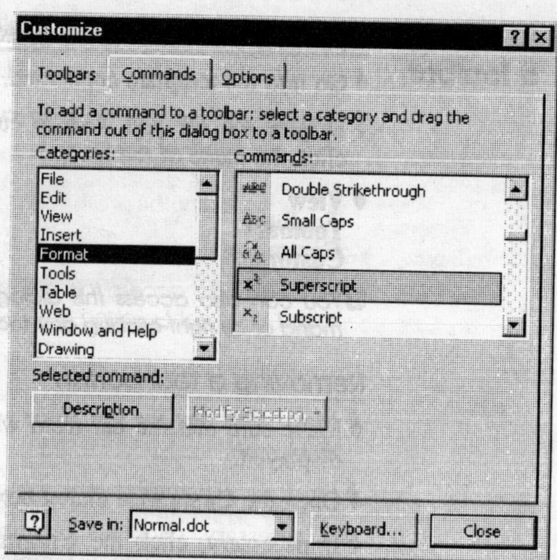

*Click the **Description** button to check what the tool does.*

♦ Drag the button you have chosen from the dialog box directly onto the appropriate toolbar (in the Word window).

♦ Choose what should be displayed with the **Modify Selection** button.

♦ Click the **Close** button on the **Customize** dialog box.

❑ *You can also add or remove tools by clicking the small black arrow visible at the very right of most toolbars then choosing **Add or Remove Buttons**.*

Customising the look of a tool button

♦ Open the **Customize** dialog box and click the **Commands** tab.

♦ On the toolbar, in the Word window, click the button you wish to customise.

♦ Click the **Modify Selection** button.

♦ Use the different options in this menu to change the presentation of the tool button.

♦ Click the **Customize** dialog box's **Close** button.

*To restore the original toolbars for a document or template, open that document, template or a document that is based on that template then use the **Tools - Customize** command and click the **Toolbars** tab. Click the name of the toolbar concerned then click the **Reset** button. In the dialog box that appears, select the name of the document or template containing the toolbar you wish to restore and click **OK**.*

Creating/deleting a custom toolbar

♦ Open the template or document in which you wish to make the toolbar available.

♦ **View**
Toolbars
Customize

♦ Click the **Toolbars** tab then the **New** button.

♦ Enter the **Toolbar name** for the bar you are creating.

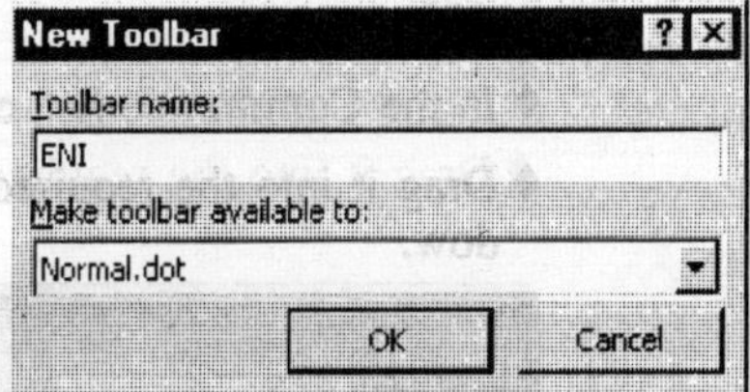

♦ In the **Make toolbar available to** text box, select the document or template concerned.

♦ Click **OK**.

*The name of your new toolbar appears at the bottom of the **Toolbars** list in the **Customize** dialog box. The new toolbar itself appears on the screen as a floating toolbar.*

♦ Add all the tools you require using the lists under the **Commands** tab.

♦ Click the **Close** button.

♦ Dock the new toolbar by double-clicking its title bar.

*To delete a custom toolbar, click its name on the **Toolbars** page of the **Customize** dialog box then click **Delete**.*

Customising menus

Deleting a menu or menu option

♦ Open the template or document concerned, then open the **Customize** dialog box with **Tools - Customize**.

♦ If it is not activated, click the **Commands** tab.

♦ To delete a menu option, open the menu in the menu bar on the application window. Point to the menu or option name that you want to remove and drag it clear of any menu.

♦ Close the **Customize** dialog box by clicking **Close**.

Adding an option to a menu

♦ Activate the template or document concerned then open the **Customize** dialog box (**Tools - Customize**).

♦ Click the **Commands** tab.

♦ Open the menu on the menu bar.

♦ In the **Categories** list, select the category which contains the option to add.

♦ In the **Commands** list, click the option.

♦ Drag it into the required position on the open menu in the Word window.

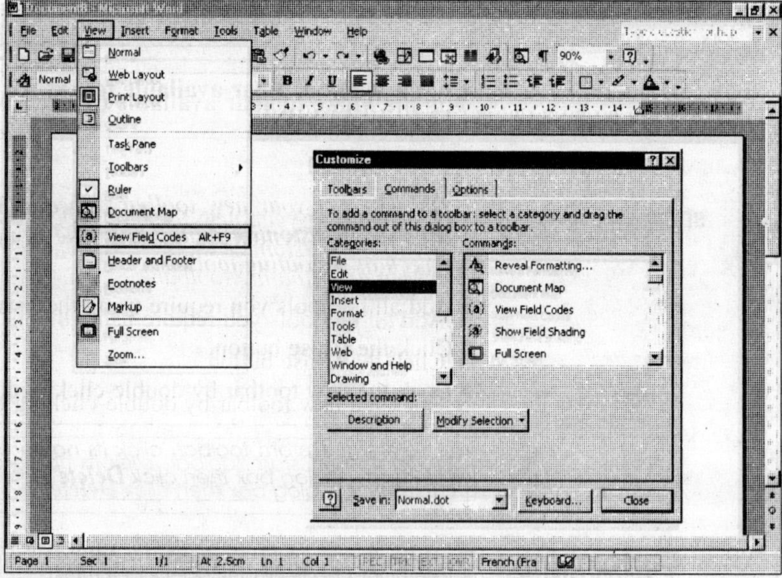

♦ Close the **Customize** dialog box by clicking **Close**.

Renaming a menu or an option

♦ Open the template or document concerned then open the **Customize** dialog box (**Tools - Customize**).

♦ If it is not activated, click the **Commands** tab.

♦ Select the menu or option you want to rename, in the Word window.

♦ Click the **Customize** dialog box's **Modify Selection** button.

♦ Type the new name into the **Name** text box (type an **&** in front of the letter which will appear underlined).

♦ Press Enter.

♦ Close the **Customize** dialog box by clicking **Close.**

Adding a new menu

♦ Open the template or document concerned then open the **Customize** dialog box (**Tools - Customize**).

♦ Click the **Commands** tab and select **New Menu** from the list of categories.

♦ Drag the **New Menu** name from the **Commands** tab to the correct position on the menu bar.

♦ Use the **Modify Selection** button to give the new menu a name.

♦ Click the new menu name to open it. Add the options of your choice.

♦ In the **Save in** list, check the template or document name then click the **Close** button.

Defining shortcut keys

Deleting a shortcut key

♦ If necessary, open the template or document concerned.

♦ Use the **Tools - Customize** command and click the **Keyboard** button.

♦ Check the name of the document or template in the **Save changes in** list.

♦ In the **Categories** list, select the required menu, or if you want to delete a shortcut key from one of the **Styles, Fonts, AutoText, Macros** or **Common Symbols,** click the appropriate option.

♦ In the corresponding list, select the **Commands, Styles, Fonts, AutoText, Macros** or **Common Symbols** whose shortcut key you wish to delete.

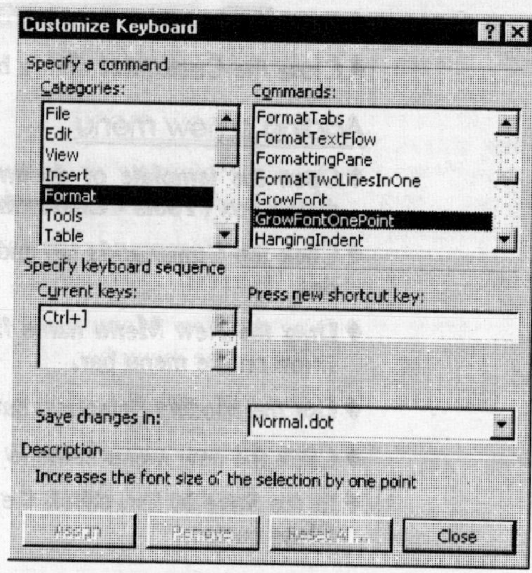

*The keyboard shortcut appears in the **Current keys** list.*

♦ In the **Current keys** box, click the shortcut you wish to delete.

♦ Click the **Remove** button.

♦ Click the **Close** button twice.

Adding a shortcut key

♦ If necessary, open the template or document concerned.

♦ Use the **Tools - Customize** command and click the **Keyboard** button.

♦ Check the name of the document or template in the **Save changes in** list.

♦ In the **Categories** list, select the required menu, or if you want to add a shortcut key to one of the **Styles**, **Fonts**, **AutoText**, **Macros** or **Common Symbols**, click the appropriate option.

♦ In the corresponding list, select the **Commands**, **Styles**, **Fonts**, **AutoText**, **Macro** or **Common Symbol** to which you wish to add a shortcut key.

♦ Click the **Press new shortcut key** text box and on the keyboard, type the new shortcut.

♦ Check that the mention **[unassigned]** appears next to the **Currently assigned to** option.

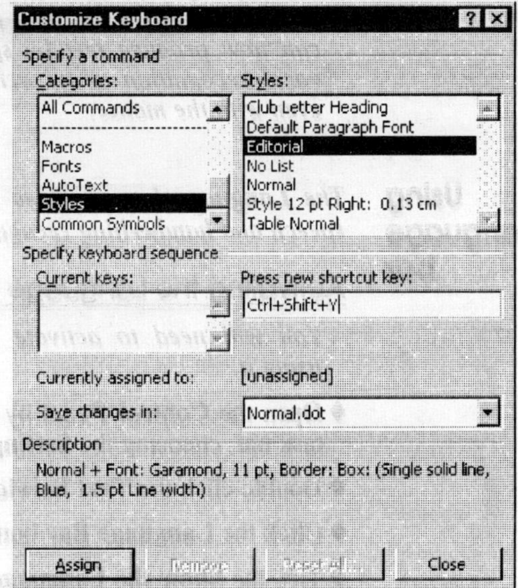

♦ Click the **Assign** button.

*The shortcut key can now be seen in the **Current keys** box.*

♦ Click the **Close** button twice.

❑ *You can restore the original Word shortcut keys for the template or document selected in the **Save changes in** list by clicking the **Reset All** button on the **Customize Keyboard** dialog box (**Tools - Customize - Keyboard** button).*

. . . . *Personal notes*. . . . .

Word 2002 offers you two new interesting ways of entering text; you can now produce text by speaking to your computer which will use vocal recognition or by writing text by hand on a graphics tablet or even with the mouse.

Using the Language bar

*The **Language** bar provides the necessary tools for working with the speech and handwriting recognition features.*

Activating the Language bar

*You will need to activate the **Language** bar before you can start using it.*

♦ Open the **Control Panel** by clicking the **Start** button on the Windows task bar, choosing the **Settings** option then **Control Panel**.

♦ Double-click the **Text Services** folder to open it.

♦ Click the **Language Bar** button.

♦ Tick the **Show the Language bar on the desktop** option.

♦ Click **OK** twice to leave the **Text Services** dialog box.

❑ *If the **Text Services** folder does not appear in the **Control Panel**, the corresponding Office component may not be installed: to remedy this, use **Start - Settings - Control Panel - Add/Remove Programs - Install/Uninstall** tab. Choose **Microsoft Office XP** in the list and click the **Add/Remove** button. Expand the **Office Shared Features** list by clicking the plus sign beside it and click the **Alternative User Input** option. Choose **Run from My Computer** and click the Update button. You may need to insert your Office XP or Word 2002 CD-ROM at this point. You can also reinstall Office XP, using a complete installation, rather than a standard one.*

Showing/hiding the Language bar

♦ To show the **Language** bar, click the EN language indicator on the status bar.

♦ Choose the **Show the Language bar** option.

*The **Language** bar appears on the screen as a floating toolbar. It cannot be docked as a normal toolbar can.*

EN English (United Kingdom) | Correction | Microphone | Tools | Handwriting | Writing Pad | ?

♦ To hide the **Language** bar, click the [-] button at the right end of it or right-click the toolbar and choose the **Minimize** option.

*This minimizes the **Language** bar into the language indicator on the status bar.*

♦ To move the **Language** bar, point to the move handle (the grey vertical line) at the left end of the bar and when the pointer takes this shape: ✥, drag it to its new position.

♦ To close the **Language** bar, right-click it and choose the **Close the Language bar** option. When you do this, the bar is deactivated and is no longer available on the status bar.

Managing other Language bar options

Adding/removing buttons from the Language bar

♦ To remove buttons from the **Language** bar, click the **Options** button [▾] at the end of the bar and click the name of the option you no longer wish to see on the bar. To restore a button, click the **Options** button and activate the option name again.

♦ The default set of buttons on the bar can be retrieved with the **Restore Defaults** option, which is also in the **Options** menu.

Using text labels on the Language bar

*By default, the buttons on the **Language** bar appear with text labels, showing the name of each function. If you wish you can use icons only, to make the bar more concise.*

♦ Right-click the **Language** bar.

♦ Activate, or deactivate the **Text Labels** option, depending on your needs.

Managing input language tool options

♦ To define which language tools should be active for each input language, click the **Options** button [▾] and choose **Settings**.

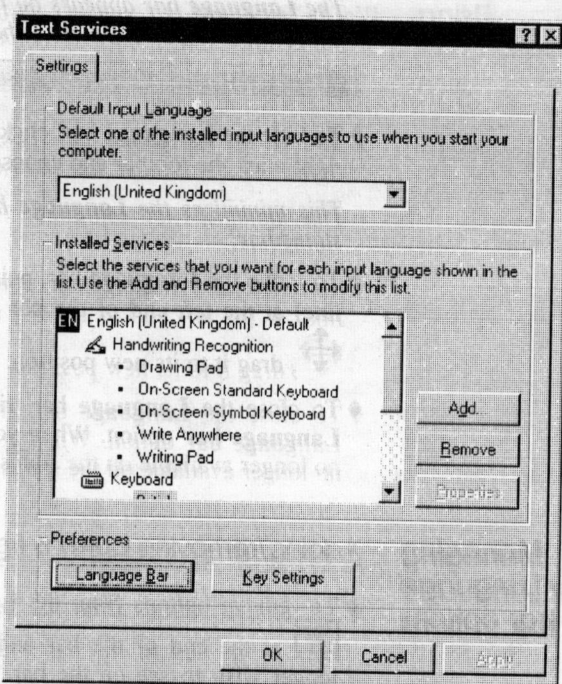

- In the **Text Services** dialog box, you can choose a **Default Input Language** for your computer from the corresponding list.
- To install handwriting tools for another input language, click the **Handwriting Recognition** option in the **Installed Services** list and click **Add.** In the **Add Input language** dialog box, choose the required language in the **Input Language** list box and click **OK.**

  The full range of handwriting recognition tools is only available for the English, Chinese, Japanese and Korean language versions of Word 2002.

- To install a keyboard layout for another language, click the **Keyboard** option in the **Installed Services** list and click **Add.** In the **Add Input language** dialog box, choose the required language in the **Input Language** list box and click **OK.**
- To remove a handwriting tool or keyboard layout, choose the appropriate option in the **Installed Services** list and click **Remove.**

Using handwriting recognition

Word's handwriting recognition feature examines text you write by hand and transforms it into either typed text or a graphic representation of your handwriting. You can write with a handwriting input device, such as a graphics tablet, but Word can even decipher text written by moving the mouse to form words.

Inserting text as handwriting

♦ In the document, place the insertion point where the handwritten text should appear.

♦ If you wish to write on the **Writing Pad**, click the **Handwriting** button [Handwriting] on the **Language** bar and choose **Writing Pad**. If you wish to write freely anywhere on the screen, using the mouse or another device, click the **Handwriting** button [Handwriting] on the **Language** bar and choose the **Write Anywhere** option.

The Writing Pad is a special dialog box which resembles lined paper. You can use it to help you write your text more easily.

♦ To insert text as handwriting, click the **Ink** button on the **Write Anywhere** bar or on the **Writing Pad**.

♦ Write on the graphics tablet (or another device), or write using your mouse by moving it on the mouse pad to make words. If you are using the **Writing Pad**, write along the line, as if it were ruled paper. The pointer, which resembles a pen, "writes" at the same time as you, either on the **Writing Pad** or if you are not using it, wherever it is positioned on the screen.

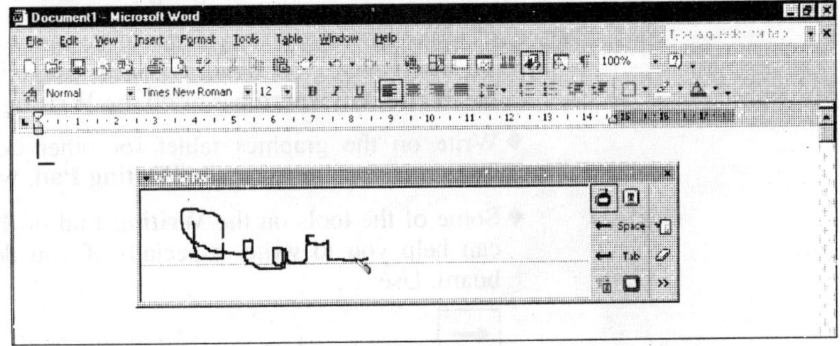

After a brief pause, Word inserts the text as you have written it. It is entered in lines, as in a standard document and the height of the line (and consequently the size of the characters) is determined by the active font size.

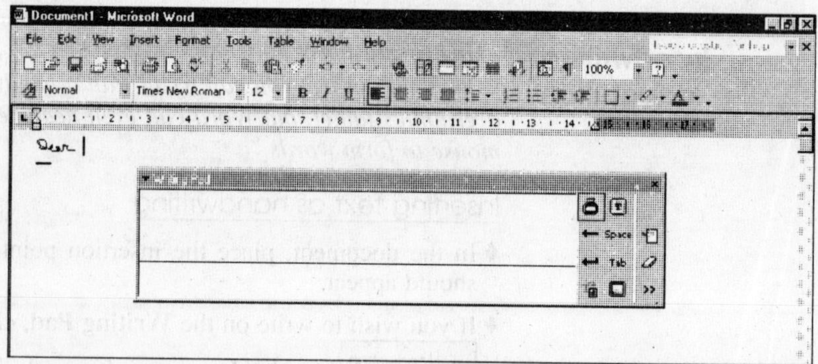

♦ When you have finished using the **Writing Pad** or the **Write Anywhere** bar, you can close it by clicking the button in its top right corner.

❑ *Handwritten text inserted in this way can be formatted like any typed text (you can change the font size or colour or apply bold type, for example) and you can also use the find and/or replace commands on handwritten text.*

Inserting typed text

♦ In the document, place the insertion point where the text should appear.

♦ If you wish to write on the **Writing Pad**, click the **Handwriting**button Handwriting on the **Language** bar and choose **Writing Pad**. If you wish to write freely, using the mouse or another device, click Handwriting on the **Language** bar and choose the **Write Anywhere** option.

♦ To insert what you write as typed text, click the **Text** button on the **Write Anywhere** bar or on the **Writing Pad**.

♦ Write on the graphics tablet (or other device), or write using your mouse. If you are using the **Writing Pad**, write along the line.

♦ Some of the tools on the **Writing Pad** or the **Write Anywhere** toolbar can help you to write, especially if you do not want to use the keyboard. Use:

to clear the last character in the typed text on the screen,

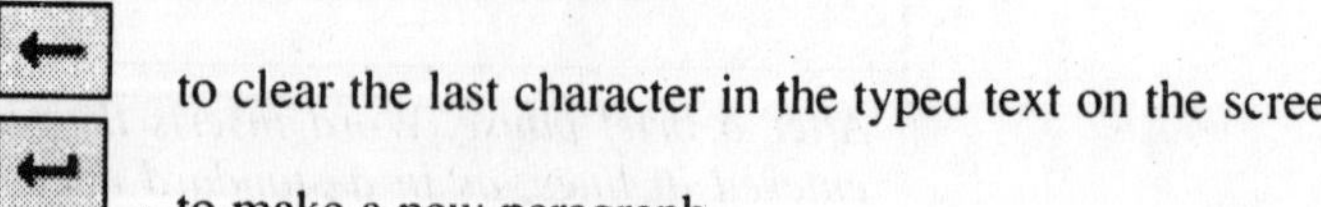

to make a new paragraph,

Space to create a space in the typed text,

Tab to insert a tab stop in the text,

↓ to move the insertion point down one line,

↑ to move the insertion point up one line,

← to move the insertion point back one character,

→ to move the insertion point forward one character.

The text you write appears in typed form at the position where you place the insertion point. This text can be formatted in the usual ways.

- When you have finished using the **Writing Pad** or the **Write Anywhere** bar, you can close it by clicking the ☒ button in its top right corner.

❑ *Word finds it easier to recognise handwritten text if you follow a few simple rules. You can use running writing or printing, or both. Be sure to write whole words, without making large gaps between each letter. Leave ample space to distinguish each separate word. In any case, if Word does not recognise your text correctly, you can correct what it has entered (cf. below).*

Correcting handwritten text

Word will recognise the vast majority of handwritten words correctly, even if you write with the mouse, which sometimes produces rather mediocre results. If, however, the text Word enters is incorrect, you can make corrections to it.

- Select the incorrect word with the mouse or the keyboard, using the normal selection techniques.
- Click the **Correction** button on the **Writing Pad** or the **Write Anywhere** bar.

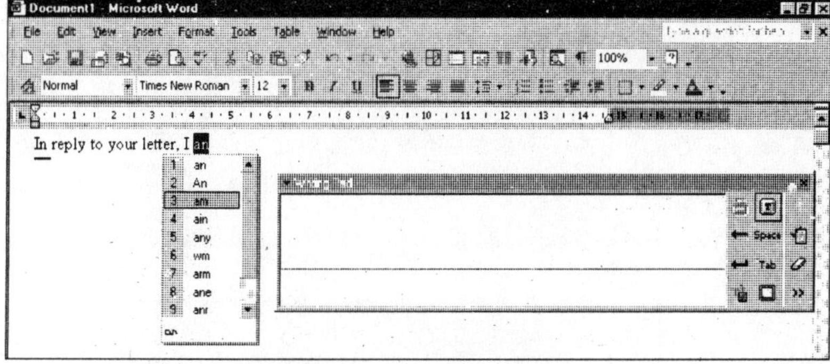

A list of suggested corrections appears below the selected mis-take: the text you wrote is reproduced at the bottom of that list.

♦ Choose the suggestion that corresponds to what you wanted to use.

The correct word replaces the selection in the document.
If the list of suggestions does not contain the text you require, you can also type the correct version in.

♦ To change text that appears as handwriting in the document, select the unsatisfactory text and rewrite the word on the screen or on the **Writing Pad** (depending on the technique you are using).

Your new text replaces the selection in the document.

♦ When you have finished your corrections, close the **Writing Pad** or the **Write Anywhere** bar by clicking the button in its corner.

Managing the Writing Pad/ Write Anywhere bar

*The **Writing Pad** and the **Write Anywhere** bar can be moved like any other toolbar but they cannot be docked. The tools described below are the same on both the **Writing Pad** and the **Write Anywhere** bar.*

♦ To clear your written text from the screen or the **Writing Pad**, click the button.

♦ If you are not working in automatic recognition mode, click the button to ask Word to recognise the handwritten item.

♦ Click the button to switch to the **Writing Pad** (when you are using **Write Anywhere** mode) or the button to switch to **Write Anywhere** mode (when you are using the **Writing Pad**).

♦ Click the button to open the **Drawing Pad**.

♦ Clicking opens the **On-Screen Standard Keyboard**.

Managing handwriting options

♦ To see the list of handwriting options, click the [▾] button on the **Write Anywhere** bar or the **Writing Pad**.

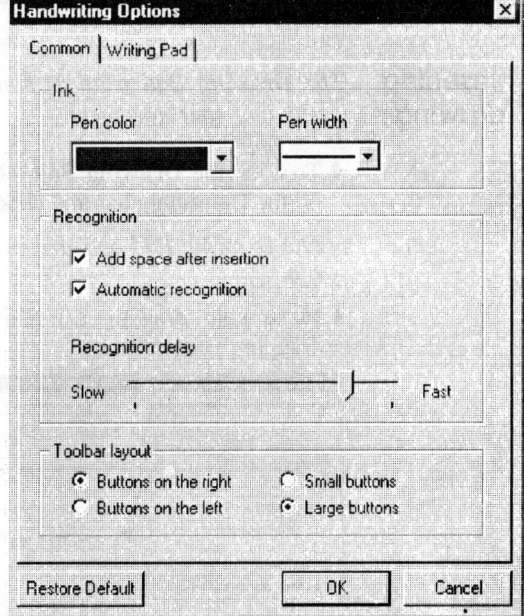

♦ To change the colour of the handwriting sample that appears as you write on the screen or in the **Writing Pad**, open the **Pen color** drop-down list and choose the required colour.

♦ To change the line weight used for the handwriting that appears as you write, open the **Pen width** drop-down list and choose another line style.

♦ Choose whether or not Word should **Add space after insertion** or if it should make an **Automatic recognition** of your writing, using the corresponding options.

*If **Automatic recognition** is not active, you will have to click the **Recognize Now** button on the **Write Anywhere** bar or the **Writing Pad** after each text you write, for Word to perform its handwriting recognition.*

♦ If you wish, choose a faster or slower **Recognition delay** by sliding the cursor.

❑ *The **Toolbar layout** options determine the size and position of the tool buttons on the **Writing Pad**.*

❑ *To change the presentation of the **Writing Pad** (its background colour, the number of lines on it etc.), use the options under the **Writing Pad** tab on the **Handwriting Options** dialog box (click the ▾ button).*

Inserting drawings

*The **Drawing Pad** features can be used to enter drawings quickly and easily into your document.*

♦ To open the **Drawing Pad**, click the **Handwriting** button on the **Language** bar and choose the **Drawing Pad** option.

The Drawing Pad appears on the screen; the pointer takes the shape of a pen.

♦ Make your drawing using a digital pen on a graphics tablet or by dragging your mouse.

♦ If you are unhappy with your drawing and you wish to clear the **Drawing Pad**, click the **Clear** button on the **Drawing Pad**.

♦ To undo the last line you drew, click the **Remove Last Stroke** button on the **Drawing Pad**.

♦ If you want to copy your drawing to the clipboard, to use it in another application for example, click the **Copy to Clipboard** button.

♦ When you are satisfied with your drawing, click the **Insert Drawing** button to insert it into the document.

*Once you have inserted your drawing, the **Drawing Pad** is cleared automatically.*

♦ To set the **Drawing Pad** options, click the button at the top left corner of its title bar and choose **Options**.

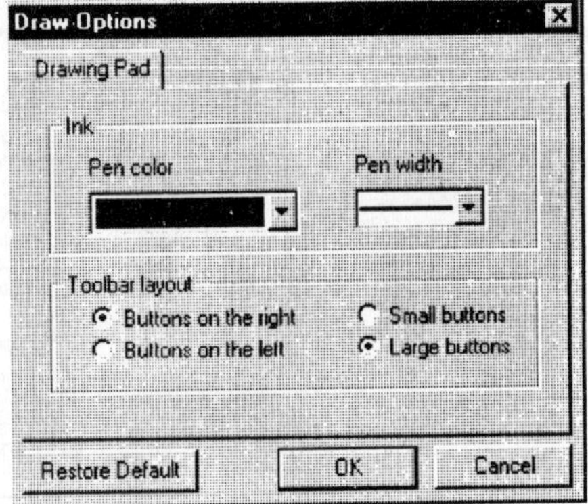

♦ Use the appropriate options to change the pen settings and the layout of the **Drawing Pad** tools.

♦ When you have finished using the **Drawing Pad**, close it by clicking the [x] button in its top right corner.

Using speech recognition

Word's speech recognition feature enables you to enter text by dictating to your computer. To use the speech recognition tools, your computer needs a sound card and a microphone. While the speech recognition feature can be very useful, you may find that you need to combine it with your keyboard and mouse to achieve an optimum result.

Setting up your microphone

♦ Make sure your microphone is plugged into your computer.

♦ Adjust your microphone's position; it should be close to your mouth but not actually touching it. Slightly off to one side is a good position. Ensure that you do not move the microphone while you are using it.

Keep the room you are in as quiet as possible, to minimise the amount of background noise which could interfere with the speech recognition.

♦ On the **Language** bar, click the **Speech Tools** button and choose the **Options** option.

♦ In the dialog box, click the **Speech Recognition** tab if necessary.

♦ Click the **Configure Microphone** button.

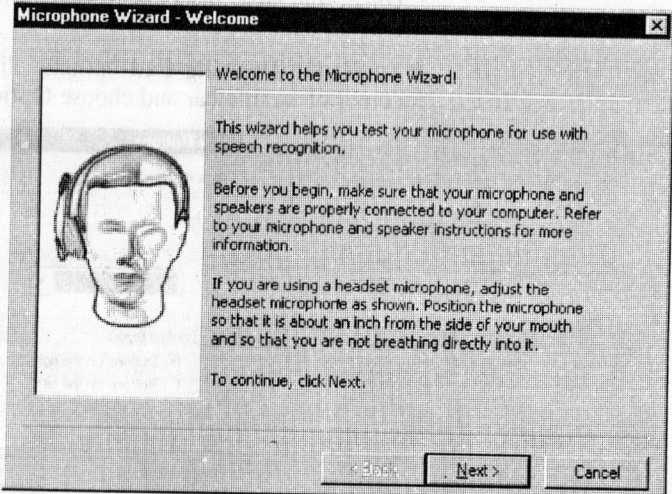

♦ Follow the instructions on the **Microphone Wizard**, speaking into the microphone where required. When you have completed all the steps, click the **Finish** button.

Your microphone should now be ready for use.

Training the speech recognition device

Before working with the speech recognition features, you need to help your computer to understand your way of speaking. To do this, your computer should undergo a training program! The aim of this is for the computer to "hear" you speaking a standard text so it can create a custom speech profile for you.

♦ Click the **Speech Tools** button on the **Language** bar and take the **Training** option.

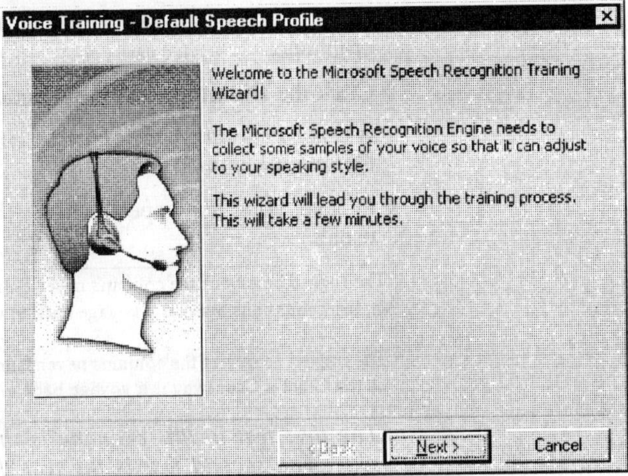

♦ Follow the steps in the **Microsoft Speech Recognition Training Wizard** that appears, speaking into the microphone when required. This takes about 10 or 15 minutes: try to ensure that you are in a quiet environment while training is underway.

This training wizard examines your speech patterns, voice tone, accent and so on, so that what you say is recognised more easily. If you are the first person to use the training wizard, your speech patterns will make up the default speech profile. Any subsequent users who wish to use speech recognition will have to create their own individual profile (cf. Creating a speech profile, below).

♦ When you have completed all the steps in the wizard, click the **Finish** button to close it and create your speech profile.

Dictating text

As you speak your text into the microphone, it appears in typed form on the screen. There may be a pause between when you speak and when Word actually converts your speech to text. If several users use the same computer, you may have to choose a profile before dictating (cf. Choosing a speech profile).

♦ If necessary, choose your personal speech profile.

♦ Position the insertion point in the document where you want the text to appear.

♦ Click the **Microphone** button on the **Language** bar to activate the microphone.

♦ Click the **Dictation** button to dictate your text.

When you wish to use a vocal command, you need to click the ***Voice Command*** *button.*

♦ Dictate your text: speak clearly but do not speak more slowly than usual.

> The rugged beauty of the columns never fails to intrigue and inspire our visitors. To stroll on the giants calls away is a voyage back in time.
>
> The rugged beauty of the columns never fails to intrigue and inspire our visitors. To stroll on the Giant's Causeway is a voyage back in time.

The first text in this example is the text produced by the dictation engine. The second text is the text that was being dictated. You can see that some features such as proper nouns, or words with apostrophes are often not reproduced correctly.

♦ Correct any errors by selecting them and retyping them or saying them again (cf. Correcting errors in dictated text).

♦ When you have finished your text, click the **Microphone** button on the **Language** bar or say the word "microphone", which turns off the microphone.

Correcting errors in dictated text

The more you use vocal recognition, the higher the amount of correct text Word produces. However, some types of text may be incorrectly interpreted. Errors made during vocal recognition are easily fixed.

♦ To correct a mistake with the mouse and/or keyboard, select the erroneous text with the mouse or the keyboard and type in the correct text.

♦ To correct a mistake by dictating it again, select the item with the mouse, keyboard or appropriate vocal command, click the **Microphone** button on the **Language** bar then the **Dictation** button and speak the text again, speaking as clearly as possible.

❑ *If you wish to delete the last word you said, say "scratch that". The word will be removed.*

Using voice commands

While you are dictating, there are certain commands you can use to simplify your work. You actually speak the names of these commands into the microphone to perform the corresponding tasks.

♦ As you dictate, say the following commands to enter punctuation or change mode:

Say this	Action performed
Colon, comma, period	Enters the corresponding punctuation mark.
Enter	Presses the [Enter] key.
Forcenum	Enters a number as a numeral not as a word.
Microphone	Turns off the microphone.
New line	Starts a new line.
New paragraph	Starts a new paragraph.
Spelling mode	Changes mode so you can spell out the word that follows (pause when you have finished to return to dictation mode).
Tab	Presses the [Tab] key.

♦ To select text with vocal commands, make sure the microphone is turned on then click the **Voice Command** button on the **Language** bar or say "voice command". Say the command required to make your selection. The table below shows the most common examples.

♦ To format text with vocal commands, make sure the microphone is on then click the **Voice Command** button on the **Language** bar or say "voice command". Say the command required to format your selection. The table below shows you the most common examples.

Commands for selecting text	Commands for formatting text
"Select next word" (to select the next word)	"Bold" (to use bold type).
"Select last word" (to select the previous word)	"Underline" (to use underlining).
"Select next line" (to select the next line)	"Italics" (to use italic type).
"Select last line" (to select the previous line)	"Font" or "Font face" followed by "name of font e.g. Arial, Tahoma" (to switch to the font named".
"Select paragraph" (to select the current paragraph)	
"Select last line" (to select the previous line)	

This list is by no means exhaustive: in Word 2002, you can use most of the menu commands and navigate in your document almost entirely with spoken commands. You can also create custom spoken commands. A detailed explanation of this can be found at the ***Microsoft Office Assistance Center*** *Web site in the article entitled* ***Speech recognition commands in Word 2002*** *(cf. Using the help).*

♦ To return to dictation mode, click the **Dictation** button on the **Language** bar or say the word "dictation".

Creating a speech profile

The default speech profile is the one created for the first person who used the speech recognition feature on that computer. Subsequent users must create their own profile.

♦ On the **Language** bar, click the **Speech Tools** button and choose the **Options** option.

♦ In the dialog box, click the **Speech Recognition** tab if necessary.

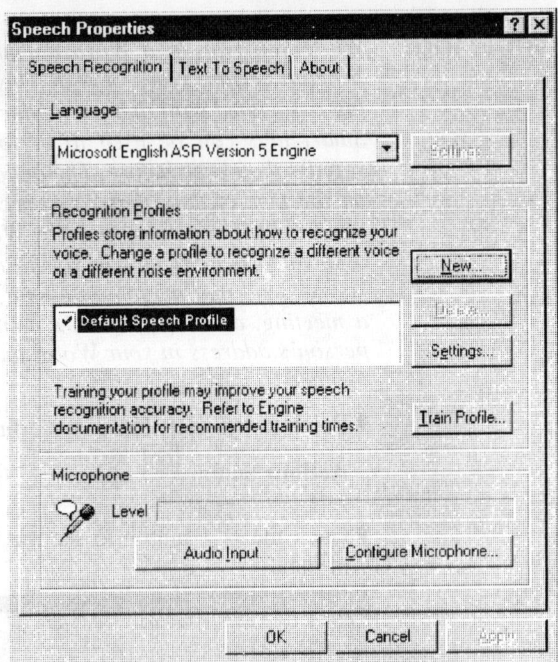

♦ In the **Recognition Profiles** frame, click the **New** button.

*The **Profile Wizard** opens: follow the instructions to create your profile.*

♦ When you have completed all the steps in the wizard, click the **Finish** button.

Choosing a different speech profile

When different users work with speech recognition on the same computer, each user should create his/her own speech profile and activate his/her custom profile before starting to work.

♦ On the **Language** bar, click the **Speech Tools** button.

♦ Point to the **Current User** option and in the list of users that appears, click the one you wish to use.

❑ *If you log in under a different user name, a new default speech profile will be created for that user name.*

Using smart tags

While you type in a Word document, a purple dotted line may appear beneath certain types of text. This indicator means that there is a ***smart tag*** *associated with that particular item of text.*
Smart tags can be used to perform certain actions within Word more rapidly than ever before. The actions proposed by each smart tag depend on the type of data that Word recognises. For example, Sandra Reid (or Sandra REID) is recognised by Word as a "person name" smart tag. The associated actions enable you to open that person's contact file, if there is one, send that person an e-mail, if he/she has an e-mail address, set up a meeting, add that person's name to your contacts or even insert that person's address in your Word document, if it can be found in your list of contacts!

♦ Point to the text that is underlined in purple to make the **Smart Tag Actions** button appear.

♦ Click the button to see the list of actions associated with this type of data.

In the example above, the text selected is Ms Barbara Nicholls. The list that opens from the button hides the selected text.

♦ Click the name of the action you wish to carry out.

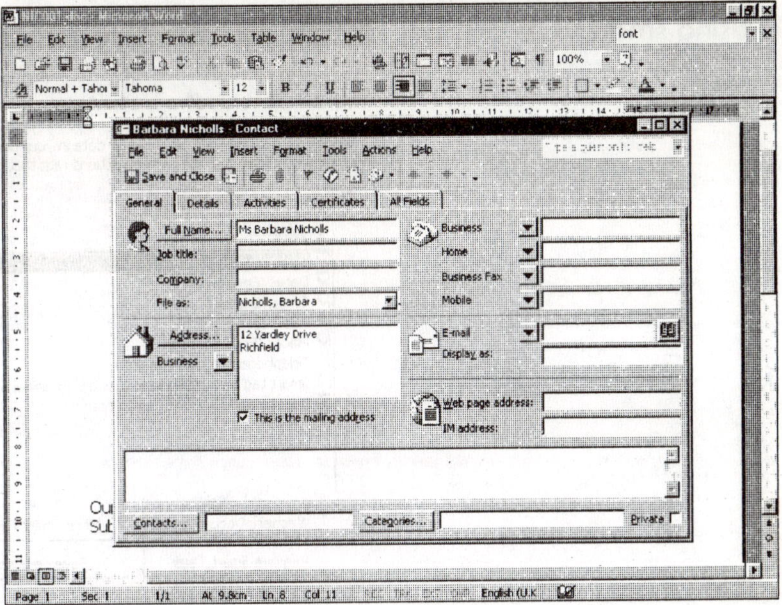

In the example above, the ***Add to Contacts*** *action has been chosen. Outlook 2002 opens a new contact form within the Word document window; you can use this form to enter all the details about the contact you wish to add. When you close and save this form, the contact will be added to those in your Outlook 2002 folder.*

♦ If necessary, use the tools and buttons in the application which opens to finish your work.

When the action has been completed, you return to the original Word document.

❑ *Smart tags are not available in a document that has been protected as a form.*

Managing smart tags

♦ **Tools**
AutoCorrect Options

♦ Click the **Smart Tags** tab.

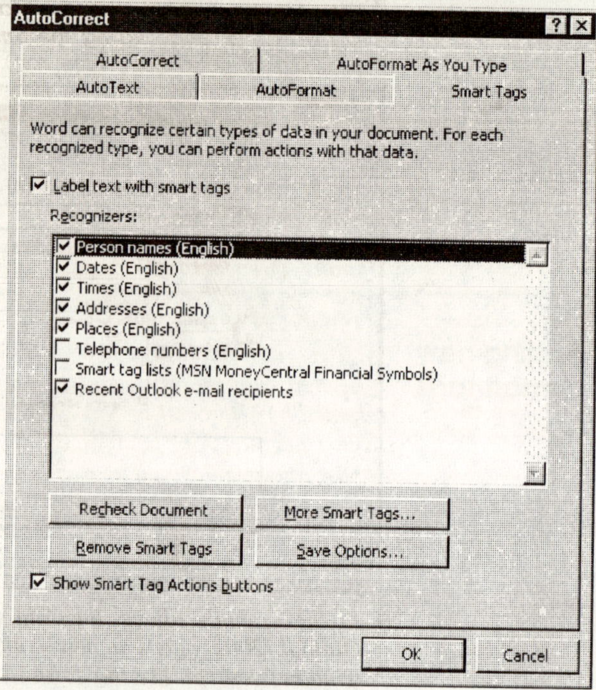

- To activate or deactivate smart tags, use the **Label text with smart tags** option.
- To choose what type of data Word should recognise and label with smart tags, activate or deactivate the options in the **Recognizers** list.

  *If the list of the type of data Word should recognise has been changed, you can apply your new choices to the active document by clicking the **Recheck Document** button.*
- To **Show Smart Tag Actions buttons** (ⓘ)in the document, make sure the corresponding option is ticked, otherwise remove the tick to hide these buttons. If you hide the buttons, you can no longer perform the actions.
- To save the smart tags when you save the document, click the **Save Options** button and activate the **Embed smart tags** option (or deactivate this option if you do not wish to save them). Click **OK**.
- Click **OK**.

❑ *You can show or hide the smart tag indicators (the purple dotted lines) by activating or deactivating the* ***Smart tags*** *option in the* ***Options*** *dialog box (****Tools - Options - View*** *tab). Hiding the indicators does not stop you using the smart tags feature. When you place the pointer over recognised text (such as a person's name) the* ***Smart Tag Actions*** *button still appears.*

❑ *Smart tags can be saved in an e-mail message so the message recipient can also use them. If you want to do this, make sure the* ***Save smart tags in e-mail*** *option is active in the* ***E-mail Options*** *dialog box (****Tools - Options - General*** *tab -* ***E-mail Options*** *button -* ***General*** *tab).*

Adding new smart tags

You can download new smart tags from Web sites to add to those already installed with the Microsoft Word application. Other smart tags may be created by Microsoft or by other IT companies and technicians.
New smart tags are being developed constantly so you can download new smart tags regularly, if you wish.

- **Tools**
  AutoCorrect Options
- Click the **Smart Tags** tab.
- Click the **More Smart Tags** option.

  A page from the Microsoft Web site appears in your Web browser window, showing the categories into which the smart tags are organised.
- Click the link that corresponds to the category that interests you then click the link to download the required smart tag application.

❑ *You can update the actions associated with each new smart tag downloaded. To do this, open the list on the* [i] *button for the smart tag concerned and choose the* ***Check for New Actions*** *option.*

Deleting smart tags

- To delete a smart tag from a text, point to the text until the **Smart Tag Actions** button [i] appears, click the [i] button and choose the **Remove this Smart Tag** option.
- To remove all the smart tags from the current document, click the **Remove Smart Tags** button on the **AutoCorrect Options** dialog box (**Tools - AutoCorrect Options - Smart Tags** tab).

The following message appears on the screen:

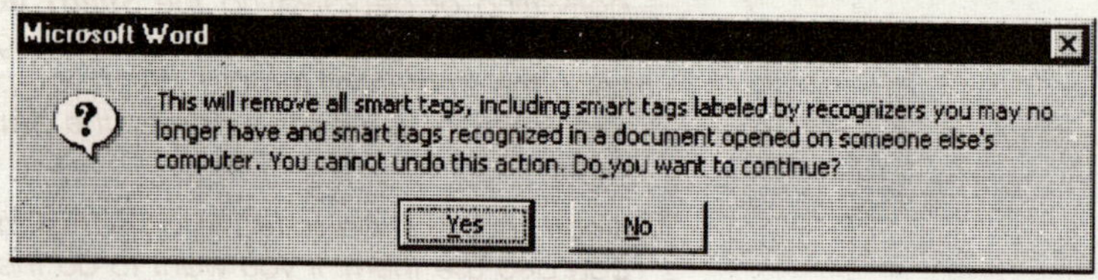

♦ Click **Yes** then click **OK** on the message informing you that the smart tags have been deleted.

Personal notes

Managing comments

Creating comments

Comments are notes or messages that you attach to text. Comments are especially useful when more than one user works on the document.

♦ Go into **Print Layout** view (**View - Print Layout**).

♦ Select the text to which the comment should refer.

♦ **Insert**
Comment

You can also create a comment by clicking the [tool button] *tool button on the **Reviewing** toolbar, if it is displayed.*

*A balloon appears in the right margin, containing the text **Comment**; the insertion point flashes in the balloon. If the **Reviewing** toolbar was not on the screen prior to this, it is now displayed.*

♦ Enter the comment text in the **Comment** balloon.

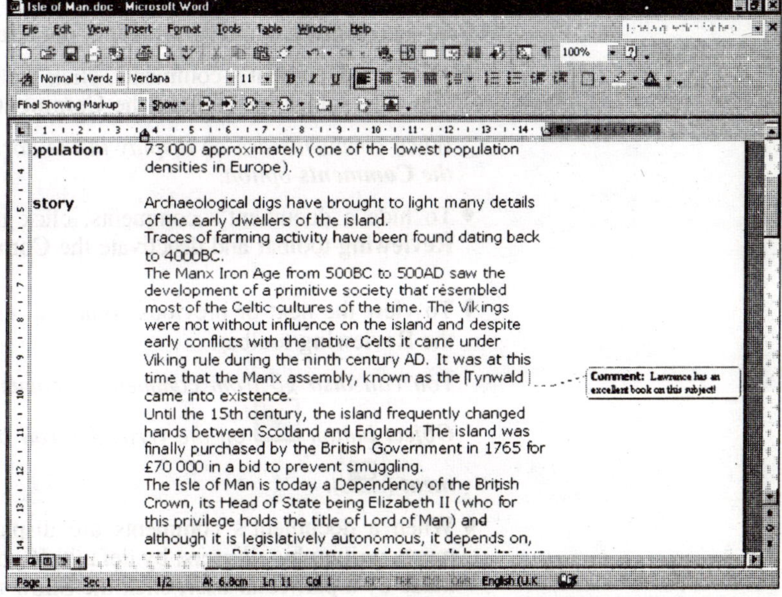

The text to which the comment refers appears in square brackets. If comments are inserted in the same document by different users, each user's comment balloons appears in a different colour.

♦ Click elsewhere in the document.

♦ Hide the comments if necessary (cf. below).

❑ *If your computer is equipped with a sound card, you can record a vocal comment. To do this, select the text to which the comment should refer, open the list on the* ***New Comment*** *button ( ) on the* ***Reviewing*** *toolbar then click the* ***Voice Comment*** *option. Record your comment using the buttons in the* ***Sound Object*** *window then close the window by clicking its button.*

❑ *In* ***Normal*** *view, comments do not appear in comment balloons but in the* ***Main document changes and comments*** *section of the* ***Reviewing Pane****. This pane appears at the bottom of the document window and can also be used to enter comment text. The* ***Reviewing Pane*** *button ( ) on the* ***Reviewing*** *toolbar hides or displays this pane.*

Showing/hiding comments

♦ If it is not on the screen, display the **Reviewing** toolbar (**View - Toolbars - Reviewing**).

♦ Go into **Print Layout** view, if it is not already active.

♦ To see a document's comments, click the **Show** tool button on the **Reviewing** toolbar and activate the **Comments** option.

When comments are on display in the document, a tick appears next to the ***Comments*** *option.*

♦ To hide a document's comments, click the **Show** tool button on the **Reviewing** toolbar and deactivate the **Comments** option.

♦ To view the next or previous comment, use the or button on the **Reviewing** toolbar.

You can also go from comment to comment using the ***Select Browse Object*** *button on the vertical scroll bar: choose* ***Browse by Comment*** *( ).*

♦ When a document's comments are displayed, you can see the comments written by all users, by default. If you wish to hide the comments made by a particular user, click the **Show** tool button on the **Reviewing** toolbar, point to the **Reviewers** option and remove the tick next to the name of each user whose comments you wish to hide. On the other hand, to view the comments of a user, tick the option corresponding to that user. Activate the **All Reviewers** option to view all users' comments once again.

❑ *When you want to show or hide comments, you can also use the **View - Markup** command. This will also hide or show the tracking of changes (text insertions and deletions as well as the formatting applied to text).*

❑ *To display in a ScreenTip the name of the user who created a comment as well as the date and time when the comment was created, check that the **ScreenTips** option is active in the **Options** dialog box (**Tools - Options - View** tab) then point (without clicking) to the relevant comment balloon.*

❑ *To modify the comment balloon options (width, margins etc), use the options in the **Balloons** frame of the **Track Changes** dialog box (click the **Show** button on the **Reviewing** toolbar then choose **Options**).*

Modifying a comment

♦ Make sure you are in Print Layout view.

♦ If the comments are not visible on the screen, display them.

♦ Click the balloon containing the comment you wish to modify.

♦ Make the required changes in the comment text.

♦ Click elsewhere in the document.

♦ Hide the comments, if you wish.

Deleting comments

♦ Make sure you are in Print Layout view and that the **Reviewing** toolbar is on display.

♦ If the comments are not visible on the screen, display them.

♦ Click the balloon containing the comment you wish to delete.

♦ To delete the active comment, click the button on the **Reviewing** toolbar or open the list on the tool button and click the **Delete Comment** option.

♦ To delete all the comments in the document, open the list on the tool button and click the **Delete All Comments in Document** option.

♦ To delete the comments of one or more users, show the comments of the users in question (cf. **Showing/hiding comments**), open the list on the tool button and click the **Delete All Comments Shown** option.

This option is unavailable if the comments of all users are on display.

♦ Hide the comments, if required.

Printing comments

♦ To print comments and the document at the same time, make sure you are in Print Layout view, show the comments in the document (you can choose to print the comments of certain users only if you wish) then print the document as usual.

♦ To print a list of the comments, use the **File - Print** command, select the **List of markup** option in the **Print what** list and click **OK.**

*Word prints all of the **Reviewing Pane**. The list of comments can be seen in the **Main document changes and comments** section.*

Tracking changes made to the document by other users

When several users work independently on the same document, they usually work on copies of that document. These copies can later be merged to form a single document.

Making a document available to several users

Before making one or more copies of a document, you must configure it in order to allow tracking of changes made to it.

♦ Open the document that you wish to make available to several users.

♦ **Tools**
Track Changes ♦ Ctrl Shift E

*You can also activate tracking by clicking the button on the **Reviewing** toolbar if it is on the screen.*

*If the **Reviewing** toolbar was not previously on the screen, it will now be displayed and the letters **TRK** appear in black on the status bar.*

♦ If you wish to modify the marks Word uses to show the different types of modification, click the **Show** button on the **Reviewing** toolbar, click the **Options** option, make your changes then click **OK**.

♦ Save the changes made to the document.

♦ You must now make the document available to other users by copying it onto your network into one or more folders that the other users can access (a shared folder on your computer or a location on the network, for example). Use the **File - Save As** command to do this, or copy the document using **Windows Explorer**.

If you wish, you can give each copy of the document a different name.

❑ *To display a message to **Warn before printing, saving or sending a file that contains tracked changes or comments**, tick the appropriate option in the **Options** dialog box (**Tools - Options - Security** tab).*

*You can also activate or deactivate the tracking of changes by double-clicking the **TRK** indicator on the status bar.*

Merging documents

Merging involves bringing together in the original document all the changes (text insertion and deletion, formatting changes etc.) and comments made by other users in the copies of that document. This is possible provided you activated tracking in the original document before making copies for the other users.

♦ Open the original document in which you wish to merge the changes and make sure you are in Print Layout view.

♦ For each copy of the document that is to be merged:

– use the **Tools - Compare and Merge Documents** command.

– Select the folder containing the document that you wish to merge with the original and select the document within that folder.

– Make sure that the **Legal blackline** option is not active. If this option is active, Word does not merge the documents but compares them and displays, in a new document, only what has changed between the original and the copy.

– Open the list on the **Merge** tool button and click the **Merge into current document** option.

*The **Merge** option shows the result of the merge in the file selected in the **Compare and Merge Documents** dialog box: the **Merge into new document** option shows the result of the merge in a new document.*
A message may appear to tell you that the documents you are about to merge contain one or more conflicting formatting changes:

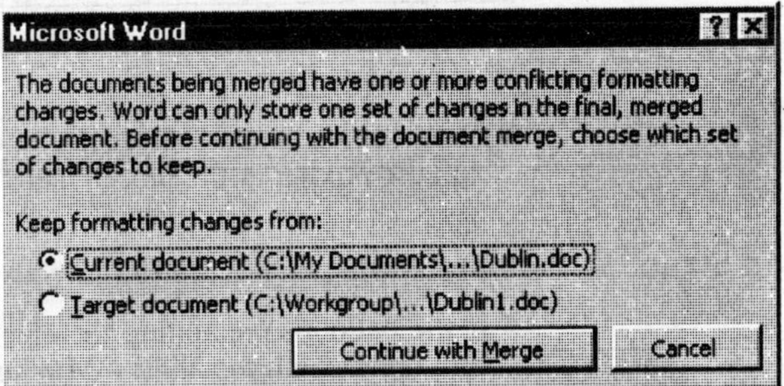

– If necessary, choose the document whose formatting changes you wish to keep then click the **Continue with Merge** button.

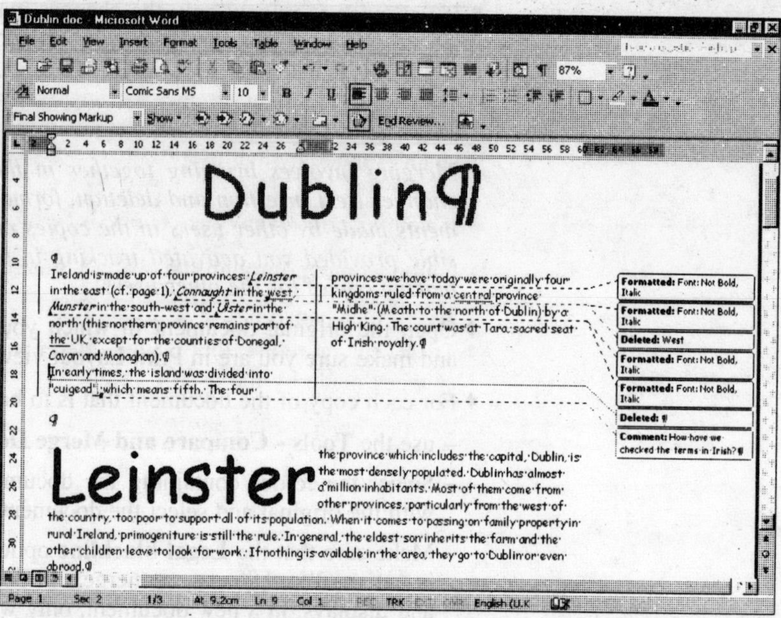

The changes and comments made by other users can now be seen in balloons: the changes and comments made by each user appear in a particular colour.

If you want to see the name of the user who modified something or created a comment, simply move the mouse pointer over the corresponding balloon.

♦ Save the changes made to the document and close it.

Accepting or rejecting changes

You can either accept or reject the changes visible in the document after merging.

♦ Open the document in which the changes have been merged and position the pointer at the place where you wish to start reviewing the changes.

♦ Make sure you are in Print Layout view.

♦ If the balloons containing the changes are not visible in the document, show them with the **View - Markup** command.

♦ Make sure the **Reviewing** toolbar is showing.

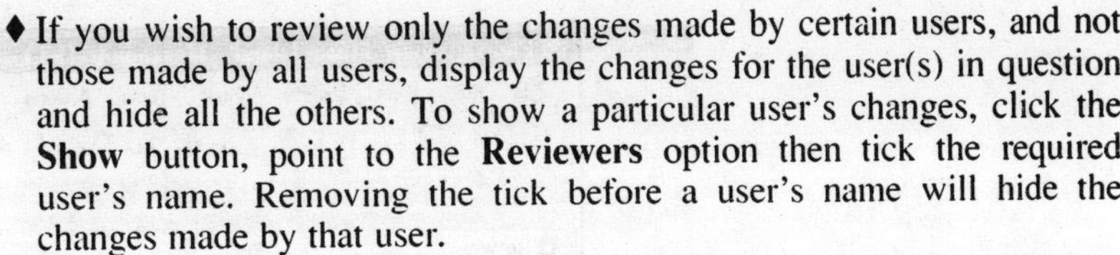

- If you wish to review only the changes made by certain users, and not those made by all users, display the changes for the user(s) in question and hide all the others. To show a particular user's changes, click the **Show** button, point to the **Reviewers** option then tick the required user's name. Removing the tick before a user's name will hide the changes made by that user.
- If you wish to review the changes one by one, use the or tool button to move through the changes then click the tool button to accept the change or the tool button to reject it.
- To accept or refuse the changes from one or several users, show the changes made by the user(s) in question (if you have not already done so) then open the list on the tool button and **Accept All Changes Shown** by clicking the appropriate option, or open the list on the tool button and **Reject All Changes Shown**.

  These two options will be unavailable if the changes made by all users are on display.
- To **Accept** or **Reject All Changes in Document**, open the list on the tool button (to accept the changes) or the list on the tool button (to reject the changes) and click the appropriate option.
- A message may appear, offering to start searching for changes from the top of the document: you can click the **Cancel** button, if you wish.
- Save the changes made to the document then close it.

❑ *You can use the options in the list on* Final Showing Markup *tool to choose how Word should display the changes and comments. You can display the* ***Original*** *document, the* ***Original Showing Markup****, the* ***Final*** *document or the* ***Final Showing Markup****.*

Sending a file for review

It is possible to send a copy of your document to one or more recipients so they can review it. This command is only available if you use the ***Outlook 2002*** *e-mail application.*

- Open the document that you wish to send for review.
- **File**
  Send To
  Mail Recipient (for Review)

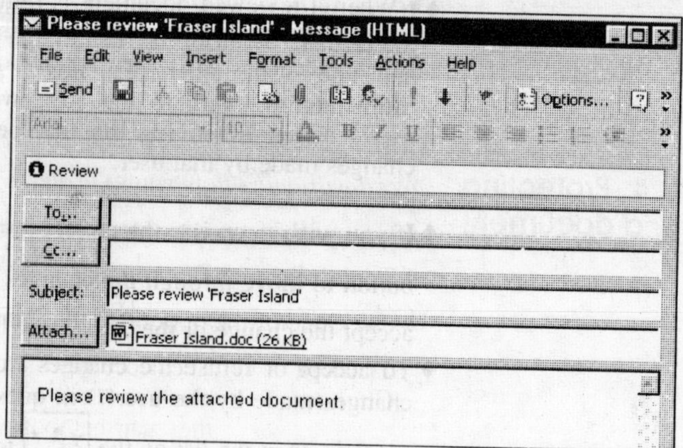

The Outlook 2002 new message window opens.

The attached document is represented by an icon and appears in the main message pane of the window or in the ***Attach*** *text box that lies below the* ***Subject*** *box.*

- In the **To** box, type the address(es) of the principal recipients of the message, separating each name with a semi-colon, or click the **To** button to select the address(es) in the address book.
- In the **Cc** (Carbon Copy) box, enter the address(es) of any recipients to whom you wish to send a copy or click the **Cc** button to select from the address book.

  A carbon copy of a message is sent for the recipient's information only and implies that you do not wish to receive a reply.

- If necessary, modify the text in the **Subject** box. By default, this box contains the text **Please review** followed by the name of the document.
- If you wish, add to or modify the text that appears in the main message pane of the window.
- Click the **Send** button.

❑ *To open and review the attached file, the message recipient will have to open the message and double-click the attachment icon. Opening this file will start the Word application; tracking changes will be activated (the letters* ***TRK*** *will appear in black on the status bar) and the* ***Reviewing*** *toolbar displayed. The recipient can review and modify the attached file then send the reviewed file back to the sender by using the* ***File - Send To - Original Sender*** *or by clicking the* ***Reply with Changes*** *tool button on the* ***Reviewing*** *toolbar (provided, of course, that he or she is working in Word 2002).*

♦ When a reviewed document is returned to you by another user, a message will appear when you open the reviewed document from the mail message. This will prompt you to merge the changes made into the original file.

Protecting a document

Word will only allow you to protect certain elements of your document.

♦ Open the document or template concerned.

♦ **Tools - Protect Document**

♦ Click one of the options in the **Protect document for** frame:

Tracked Changes	The document's contents can be modified but any changes made are highlighted (as tracked changes) so they can be spotted easily. Tracking changes is activated and you cannot deactivate it. In addition, you can no longer accept or reject changes made to the document.
Comments	The document's contents cannot be modified but you can insert comments.
Forms	Users of a form can only access the form fields: modifications are prohibited in the rest of the document. The **Sections** button becomes available when a form contains several sections. Click it to indicate which sections to protect.

♦ If required, give a password (of up to 15 characters) in the corresponding text box.

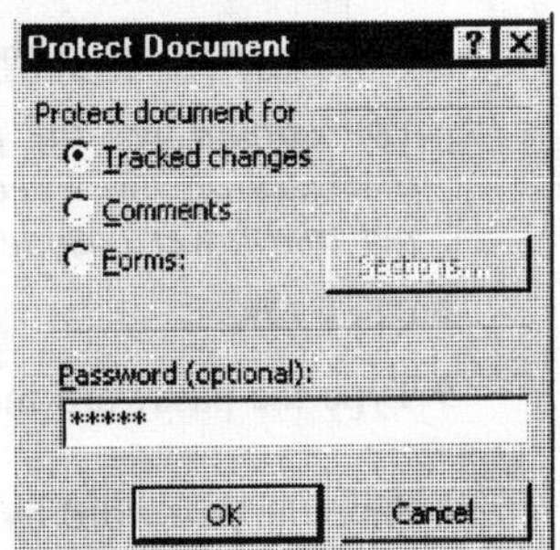

Asterisks replace the characters you type in. Be careful, as Word distinguishes between upper and lower case letters.

♦ Click **OK**.

For security reasons, Word will ask you to type the password again.

♦ Enter the password in the text box again and click **OK**.

♦ To remove the protection from a document, use the **Tools - Unprotect Document** command and, if requested, enter the **Password** in the text box and click **OK**.

Associating a password with a document

The document can no longer be modified without the password.

♦ Open the document concerned.

♦ **Tools**
Options
Security tab

♦ If the password is to be required before the document will even open, enter a password in the **Password to open** text box.

♦ Tick the **Read-only recommended** option if you want Word to validate the password then prompt the user to open the document in read-only mode.

♦ If you wish to prevent unauthorised users modifying or saving the document, enter a password in the **Password to modify** box. If the user does not know the password, he/she will only be able to open the document and read it.

You cannot see the password as you type it in, as it is replaced by asterisks on the screen. Be careful as Word differentiates between upper and lower case letters.

♦ Click **OK**.

♦ Type the password in the text box again to confirm it then click **OK**.

♦ Save the password by clicking the tool button.

❑ *To remove a password associated with a document, delete the asterisks (*) from the corresponding text box in the dialog box (**Tools - Options - Security** tab).*

Creating several versions of a document

A version is a "snapshot" that Word can take of your document, without creating a new file. The different versions are saved in the document, saving on disk space.

♦ Open the document concerned.

♦ **File**
Versions

♦ Click the **Save** button.

♦ Enter a comment.

♦ Click **OK**.

❑ *To create a version each time you close the document, activate the **Automatically save a version on close** option in the **Versions** dialog box (**File - Versions**).*

Managing versions of a document

Opening a version

♦ Open the document concerned.

♦ **File**
Versions

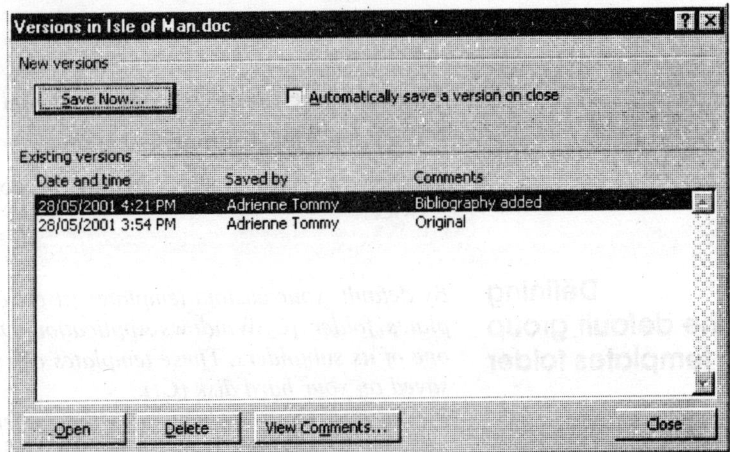

♦ Select the version you wish to consult then click the **Open** button or simply double-click the version name.

❑ *To save a version as a separate file, open it then use the **File - Save As** command.*

Deleting a version

♦ Open the document concerned.

♦ **File**
Versions

♦ Select the version you wish to delete.

♦ Click the **Delete** button.

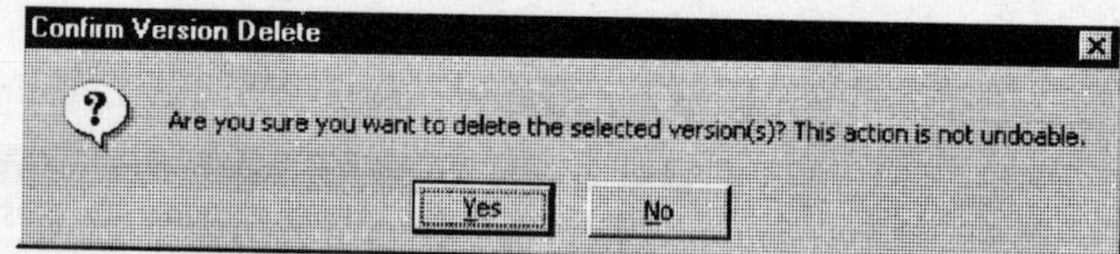

Word prompts you to confirm your deletion.

♦ Confirm by clicking the **OK** button.

♦ Click the **Close** button.

Viewing a version's comments

♦ Open the document concerned.

♦ **File**
Versions

♦ Select the version whose comments you wish to see.

♦ Click the **View Comments** button.

♦ When you have finished reading the comments, click the **Close** button twice.

Defining the default group templates folder

By default, your custom templates (user templates) are saved in the Templates folder (C:\Windows\Application Data\Microsoft\Templates) or in one of its subfolders. These templates can only be used by you as they are saved on your hard disk (C:).
If you wish to create templates that others can use (workgroup templates), you should save them on the network, in a folder that the other users can access then define the default folder for the workgroup templates.

♦ **Tools**
Options
File Locations tab

♦ In the **File types** list, click the **Workgroup templates** option.

*By default, there is no initial **Location** specified for **Workgroup templates**.*

♦ Click the **Modify** button.

*A dialog box resembling the **Open** and **Save As** dialog boxes appears on the screen.*

♦ If the folder already exists, go to the network and double-click the folder concerned.

♦ If the folder does not exist, go to the place in the network where you want to create the folder and click the tool button. Enter the **Name** of the folder in the corresponding text box and click **OK**.

♦ Click **OK** to close the **Modify Location** dialog box.

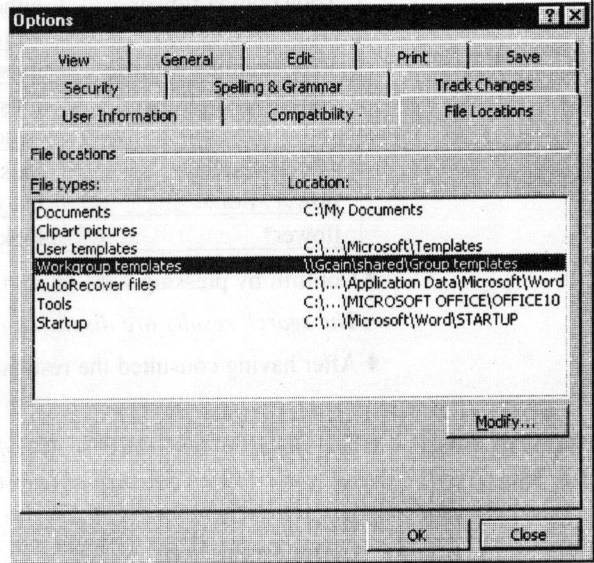

*The file path to the folder appears in the **Workgroup template** row.*

♦ Click **OK**.

❑ *When you save a template, the user template folder (C:\Windows\Application Data\Microsoft\Templates) is suggested by default in the **Save As** dialog box. To save a template in the Workgroup templates folder, select this folder in the **Save in** list in the **Save As** dialog box.*

❑ *Templates saved in the Workgroup templates folder can be seen on the **General** tab of the **Templates** dialog box (**File - New** then click the **General Templates** link in the task pane).*

Searching for Internet sites

♦ Display the **Web** toolbar.

♦ Click the **Search the Web** tool button ( ).

The search page of the MSN Microsoft site opens in your computer's default browser.

♦ Type the keyword(s) into the appropriate text box(es).

To make the search easier, you can use the following techniques with most search engines:

This request	will find pages or themes containing
Toowoomba flower	either the word "Toowoomba" or the word "flower"
+Toowoomba +flower	must find both words
"Toowoomba flower"	must find the expression "Toowoomba flower"
+Toowoomba + flower -florist	looks for "Toowoomba" and "flower" but excludes the word "florist"
flower*	looks for flower, flowers etc.

♦ Confirm by pressing Enter to start searching.

The search results are displayed in a new window.

♦ After having consulted the results, close the browser window.

Consulting help on the Microsoft site

When the help integrated in Word cannot provide the information you need, you can look for further help on the Microsoft site.

♦ **Help**
Office on the Web

*The **Microsoft Tools on the Web** site opens in the Web browser window.*

♦ Search for the help you need.

♦ After you have finished, close the browser window.

Creating a Web page

You can create a Web page that you can publish on an Internet/intranet site.

♦ Open the document you want to use to create your Web page.

♦ **File**
Save as Web Page

♦ If necessary, in **File Name**, type in a new name or modify the current name for the document.

♦ Click the **Change Title** button if you want to change the page heading.
The page heading is displayed on the title bar of the browser.

♦ Select the folder in which to save the document.

♦ Click the **Save** button.

A confirmation window may appear if the browser does not support some of the document functions.

❑ *When a Web page is composed of elements (bullets, background, pictures...), Word groups them by default into a folder called a supporting files folder. This folder's name is the name of the Web page followed by **_files**. It is created in the folder containing the Web page. If you need to move or copy your Web page, you must also move this folder in order to preserve its links with the Web page.*

❑ *To publish a Web page so that it can be viewed on a network (the Internet and/or an intranet), open Windows Explorer, select the Web page (.htm file) and its folder of supporting files (a folder with the same name as the .htm file plus **_files**) if it has one and copy them onto a Web server.*

Viewing a Web page

♦ Use Word's **File - Open** command to open the Web page (.htm file) you want to view in a browser.

♦ **File**
Web Page Preview

The Web page opens in the default browser and you see it as it would be displayed on an Internet/intranet site.

♦ Once you have seen the page, close the browser.

♦ Close the Web page (.htm file) in the same way as you would close any document.

Managing Web pages

Deleting a Web page

A Web page must be closed before it can be deleted.

♦ To delete a Web page (.htm file) and its supporting files (the folder with the same name as the htm file plus **_files**), use **File - Open** then select the folder containing the Web page you want to delete.

♦ Select the Web file (.htm extension) then press Del.

♦ Click **Yes** to confirm.

The supporting files folder associated with the page (NameofWebPage_files) is deleted automatically.

♦ Close the **Open** dialog box by clicking ☒.

❑ *To delete a Web page (and its supporting files) from a Web server, use the Windows Explorer to access the server and (if appropriate) the folder containing the Web page. Select the Web file (.thm) and press Del.*

❑ *Deleting items from your computer's hard disk does not affect the items on the Web server and vice versa.*

Modifying a Web page

♦ Open the Web page to be modified (**File - Open**).

♦ Modify the document normally using Word's editing tools.

♦ **File**
Save

♦ Ctrl S

♦ Close the Web page by clicking ☒.

❑ *If you need to update a Web page on a Web server, copy a revised version of the file (and any supporting files folder) onto the Web server to replace the old one.*

Interaction between Word and your Internet browser

Editing an HTML page in Word

While you are working in your Internet browser (Internet Explorer for example), it is possible to get the Web page you are viewing to open in Word so that you can save it on your disk and use Word's tools to edit it if necessary.

♦ Start your Internet browser. In the **Address** box, give the address of the Web page you want to see and press Enter.

♦ **File**
Edit with Microsoft Word

A message might appear, prompting you to use Word as your default Web page editor.

♦ Click **Yes** if appropriate. If in doubt, click **No.**

The Web page appears in the Microsoft Word application.

♦ Use Word's **File - Save** command to save the Web page on one of your computer's drives.

Unless you have no interest in preserving the links with the document's style sheets, choose the ***Web Page (*.htm; *.html)*** *format.*

♦ When you are ready to close the file, use Word's **File - Close** command.

Switching between Word and an Internet browser

Using a hyperlink, you can switch easily between Word and your browser (e.g. Internet Explorer). When an HTML file open in Word contains a hyperlink to another HTML file, you can activate the link to open the other file in the browser. From the browser you can then return quickly and easily to the original document in Word.

♦ In the Word application, open the HTML file concerned and, if it does not already exist, create a hyperlink towards anoher HTML file.

You can do this with the ***Insert - Hyperlink*** *command or* Ctrl ***K***.

♦ Ctrl-click the hyperlink to activate it.

The HTML file appears in the browser.

♦ To return to the original document in Microsoft Word, simply click the Back tool button.

The browser window closes.

Inserting a frames page

To show several Web pages on a single screen you need to use frames. A group of frames is called a ***frames page****. A frames page is itself a special Web page which defines the size and the position of each frame it contains.*

♦ Open the Web page from which you want to create a frames page.

♦ **Format**
Frames
New Frames Page

The ***Frames*** *toolbar is now visible on the screen.*

♦ Save the frames page:
File
Save as Web Page

♦ Activate the folder in which you want to save your frames page.

♦ Type in the **File Name**.

♦ Click **Save**.

♦ Close the frames page by clicking the [X] button.

Inserting a table of contents in a frame

♦ Open the Web page that contains the text to which the table of contents will refer.

♦ **File**
Frames
Table of Contents in Frame

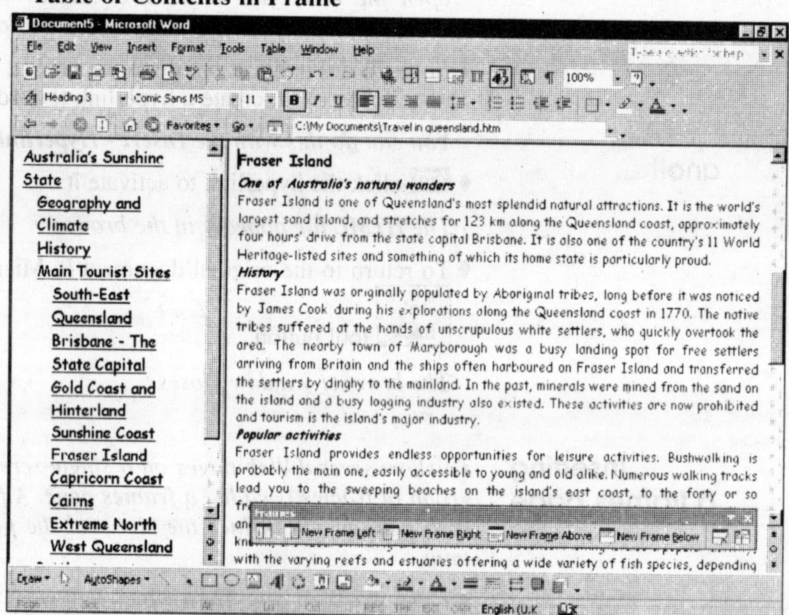

Notice that Word creates a new document. It is made up of two frames.

To show one of the titles in the right frame, hold down the [Ctrl] *key and click the corresponding titles in the table of contents.*

♦ Save the new Web page (in htm format) and close it.

Creating a new frame in a frames page

♦ Open the frames page in which you wish to create a frame.

♦ Click in the frame adjacent to where the new frame will be placed.

♦ **Format**
Frames

♦ Click one of the four **New Frame** options depending on the position you want it to have.

♦ Save the changes made to your frames page then close it.

❑ *To resize a frame, point to its border and drag it or click inside the frame then change the* ***Size*** *options shown in the* ***Frame Properties*** *dialog box (****Format - Frames - Frame Properties - Frame*** *tab).*

You can also create an empty frame using the ***Frames*** *toolbar.*

Creating a hyperlink to display a page in another frame

Once you have created a frames page, you can put it to use: clicking one of the hyperlinks will display the corresponding page in one of the other Web page frames.

♦ Open the Web page in which you want to create a hyperlink that will display a page in another frame.

♦ Click in the frame where you wish to insert the hyperlink.

♦ **Insert**
Hyperlink  ♦  K

♦ Click the **Existing File or Web Page** shortcut on the **Link to** Places Bar (cf. Inserting a hyperlink in the ENTERING/EDITING TEXT chapter).

♦ Select the **Address** of the file (or page) to which the hyperlink will refer, or activate one of the buttons (**Current Folder**, **Browsed Pages** or **Recent Files**) and select the file/page in the central area of the dialog box.

♦ If you need to, click the button to choose another **Target Frame**.

If you choose **Page Default (None)**, the target file (or Web page) will appear in a new window.

♦ If you need to, change the **Text to display** for the hyperlink.

♦ Click **OK**.

By default, the hyperlink appears in blue. When you point to the link, without clicking, the address of the target file/page appears in a screen tip.

♦ Hold down Ctrl and click the hyperlink to see the linked page.

*Word displays the file (or Web page) in the **Target Frame** you chose in the previous step. If you chose **Page Default None**, it appears in a new window.*

♦ When you have finished looking at the file (or Web page) displayed by the hyperlink, go back to the previous frames page by clicking the button if the file/page appears in a frame, or the button if it appears in a separate window.

The hyperlink will now be purple, as the linked page has been visited.

♦ Save the changes made to the Web page and close it.

Modifying frame border properties

♦ Open the Web page whose frame border properties you wish to modify.

♦ **Format**
Frames
Frame Properties

♦ Activate the **Borders** tab.

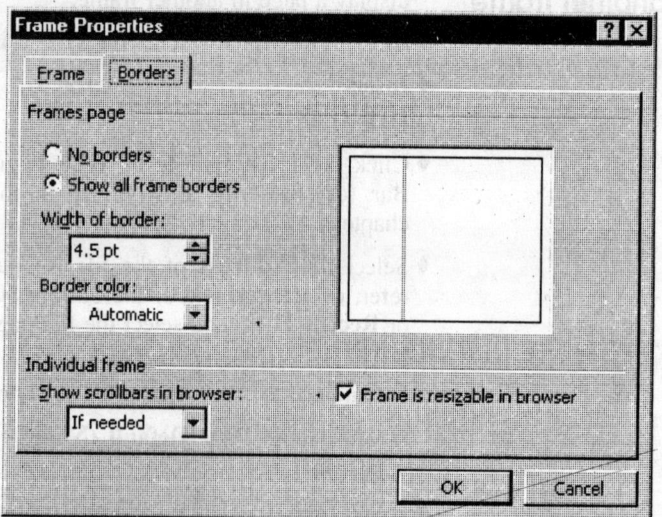

♦ Click the **No borders** option if you do not want to see the frame borders.

♦ If you wish, use the text boxes under **Frames page** to modify the **Width of border** and the **Border color**.

♦ Define when you want to **Show scrollbars in browser** using the drop-down list under **Individual frame.**

♦ Deactivate the **Frame is resizable in browser** option if you do not want the position of the borders to change when the page appears in a browser.

*The options under **Individual frame** only apply to the active frame and not to all the frames on the frames page.*

♦ Click **OK**.

♦ Save the changes made to the frames page and close it.

Deleting a frame

♦ Click in the frame you want to delete.

♦ **Format**
Frames
Delete Frame

♦ Save the changes you made to the frames page and close it.

Applying a theme to a Web page

A theme is a group of formatting elements and colours that can be applied to the active frame of a Web page.

♦ Open the Web page or frames page concerned.

♦ Click in the frame where the theme will be applied.

♦ **Format**
Theme

♦ In the **Choose a theme** list, click the desired theme.

♦ Activate the **Vivid Colors** option to intensify the colour of headings and table borders and create a brighter background colour.

♦ Activate the **Background Image** option to use the background specified in the active theme for the document or file. Deactivate this option to apply the grey background colour.

♦ If the theme contains **Active Graphics**, activate this option to see the animation effect when the page comes up in your browser (Internet Explorer, for example).

♦ Click **OK**.

♦ Save the page and close it.

Applying a background

A background can only be seen in Web Layout view (this is the view which shows you what will be displayed in a Web browser) and does not print with the document.

A background colour

- Open the Web page (possibly a frames page) to which you want to apply the background.
- If necessary, click a frame to apply the background to that frame.
- **Format**
  Background
- Choose a background colour or define your own colour with the **More Colors** option.
- Save the changes made to the page and close it.

A gradient/pattern/texture or background picture

- Open the Web page (possibly a frames page) to which you wish to apply the background.
- If necessary, click a frame to apply the background to that frame.
- **Format**
  Background
- Click the **Fill Effects** option.
- Choose the **Gradient**, **Texture**, **Pattern** or **Picture** tab, depending on what you want to apply to the background.
- Make your choice and click **OK**.
- Save the changes made to the page and close it.

Formatting

Characters

Keys	Action
Ctrl Shift F	Selecting a font
Ctrl Shift P	Selecting the character size
Ctrl Shift >/Ctrl Shift <	Next size up/down
Shift F3	Change the case of letters
Ctrl B	Bold formatting
Ctrl Shift H	Activate/deactivate hidden text
Ctrl I	Italic formatting
Ctrl Shift K	Format as small capitals
Ctrl U	Underline
Ctrl Shift W	Underline individual words
Ctrl Shift D	Double underline
Ctrl Shift +	Superscript
Ctrl =	Subscript
Ctrl space	Normal character
Ctrl Shift Q	Symbol font

Paragraphs

Keys	Action
Ctrl 1/Ctrl 2	Single/double line spacing
Ctrl 5	1.5 line spaces between lines
Ctrl 0 (zero) on the main keyboard	Add/delete a space before the paragraph
Ctrl E	Centre a paragraph
Ctrl L	Left align
Ctrl R	Right align
Ctrl J	Justify a paragraph
Ctrl M /Ctrl Shift M	Increase/decrease left indent
Ctrl T/Ctrl Shift T	Increase/decrease hanging indent of first line
Ctrl Q	Standard paragraph

Various

Keys	Action
Ctrl Shift N	Return to Normal style
Ctrl Shift C	Copy formatting
Ctrl Shift V	Paste formatting
Alt Ctrl K	Run autoformat
Alt Ctrl 1 (on the main keyboard)	Apply style Heading1
Alt Ctrl 2	Apply style Heading2
Alt Ctrl 3	Apply style Heading3

Moving/selecting/entering text

Entering

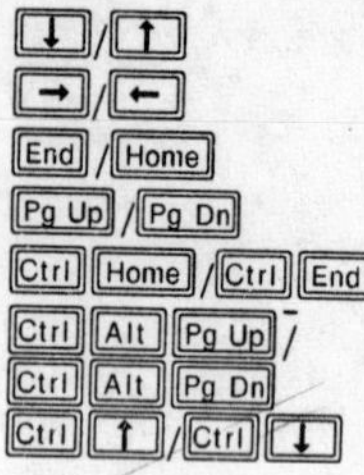

Delete the word to the left of the insertion point
Delete the word to the right of the insertion point
Overtype/insertion modes

Moving

Following/preceding line
Following/preceding character
End/beginning of a line
Previous/following screen
Beginning/end of the document
Top/bottom of the window

Previous/following paragraph

Selecting

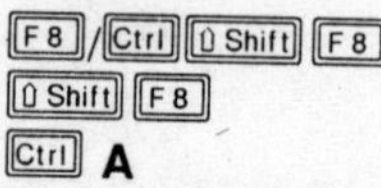

Select text/columns
Return to previous selection
Select whole document

Inserting special characters/contents

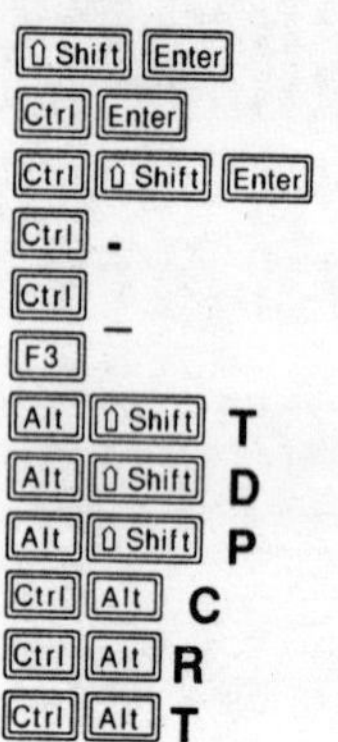

Line break
Page break
Column break
Conditional hyphen
Non breaking hyphen
Insert AutoText entry
Insert time field
Insert date field
Insert page field
Copyright symbol
Registered Trademark symbol
Trademark symbol

Specific shortcut keys

Fields

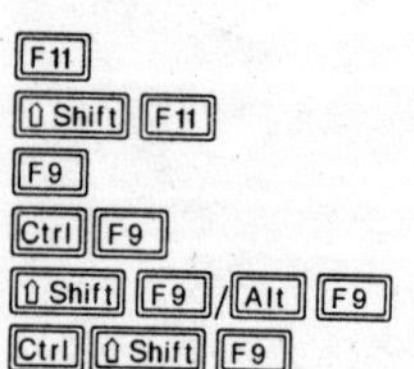

Move to next field
Move to previous field
Update selected field
Insert a field
Display (hide) a selected field code/all field codes
Replace a field by the information it displays

Tables

Keys	Action
Tab / Shift Tab	Select next/previous cell
Alt 5	Select whole table
Alt End / Alt Home	Go to the last/first cell of the line
Alt Pg Dn / Alt Pg Up	Go to the last/first cell of the column
Ctrl Tab	Use a tab in a table (except decimal tabs)
Alt click	Select a column

Outlines

Keys	Action
Alt Shift ←	Level +1
Alt Shift →	Level -1
Alt Shift 1 - 9	Display by heading level
Alt Shift +	Expand a heading
Alt Shift -	Collapse a heading
Alt Shift A	Display whole document (heading, sub-heading, texts)
Alt Shift ↑	Move a heading towards the one before
Alt Shift ↓	Move a heading towards the one after

Mail Merges

Keys	Action
Alt Shift N	Merge to a new document
Alt Shift M	Print a merged document
Alt Shift E	Modify the data file

Menu shortcut keys

File

Keys	Action
Ctrl N	New
Ctrl O	Open
Ctrl W	Close
Ctrl S	Save
Ctrl P	Print
Alt F4	Exit
Ctrl F2	Print preview
F12	Save As

Edit

Keys	Action
Ctrl Z	Undo
Ctrl Y	Repeat
Ctrl X	Cut
Ctrl C	Copy
Ctrl V	Paste
	Clear
Del	Contents

Keys	Action
Ctrl A	Select all
Ctrl G	Go To
Ctrl F	Find
Ctrl H	Replace

View

Keys	Action
Ctrl Alt N	Normal
Ctrl Alt O	Outline
Ctrl Alt P	Print Layout

AutoText

Keys	Action
Alt F3	Insert new

Insert

Keys	Action
Ctrl Alt F	Footnote
Ctrl Alt E	Endnote
Alt ⇧Shift X	Mark index entry
Ctrl K	Hyperlink

Format

Keys	Action
Ctrl D	Font
Alt Ctrl K	AutoFormat

Tools

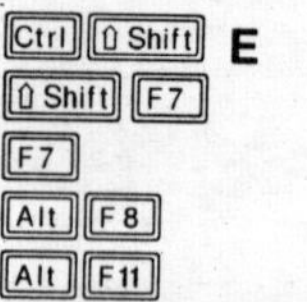

Keys	Action
Ctrl ⇧Shift E	Track changes
⇧Shift F7	Thesaurus
F7	Spelling check
Alt F8	Macros
Alt F11	Visual Basic Editor
Alt ⇧Shift F11	Microsoft Script Editor

Table

Keys	Action
Alt 5	Select table

Various shortcut keys

Keys	Action
⇧Shift F10	Displays a shortcut menu
⇧Shift F5	Return to last three positions
⇧Shift F4	Reruns a search
⇧Shift F2 / F2	Copy/move text without using clipboard
F6 / ⇧Shift F6	Move to next/previous pane
Ctrl ⇧Shift *	Display non-printing characters
F1 / ⇧Shift F1	Summary of Help/On line Help

A

B

C

P

R

FIREWALL MEDIA

(An imprint of Laxmi Publications Pvt. Ltd.)

Computer Books *for School, BCA, MCA, IGNOU, DOEACC and Engineering Students and Professionals*

ISBN	TITLE	AUTHOR	PRICE	PAGES
	.NET			
8170087155	**Building Business Intelligence Applications with .Net**	Robert Ericsson	Rs. 295.00	404
8170083567	**Learning VB.Net Through Applications**	Clayton Crooks	Rs. 295.00	450
8131800865	**Magic of C# with .Net Frame Work**	Shibi Panikkar, Kumar Sanjeev	Rs. 495.00	950
8170082471	**Magic of ASP.Net with C#**	Shibi Panikkar, Kumar Sanjeev	Rs. 395.00	828
8170089662	**ASP.Net Interview Questions and Answers**	J. Rajaram	Rs. 95.00	175
	A TO Z SERIES			
8170083214	**Access 2002 from A to Z**	Julia Kelly, Stephen L. Nelson	Rs. 75.00	185
8170083222	**Excel 2002 from A to Z**	Stephen L. Nelson	Rs. 75.00	193
8170083230	**Front Page 2002 from A to Z**	Heather Williamson	Rs. 85.00	219
8170083249	**Outlook 2002 from A to Z**	Stephen L. Nelson	Rs. 75.00	202
8170083257	**Page Maker 7 from A to Z**	Marc Campbell	Rs. 75.00	202
8170083265	**PowerPoint 2002 from A to Z**	Stephen L. Nelson	Rs. 75.00	202
8170083273	**Windows XP from A to Z**	Pat Coleman	Rs. 95.00	249
8170083281	**Word 2002 from A to Z**	Stephen L. Nelson	Rs. 75.00	199
817008329X	**XML from A to Z**	Heather Williamson	Rs. 75.00	200
8170083303	**Dreamweaver 4 from A to Z**	Heather Williamson	Rs. 85.00	215
	BEGINNERS & GENERAL INTEREST			
817008248X	**Shortcuts to Success in Computing**	Dheeraj Mehrotra	Rs. 55.00	110
8170083311	**Pictorial Computer Dictionary**	Dheeraj Mehrotra	Rs. 45.00	156
8170083486	**Pocket Net Browser**	Dheeraj Mehrotra	Rs. 95.00	302
8170084261	**1000 IT Quizzes**	Dheeraj Mehrotra	Rs. 75.00	120
8131800679	**Information Technology Bible**	Remesh Bangia	Rs. 295.00	567

Please write for a free color Firewall Media Catalog for details on the above books.

ISBN	TITLE	AUTHOR	PRICE	PAGES
8131800377	**Fundamentals of Information Technology Including MS Office**	Dinesh Maidasani, Jai Narayan Yadav	Rs. 175.00	356
813180089X	**Fundamentals of Information Technology Including MS Office (Hindi Medium)**	Dinesh Maidasani, Jai Narayan Yadav	Rs. 175.00	425
8170089719	**Foundations of Computer Science**	Ashok Arora	Rs. 250.00	386

CALL CENTERS

ISBN	TITLE	AUTHOR	PRICE	PAGES
8170082196	**Call Centers Made Easy**	Stephen Medcroft	Rs. 195.00	310

CISCO

ISBN	TITLE	AUTHOR	PRICE	PAGES
8170087481	**Enabling IP Routing with Cisco Routers**	R. Das, K. Chakrabarty	Rs. 295.00	486
817008749X	**Designing Networks with Cisco**	H. Pasricha, D. Jagu	Rs. 195.00	316
8170087503	**Cisco IP Routing Protocols: Troubleshooting Techniques**	V. Anand, K. Chakrabarty	Rs. 295.00	409

DATABASES

ISBN	TITLE	AUTHOR	PRICE	PAGES
8170089530	**DBMS—Complete Practical Approach**	Sharad Maheshwari, Ruchin Jain	Rs. 350.00	656
8170082404	**Learn to Program Visual Basic-Examples**	John Smiley	Rs. 295.00	482
8170082412	**Learn to Program Visual Basic-Databases**	John Smiley	Rs. 325.00	653
8170082420	**Learn to Program Visual Basic-Objects**	John Smiley	Rs. 325.00	670
817008475X	**IT Resources-Access 2002 VBA Programming Access**	Michele Amelot	Rs. 195.00	424
8170084512	**The Power of Oracle 9i**	Rajiv Parida, Vinod Sharma	Rs. 475.00	1035
8170088518	**Principles and Implementation of Data Warehousing**	Rajiv A. Parida	Rs. 295.00	487
817008864X	**DBA Study Guide OCP Prep Guide**	Nazar Abdul	Rs. 295.00	474
8170088658	**Oracle 11i—The Complete Reference**	Rashmi Anandi	Rs. 495.00	975
8131800067	**Toxonomy of Database Management System**	Aditya Kumar Gupta	Rs. 75.00	146
8131800385	**Introduction to SQL and PL/SQL**	Sharad Maheshwari, Ruchin Jain	Rs. 200.00	389

ISBN	TITLE	AUTHOR	PRICE	PAGES
	DOEACC 'O' LEVEL			
8170088089	**DOEACC 'O' Level Model Test Papers**	Ramesh Bangia	Rs. 175.00	296
8170089115	**DOEACC 'O' & 'A' Level Programming & Problem Solving Through 'C' Language (Model Test Paper with Solutions)**	Mukesh Sharma	Rs. 95.00	213
8170089069	**DOEACC 'O' & 'A' Level Business Systems (Model Test Paper with Solutions)**	Mukesh Sharma	Rs. 100.00	252
8170085640	**Programming and Problem Solving Through "C" Language**	Harsha Priya, R. Ranjeet	Rs. 95.00	306
8170084474	**IT Tools and Applications**	Ramesh Bangia	Rs. 145.00	370
8170085594	**Business Systems**	Ramesh Bangia	Rs. 175.00	452
8170089514	**Internet & Web Design**	Ramesh Bangia	Rs. 150.00	300
	ELECTRONIC COMMERCE			
8170085497	**Electronic Commerce**	Pete Loshin, John Vacca	Rs. 295.00	472
817008119X	**E-Commerce**	Mamta Bhusry	Rs. 95.00	215
8170083524	**Marketing in the Cyber Age**	Kurt Rohner	Rs. 295.00	223
	HARDWARE/EMBEDDED SYSTEMS			
8170087473	**Essential Electronics for PC Technicians**	John W. Farber	Rs. 295.00	546
8170086264	**Grid Computing: A Practical Guide to Technology and Applications**	Ahmar Abbas	Rs. 295.00	408
8170088186	**CD Cracking Uncovered Protection Against Unsanctioned CD Copy**	Kris Kaspersky	Rs. 295.00	422
8170083435	**Practical Linux Programming: Device Drivers, Embedded Systems and the Internet**	Ashfaq A. Khan	Rs. 295.00	420
8170083575	**TCP/IP Application Layer Protocols for Embedded Systems**	M. Tim Jones	Rs. 295.00	460
8131800520	**PC Repair and Maintenance : A Practical Guide**	Joel Rosenthal, Kevin Irwin	Rs. 195.00	362

ISBN	TITLE	AUTHOR	PRICE	PAGES
8131800768	**The A+ Certification and PC Repair Handbook**	Christopher A Crayton, Joel Z. Rosenthal	Rs. 495.00	888

INTERNET & WEB TECHNOLOGY

ISBN	TITLE	AUTHOR	PRICE	PAGES
8170083206	**The Internet Handbook for Writers, Students and Teachers**	Mary McGuire, Linda Stilborne	Rs. 195.00	276
8170084776	**Way in-Internet Getting Started**	Elizabeth Bramire	Rs. 95.00	165
8170088976	**Web Technology**	Ramesh Bangia	Rs. 250.00	560
8170087163	**Web Design with Macromedia Studio MX 2004**	Eric Hunley	Rs. 295.00	558
8170083400	**Professional Web Design (Techniques and Templates)**	Clint Eccher	Rs. 295.00	425
8170088046	**HTML, XHTML, CSS and XML**	Teodoru Gugoiu	Rs. 195.00	355
8170083583	**FrontPage 2000 for Visual Learners**	Chris Charuhas	Rs. 95.00	200
8170083591	**HTML & Java Script for Visual Learners**	Chris Charuhas	Rs. 95.00	200
8170083605	**The Visual Learners Guide to Managing Web Projects**	Chris Charuhas	Rs. 95.00	130
8170083613	**Dreamweaver 4 for Visual Learners**	Chris Charuhas	Rs. 95.00	200
8170084768	**IT Resource-Implementing XML: Managing and Formatting Data**	Johhny Brochard	Rs. 125.00	279
8170089476	**Design Your Web World**	Sunil Jalota	Rs. 75.00	146

KEEPING AHEAD SERIES

ISBN	TITLE	AUTHOR	PRICE	PAGES
8170084652	**Keeping Ahead-Exchange 2000 Server**	Philippe Levesque	Rs. 145.00	285
8170084660	**Keeping Ahead-Windows 2000 Professional**	Jose Dardoigne	Rs. 175.00	388
8170084679	**Keeping Ahead-Windows 2000 Server**	Philippe Mathon	Rs. 175.00	360
8170084687	**Keeping Ahead-Linux Administration Kernel Version 2.0 to 2.2**	Bruno Guèrin	Rs. 125.00	240

Please write for a free color Firewall Media Catalog for details on the above books.

ISBN	TITLE	AUTHOR	PRICE	PAGES
8170084695	**Keeping Ahead-Using Linux Kernel Version 2.0 to 2.2**	Bruno Gùerin	Rs. 125.00	258
8170084709	**Keeping Ahead-Java 2**	Benjamin Aumaille	Rs. 145.00	284
8170084717	**Keeping Ahead-SQL Server 7**	Joelle Mosset	Rs. 145.00	329
8170084725	**Keeping Ahead-JavaScript and VBScript**	Benjamin Aumaille	Rs. 145.00	313
8170084733	**Keeping Ahead-C++ Programming Language**	Bruno Dubois	Rs. 125.00	234
8170084741	**Keeping Ahead-TCP/IP in the NT Environment**	Bruno Ferec	Rs. 125.00	230

MCSE

ISBN	TITLE	AUTHOR	PRICE	PAGES
817008489X	**MCSE-Administering SQL Server 7.0**	Jerome Gabillaud	Rs. 295.00	580
8170084903	**MCSE-Networking Essentials**	Jose Dordoigne	Rs. 245.00	453
8170084911	**MCSE-Windows 2000 Professional**	Jose Dordoigne	Rs. 325.00	665
817008492X	**MCSE-Windows 2000 Server**	Phillippe Mathon	Rs. 345.00	712

MULTIMEDIA AND ANIMATION

ISBN	TITLE	AUTHOR	PRICE	PAGES
8170088208	**3DS Max 6 Animation with Character Studio 4 and Plug-Ins**	Boris Kulagin, Dmitry Morozov	Rs. 175.00	216
8170088216	**Adobe Audition: Soundtracks for Digital Video**	Roman Petelin, Yury Petelin	Rs. 195.00	278
8170086205	**Building A Digital Human**	Ken Brilliant	Rs. 295.00	380
8170086213	**Making Digital Videos**	Ben Long	Rs. 295.00	284
8170087171	**Illustrating with Macromedia Flash ™ MX2004**	Robert Firbaugh	Rs. 245.00	366
8170082439	**Multimedia Basics-Technology (Vol. I)**	Andreas Holzinger	Rs. 195.00	312
8170082447	**Multimedia Basics-Learning (Vol. II)**	Andreas Holzinger	Rs. 195.00	326
8170082455	**Multimedia Basics-Design (Vol. III)**	Andreas Holzinger	Rs. 195.00	280
8170083532	**Maya Feature Creature Creations**	Todd Palamar	Rs. 295.00	376

Please write for a free color Firewall Media Catalog for details on the above books.

ISBN	TITLE	AUTHOR	PRICE	PAGES
8170083540	**Sound Forge Power**	Scott R. Garrigus	Rs. 195.00	344
8131800288	**Multimedia and Web Technology**	Ramesh Bangia	Rs. 395.00	878
813180044X	**Photoshop CS**	Shruti Lal	Rs. 195.00	434
	NETWORKING			
817008721X	**Networking Essentials**	Jose Dordoigne	Rs. 195.00	453
8170089328	**TCP/IP Distributed System**	Vivek Acharya	Rs. 250.00	474
8170087023	**Computer Networks**	Ajit Kumar Singh	Rs. 95.00	181
8131800148	**The Real—world Network Troubleshooting Manual**	Alan Sugano	Rs. 295.00	396
817008203X	**Telecom & Networking Glossary**	Robert Mastin	Rs. 300.00	250
8170082048	**Data Networking Made Easy**	Karen Patten	Rs. 360.00	350
8170082056	**Digital Convergence**	Andy Covell	Rs. 300.00	234
	OFFICE AUTOMATION			
8170089891	**Desk Top Publishing**	Dinesh Maidasani	Rs. 150.00	311
8170087805	**Learning Computer Fundamentals, MS Office and Internet & Web Technology**	Dinesh Maidasani	Rs. 95.00	301
8170087686	**MS-Word 2000 Thumb-Rules and Details**	Snigdha Banerjee	Rs. 175.00	390
8170089239	**Computer Accounting with Tally 7.2**	Firewall Media	Rs. 195.00	330
	ON YOUR SIDE SERIES			
8170084830	**On your Side-Powerpoint 2002**	Andrew Blackburn	Rs. 145.00	282
8170084849	**On your Side-Excel 2002**	Adrienne Tommy	Rs. 125.00	275
8170084857	**On your Side-Word 2002**	Adrienne Tommy	Rs. 125.00	289
8170084865	**On your Side-Access 2002**	Adrienne Tommy	Rs. 125.00	303
8170084873	**On your Side-Frontpage 2002**	Andrew Blackburn	Rs. 95.00	245
8170084881	**On your Side-Windows XP**	Adrienne Tommy	Rs. 125.00	310

Please write for a free color Firewall Media Catalog for details on the above books.

ISBN	TITLE	AUTHOR	PRICE	PAGES
	OPERATING SYSTEMS			
8170087236	**Linux—A Practical Approach**	B. Mohamed Ibrahim	Rs. 95.00	187
8170088623	**Red Hat Linux Study Guide**	Vijay Shekhar	Rs. 350.00	635
8170088631	**Red Hat Linux-The Complete Bible**	Vijay Shekhar	Rs. 545.00	1176
8170089581	**Unix and Shell Programming**	Archana Verma	Rs. 80.00	137
8170089131	**Operating System Concepts**	P.S. Gill	Rs. 95.00	181
8170083427	**The MS-Windows XP Professional Handbook**	Louis Columbus	Rs. 295.00	330
8170084784	**Way in-Windows XP Home Edition**	Andrew Blackburn	Rs. 95.00	183
8170086221	**Cyber Rookies—Operating System Fundamentals**	D. Irtegov	Rs. 295.00	498
	PROGRAMMING			
8170087791	**The Art of Programming Through Flowcharts & Algorithms**	Anil Bikas Chaudhuri	Rs. 95.00	160
8170086248	**Preventative Programming Techniques: Avoid and Correct Common Mistakes**	Brian Hawkins	Rs. 295.00	322
8170083443	**Learning Computer Programming : It's not about Languages**	Mary Farrell	Rs. 295.00	375
8170086256	**Object-Oriented Programming: From Problem Solving to Java**	José M. Garrido	Rs. 295.00	360
817008931X	**Object-Oriented Programming-Concept and Implementation**	A. Rajesh	Rs. 95.00	182
8170089107	**Java: J2SE-5 A Practical Approach**	B. Mohammad Ibrahim	Rs. 175.00	332
8170089409	**Advance Java**	Gajendra Gupta	Rs. 175.00	305
8170088038	**Assembly Language Programming for Intel Processors Family**	Vasile Lungu	Rs. 295.00	577
8170088178	**The Assembly Programming Master Book**	Vlad Pirogov	Rs. 395.00	726
813180075X	**Java Messaging**	Eric Bruno	Rs. 295.00	480

Please write for a free color Firewall Media Catalog for details on the above books.

ISbN	TITLE	AUTHOR	PRICE	PAGES
	PROGRAMMING - C#, C, C++			
8170083702	**The Power of C#**	Rajiv Parida	Rs. 295.00	576
8170085632	**Mastering Graphics Programming in 'C'**	Sudhir Dawra	Rs. 145.00	286
8170088879	**Programming in C and Numerical Analysis**	J.B. Dixit	Rs. 350.00	355
8170087074	**Mastering C Programs**	J.B. Dixit	Rs. 195.00	434
8170081262	**Programming in C**	J.B. Dixit	Rs. 295.00	506
8170087619	**Unix and C Programming**	Ashok Arora, Shefali Bansal	Rs. 295.00	606
817008878X	**C Interview Questions and Answers**	J. Rajaram	Rs. 75.00	139
8170089034	**Pragmatic C**	R.K. Jangda	Rs. 150.00	258
8170086140	**Data Structure for 'C' Programming**	Ajay Kumar	Rs. 145.00	290
8170081270	**Programming in C++**	J.B. Dixit	Rs. 260.00	602
8170088194	**Hackish C++ Pranks & Tricks**	Michael Flenov	Rs. 245.00	326
8170082889	**Basics of C++ Programming**	Nishant Kundalia	Rs. 95.00	168
8170083648	**Mastering C++ Programs**	J.B. Dixit	Rs. 295.00	598
817008623X	**Cyber Rookies—C++ Programming Fundamentals**	Chuck Easttom	Rs. 295.00	417
8131800202	**Data Structure using C++**	N. Jayalakshmi	Rs. 65.00	126
8170089123	**C++ Made Easy**	T.D. Malhotra	Rs. 250.00	449
8131800393	**C++ & Introduction to C#**	T.D. Malhotra, Rajeev A. Parida, A. Rajesh	Rs. 200.00	440
8131800350	**OOPS with C++**	M. Jaya Prasad	Rs. 150.00	317
	SECURITY			
8170083419	**Computer Forensics : Computer Crime Scene Investigation**	John Vacca	Rs. 445.00	731
8131800156	**Computer Evidence (Collection and Preservation)**	Christopher L.T. Brown	Rs. 295.00	394
8170083494	**Firewall Architecture for the Enterprise**	Norbert Pohlmann, Tim Crothers	Rs. 295.00	480
8170086272	**Net Spies**	Andrew Gauntlett	Rs. 195.00	210
3826607546	**Firewall Systems**	Norbert Pohlmann	Rs. 1630.00	544
8131800504	**Homeland Security Techniques and Technologies**	Jesus Mena	Rs. 295.00	346

ISBN	TITLE	AUTHOR	PRICE	PAGES

ENGINEERING AND TECHNOLOGY

ISBN	TITLE	AUTHOR	PRICE	PAGES
817008718X	**Human Aspects of Software Engineering**	James E. Tomayko, Orit Hazzan	Rs. 195.00	338
8131800032	**Management Information Systems**	Avdhesh Gupta, Anurag Malik	Rs. 195.00	400
8170087953	**Human Computer Interaction**	Rajendra Ranjan Kumar	Rs. 95.00	210
8170088097	**Structured System Analysis and Design**	Preeti Gupta	Rs. 125.00	192
817008802X	**Autocad 2005 for Engineers**	Ionel Simion	Rs. 175.00	271
8170088054	**Digital Signal Processing Fundamentals**	Ashfaq A. Khan	Rs. 295.00	391
8131800164	**Digital Communication System Using System VUE**	Dennis Silage	Rs. 295.00	365
8170089719	**Foundations of Computer Science**	Ashok Arora	Rs. 250.00	386
817008363X	**Practical Project Management**	Ivan Bayross	Rs. 195.00	342
8131800806	**Digital Signal Processing using MATLAB and Wavelets**	Michael Weeks	Rs. 350.00	452
8131800792	**Classical Electrodynamics**	Hans C. Dhanian	Rs. 395.00	620
8131800512	**The Software Vulnerability Guide**	Herbert H. Thompson, Scott G. Chase	Rs. 195.00	368
8131800776	**Robot Modelling and Kinematics**	Rachid Manseur	Rs. 295.00	380
8131800369	**System Software**	M. Joseph	Rs. 95.00	185

STRAIGHT TO THE POINT SERIES

ISBN	TITLE	AUTHOR	PRICE	PAGES
8170084601	**STTP : Word 2002**	Corinne Hervo	Rs. 45.00	154
817008461X	**STTP : Excel 2002**	Corinne Hervo	Rs. 45.00	153
8170084628	**STTP : Dreamweaver 4**	Corinne Hervo	Rs. 45.00	135
8170084636	**STTP : Flash 5**	Corinne Hervo	Rs. 45.00	183
8170084644	**STTP : Photoshop 6**	Corinne Hervo	Rs. 45.00	152
817008881X	**STTP : MS Office 2000**	Dinesh Maidasani	Rs. 125.00	290
8170086100	**STTP : MS Office 2003**	Dinesh Maidasani	Rs. 145.00	288
8170087651	**STTP : MS Word 2003**	Firewall Media	Rs. 60.00	150
8170088011	**STTP : Photoshop CS**	Firewall Media	Rs. 60.00	150
8170088143	**STTP : MS Excel 2003**	Firewall Media	Rs. 60.00	150
8170088151	**STTP : CorelDraw 12**	Firewall Media	Rs. 60.00	150
8131800105	**STTP : 3ds MAX 7**	Dinesh Maidasani	Rs. 95.00	182

Please write for a free color Firewall Media Catalog for details on the above books.

ISBN	TITLE	AUTHOR	PRICE	PAGES
8131800083	**STTP : Auto CAD 2006**	Dinesh Maidasani	Rs. 95.00	190
8131800245	**STTP : CorelDraw X3**	Dinesh Maidasani	Rs. 75.00	188
8131800253	**STTP : Dreamweaver 8**	Dinesh Maidasani	Rs. 75.00	148
8131800237	**STTP : Photoshop CS2**	Dinesh Maidasani	Rs. 75.00	172
8170088380	**STTP : Tally 7.2**	Firewall Media	Rs. 175.00	322
8131800091	**STTP : Flash 8**	Dinesh Maidasani	Rs. 95.00	180
8131800407	**STTP : My SQL 5.0**	Dinesh Maidasani	Rs. 85.00	166
8131800458	**STTP : Microsoft Power Point 2003**	Dinesh Maidasani	Rs. 75.00	142

STUDIO FACTORY

ISBN	TITLE	AUTHOR	PRICE	PAGES
8170084792	**Studio Factory—Photoshop 6**	Christophe Aubry	Rs. 175.00	364
8170084806	**Studio Factory—Flash 5**	Sami Ben Yahiya	Rs. 145.00	314
8170084814	**Studio Factory—Dreamweaver Ultradev 4**	Phillippe Chatellier	Rs. 95.00	240
8170084822	**Studio Factory—Dreamweaver 4**	Christophe Aubry	Rs. 175.00	373
8170087643	**Studio Factory—Dreamweaver MX**	Christophe Aubry	Rs. 195.00	407
8170087627	**Studio Factory—Flash MX**	Arnaud Blanche	Rs. 145.00	337
817008766X	**Studio Factory—Photoshop 7**	Cyril Guerin	Rs. 195.00	420

LAXMI PUBLICATIONS (P) LTD

113, Golden House, Daryaganj, New Delhi-110002

Phone : **011 - 43 53 25 00**

Fax : **011 - 43 53 25 28**

EMAIL : info@laxmipublications.com

Website : www.laxmipublications.com

BRANCHES

- 129/1, IIIrd Main Road, IX Cross, Chamrajpet, **Bangalore** (*Phone* : 080-26 61 15 61)
- 26, Damodaran Street, T. Nagar, **Chennai** (*Phone* : 044-24 34 47 26)
- 43/1394D, St. Benedict's Road, Ernakulam North, **Cochin** (*Phone* : 0484-239 70 04)
- Pan Bazar, Rani Bari, **Guwahati** (*Phones* : 0361-254 36 69, 251 38 81)
- 4-2-453, Ist Floor, Ramkote, **Hyderabad** (*Phone* : 040-24 75 02 47)
- Adda Tanda Chowk, N.D. 365, **Jalandhar City** (*Phone* : 0181-222 12 72)
- 106/A, Ist Floor, S.N. Banerjee Road, **Kolkata** (*Phones* : 033-22 27 37 73, 22 27 52 47)
- 18, Madan Mohan Malviya Marg, **Lucknow** (*Phone* : 0522-220 95 78)
- 142-C, Victor House, Ground Floor, N.M. Joshi Marg, Lower Parel (W), **Mumbai** (*Phones* : 022-24 91 54 15, 24 92 78 69)
- Radha Govind Street, Tharpagna, **Ranchi** (*Phone* : 0651-230 77 64)